Witchcraft: European and African

by the same author

*

AVATAR AND INCARNATION

JESUS IN THE QUR'AN

UPANISHADS, GITA AND BIBLE

WORSHIP IN THE WORLD'S RELIGIONS

WITCHCRAFT:
EUROPEAN AND AFRICAN

by

GEOFFREY PARRINDER

FABER AND FABER
London

First published by Penguin Books Ltd in 1958
This edition first published 1963
by Faber and Faber Limited
24 Russell Square London W.C.1
Reprinted 1968, 1970
Printed in Great Britain by
Latimer Trend & Co Ltd Whitstable
All rights reserved

ISBN O 571 09060 5 (cloth edition)
ISBN O 571 06416 7 (paper covered edition)

BF
1566
.P3
1970

60617

Contents

CHAPTER 1

Introduction

Belief in witchcraft is one of the great fears from which mankind has suffered. It has taken its toll literally in blood. The belief has appeared in many parts of the world, in one form or another. It became particularly prominent and developed in Europe, in the later Middle Ages and Renaissance periods. Still in modern Africa belief in witchcraft is a great tyranny spreading panic and death.

Interest in witchcraft is still widespread in Europe and America. Passionately believed in and causing terrible persecutions from the fifteenth to the eighteenth centuries, rejected as an illusion in the last century, the subject fascinates modern men with that appeal which the mysterious exercises on the mind. The literature of witchcraft is immense. Moreover, from its experiences of the Nazi horrors, this generation can understand better than the last one the despotism of false ideas, the worthlessness of forced confessions, and the torture of scapegoats. And even in western Europe the revival of superstition, as seen in newspaper astrology and the like, following upon the decline in Christian faith, is favourable to the recurrence of dabbling in the black arts.

In other continents, from India to the Pacific, various forms of witchcraft belief appear. But it is in Africa that it is now most widespread. Witch-hunts are common there and witch-doctors are important members of society. The coming of education seems to have done little as yet to shake the belief, and there are signs that many of the educated increase their convictions in the reality of witchcraft when the power of the old gods is broken.

The present book is in the main a study of belief in witchcraft in

9

bygone Europe and America and modern Africa. European and African witchcraft beliefs are easily comparable, since certain ideas found in both continents are similar. By far the best studies of witchcraft are those which have been made of the earlier European beliefs and those made in recent years by field workers in many African societies.

A new study of European witchcraft is necessary because of a prevalent modern theory that witchcraft was a relic of old pagan cults, which are said to have survived until the eighteenth century in Europe. This is a complete reversal of the previous theory held by most scholars that European witchcraft was an illusion. Because of its important bearing upon the whole question of the nature of witchcraft in other lands, this new theory will be studied extensively in the following chapters. Ancient and modern authorities will be quoted in an endeavour to establish what was the true nature of European witchcraft.

The interpretation of ancient European witchcraft (and of some modern mass-hysterias) may be clarified also by the findings of trained anthropologists in Africa. Their conclusions have great significance as well for those educated people in Africa who still believe in witchcraft. The results of these investigations are known to specialists, but the general reader is not likely to know the names of Evans-Pritchard, Margaret Field, or S. F. Nadel. Their works are expensive and rare, stocked by few public libraries, and rapidly go out of print. Therefore a more popular work of this kind, which seeks to link European and African beliefs, but is based on the best authorities, should be of value to the general reader. To the subject of witchcraft I have given five years' intensive study and much longer general interest during twenty years in Africa.

POSSIBLE DEFINITIONS

Few subjects can have been more misunderstood than witchcraft. Many things have passed under that name which are not witchcraft at all. A great deal of wood has to be cleared away before it is possible to treat of witchcraft seriously and intelligibly.

The Shorter Oxford English Dictionary defines a male witch as 'a man who practises witchcraft or magic; a magician, sorcerer, wizard'. Not very helpfully it then defines witchcraft as 'the practice of a witch or witches', amplifying this however to 'the exercise of super-natural power supposed to be possessed by persons in league with the devil'. The female witch is called 'a female magician, sorceress; in later use, especially, a woman supposed to have dealings with the devil or evil spirits and to be able by their co-operation to perform supernatural acts.'

This does stress the 'later use' when the notion of diabolical power became current, a matter that we shall refer to later. But the defini-tion does not distinguish clearly enough between magic, sorcery, and witchcraft. It is perhaps expecting too much of a general dictionary to make the distinctions that a specialist work must establish.

The dictionary indicates the general point of view, and the con-fusions that arise in common speech, for example, between a witch as either 'a young woman or girl of bewitching aspect or manners', or 'a contemptuous appellation for a malevolent or repulsive-looking old woman'.

Further confusion is introduced into the definition of witchcraft by linking it with spiritualism, as some writers have done. This identification is made by Father Montague Summers, author of a number of diffuse and fanatical books on witchcraft. He says bluntly 'Modern Spiritism is merely Witchcraft revived'. And again, 'This "New Religion" is but the Old Witchcraft. There is, I venture to assert, not a single phenomenon of modern Spiritism which can-not be paralleled in the records of the witch trials and examina-tions.'[1]

This statement proves nothing, for the records of the witch trials are wonderfully comprehensive. But we shall see in due course that spiritualism has none of the distinctive marks of classical witchcraft, and must be firmly excluded from the definition of witchcraft.

One popular writer, Pennethorne Hughes, gives as his description: 'Witchcraft, as it emerges into European history and literature, represents the old palaeolithic fertility cult, *plus* the magical idea, *plus* various parodies of contemporary religions.'[2] The idea that witchcraft was an ancient cult is the modern hypothesis that we are going to examine. The inclusion of magic under witchcraft adds undue complications, and it will be the first part of our task to separate witchcraft properly so-called from magic.

[1] *The History of Witchcraft and Demonology*, 1926, pp. 156 and 269.
[2] *Witchcraft*, 1952, p. 24.

Introduction

WITCHCRAFT AND MAGIC

In one of the most outstanding modern books on witchcraft, Dr. Margaret Murray makes a clear distinction between what she terms Operative Witchcraft and Ritual Witchcraft. Operative Witchcraft she takes to be 'all charms and spells, whether used by a professed witch or by a professed Christian, whether intended for good or for evil, for killing or for curing. Such charms and spells are common to every nation and country, and are practised by the priests and people of every religion.'[1] This distinction would separate witchcraft off entirely from that magic and superstition which so confuse the writers and readers of articles in the popular press.

Ritual Witchcraft, which Miss Murray calls the Dianic Cult, she says, 'embraces the religious beliefs and ritual of the people known in late medieval times as "witches"'. She then proceeds to expound her hypothesis of witchcraft as a cult or resurgence of paganism.

The distinction of witchcraft from magic is useful. Indeed something like it must be found if witchcraft is to be spoken of at all usefully apart from sorcery and black magic. But it must be said that the distinction was often far from clear in the olden days, and that many people were executed as witches during the persecutions in Europe for using charms and spells, rather than for supposedly attending pagan cults. Even though the diabolical side of witchcraft was often stressed by the writers of those times, yet they included magical practices as well. Thus Michael Dalton in 1618, in his *Discovery of Witches*, intended to serve as a guide to jurymen, lists both the witches' compacts with devils and familiars, and also the necessity of searching their houses 'for pictures of clay, or wax, &c., cut hair, bones, powders, books of witchcraft, charms, and for pots or places where their spirits may be kept, the smell of which will stink detestably'.[2]

The laws of Europe made sporadic attempts at distinguishing witchcraft from other evil practices. In England, by the time the full-

---

[1] *The Witch-cult in Western Europe*, 1921, pp. 11 f. I should say here that although I have felt obliged to criticize Miss Murray's theory of the witch-cult in detail, yet I have a great respect for the breadth of her learning. It is the interpretation of her material that is in question.

[2] Quoted in C. L'Estrange Ewen's *Witch Hunting and Witch Trials*, 1929, Appendix II.

scale persecutions began in the Tudor and early Stuart periods, some clarifications had been made. William West, a lawyer of the Inner Temple in the time of the first Elizabeth, published a treatise called *Symbolaeographie* in which he distinguishes the various kinds of black arts as magic, soothsaying, wizards, divination, juggling, enchanting and charming, and finally witchery. There was rather much of the devil in all of them. Magicians were said to bring forth dead men's ghosts and to make compacts with the devil written in their own blood. Charmers were thought to use images and herbs as taught by the Devil. But witches in particular had made a league with the Devil not only to cause tempests and ruin crops, but to fly to distant places upon their staffs and spend all night in devilish lusts and monstrous mockeries.[1]

AFRICAN WITCHCRAFT AND SORCERY

The modern anthropologist in Africa makes a similar distinction of witchcraft from magic as suggested above, though he generally avoids the ambiguity of using the name of witchcraft for both classes as Miss Murray has done. He bases it upon a distinction often to be found in African languages. Seeing that African peoples present some of the clearest examples of belief in witchcraft today, it is of value to refer to them, and we may learn from them useful differences which may be concealed in European records, which are susceptible of interpretation in a variety of ways.

In October 1935 the learned journal *Africa* devoted the whole of its quarterly issue to a consideration of witchcraft in various parts of Africa. Unfortunately this publication did not appear in book form, else it would have been more easily accessible and better known. In an introductory article Professor Evans-Pritchard, one of the foremost authorities on African witchcraft, defined the field of study. 'There is much loose discussion about witchcraft. We must distinguish between bad magic (or sorcery) and witchcraft. Many African peoples distinguish clearly between the two and for ethnological purposes we must do the same.'

Evans-Pritchard defines witchcraft first as 'an imaginary offence because it is impossible. A witch cannot do what he is supposed to do and has in fact no real existence.' In his major book on the subject

[1] Ewen, pp. 22–4.

the same author amplifies this statement. 'A witch performs no rite, utters no spell, and possesses no medicine. An act of witchcraft is a psychic act.'[1]

This description of witchcraft is astonishing at first sight. Its applicability to Europe will be challenged by those who believe European witchcraft to have been an ancient pagan ritual. Its justification in Africa will be doubted by most Africans. Yet it is the considered opinion of the great majority of European scholars who have studied African witchcraft at first hand. It is not impossible that it may throw some light on European beliefs. It is known that some of the inquisitors, Reformers, and later rationalists, came to the conclusion that some witches, at least, imagined the deeds to which they had confessed, for their bodies had been observed to lie in one place all night.

For the moment, however, we will confine our attention to the distinction of witchcraft from sorcery. 'The sorcerer, on the other hand,' continues Evans-Pritchard, 'may make magic to kill his neighbours. The magic will not kill them but he can, and no doubt often does, make it with that intention.' Clearly the sorcerer is an evil magician, who deliberately and consciously makes harmful potions against his fellows and is duly hated for it.

The distinction of the witch, who says that she assists at nocturnal feasts, from the sorcerer who makes harmful magic, is most helpful. It clears away some of the jungle of confused beliefs that entangle our subject. People have included witchcraft under the same heading as magic. But the two are essentially distinct, and no progress can be made in understanding what witchcraft is about until the consideration of magic in the same category is abandoned. For this reason it is preferable not to take up Murray's term Operative Witchcraft, but to speak of Black Magic or Sorcery instead.

The modern African dislikes and fears both the witch and the sorcerer. Against both of them he employs diviners, oracles, and magical medicines. The witch-doctor (a title often misapplied) is a person who seeks to doctor and cure those who are believed to have been bewitched. He is honoured and works in public, whereas the witch is supposed to work in secret and is greatly feared.

Some distinction may also be made in the definition of a magician. For a magician may be good or bad. In African society, as in many

[1] *Witchcraft, Oracles and Magic among the Azande,* 1937, p. 21.

others, everybody uses lucky charms, like our rings and mascots. These charms need preparing and blessing by a magician or diviner, and there are known persons whose task it is to help other people. There are, however, those who work in secret and who may be consulted at night. There are the evil magicians or sorcerers, whose work is to harm enemies by magical or material means. They are anti-social and are hated for their nefarious practices. They may use spiritual or magical devices, spells or charms, or imitative methods such as sticking thorns in dolls. Or they may use real poisons which are dropped into the cooking pot. These magicians do not concern us here, for they are not witches.

This book combines, I think for the first time, a survey of European witchcraft with an account of African witchcraft. Whether they were at all related to one another in the far distant past nobody can say, though some of the ideas have a family likeness because they are of almost universal occurrence. But in the interpretation of witchcraft today European and African beliefs are often cited together. The witch-cult theory of Europe is often said to have African parallels, and so the truths about African witchcraft need to be made plain. On the other hand, Africans often say that witchcraft must be true since Europeans believed in it once. If there was a European witch-cult, that might strengthen their contention, and so this theory needs examination.

Just as modern African practices can throw light on some old European beliefs, so the latter properly studied may help to dispel the illusions of Africa. To some Europeans the subject of witchcraft may be simply curious or of antiquarian interest, though there are features of our modern life that are comparable with the ancient witch-hunts. To most Africans the subject is one of life and death.

Governments, missions, and native leaders of thought and politics in Africa are faced with recurrent witch-hunts which, as one authority says, seem to appear as it were from nowhere, flourish for a time, and then subside again. In 1951, Nigeria, the largest African state, and one of the most advanced, suffered from a witch mania that caused death to some unfortunate women and terror to thousands. Anything which can help to explode this dangerous illusion should be welcome to both rulers and people.

A study of witchcraft at first hand over the years has impressed upon me the importance of a new and comparative study of the subject. This has led to a scrutiny of much of the literature of both African and European beliefs in witchcraft, because they are now so well documented. A study of biblical literature has prompted the addition of a chapter on Palestine and the Near East, as a possible link between Europe and Africa. The verse 'Thou shalt not suffer a witch to live', has been quoted as a justification of persecution by both old European and some modern African witch-finders. How inappropriately the biblical evidence has been used I hope to show.

It will be our conclusion that the belief in witchcraft is a tragic error, a false explanation of the ills of life, and one that has only led to cruel and baseless oppression in which countless innocent people have suffered. The psychological and the social significance of the belief will be indicated.

We shall study first the records of European witchcraft. Then, having shown the hollowness of this pathetic fallacy, we shall apply our conclusions to the witchcraft belief that grips a continent which is ever more closely brought into contact with Europe. We have exported good things and bad to Africa. If some light can help to dispel the gloom and fear of witchcraft, a little more may be placed to the credit of our account.

CHAPTER 2

European Witch-hunting

EARLY LEGISLATION

Those who maintain that Western European witchcraft was a cult are not sure whether it was the remains of Druidic religion or of some more ancient fertility cult. Dr. Murray says, 'Whether the religion which survived as the witch cult was the same as the religion of the Druids, or whether it belonged to a still earlier stratum, is not clear.'[1] But she holds that in any case Christianity labelled it all as diabolical and took centuries to root it out.

However that may be, it is true that the Church fought against other gods from the time of the introduction of Christianity into Roman Britain, about the fourth century onwards. Cults or no, there were many practices which the Church condemned. Witchcraft was classed together with sorcery, enchantment, and invocations of the magic arts from early times.

In 690 Theodore of Canterbury legislated against those who sacrificed to demons, destroyed other people by spells, or used divinations of devilish witchcrafts. The penalty for the latter offence was one year's penance. Ecgberht of York in 766 decreed fasting for a woman who practised the magic art, witchcrafts, and evil spells, and seven years fasting if the spells were fatal. Witches (*wiccan*), diviners, death-workers, and adulteresses were to be driven from the land by the laws of Edward (901). Ethelstan in 940 decreed death for witchcrafts or death-deeds that were fatal, if the accused could not deny it, but prison if the guilt was proved by ordeal.[2]

So the laws went on, forbidding a mixed company of anti-social

---

[1] *The Witch-cult*, p. 19.
[2] Ewen, *Witch Hunting and Witch Trials*, pp. 2 ff.

and anti-Christian practices. At first pagan cults and magic are clearly in mind, as might be expected. Edgar in 959 enjoined 'that every priest zealously promote Christianity, and totally extinguish every heathenism; and forbid well-worshippings, and necromancies, and divinations and enchantments.' And Cnut (1038) decreed, 'we earnestly forbid every heathenism: heathenism is, that men worship idols'.[1]

But laws against heathenism gradually disappear, and witchcraft is classed with sorcery and poisoning in the laws of William the Conqueror and Henry I. Public court records are not available before the thirteenth century in England. There were few civil prosecutions for witchcraft or magic, such offences being dealt with by the Church courts.[2]

The confusion between witchcraft and sorcery runs right through the early references. The Anglo-Saxon *wicce-craeft* can be interpreted as either witchcraft or sorcery, and the Latin *veneficium* could be translated sorcery or poisoning. For many centuries there was no clear distinction, and even later on when some sort of definition of witchcraft had been arrived at the witch was liable to be accused of offences which were properly magical.

It is difficult to find a clear definition of witchcraft in England before 1594, when William West the lawyer wrote thus: 'A Witch or hag is she which being eluded by a league made with the devil through his persuasion, inspiration and juggling, thinketh she can design what manner of things soever, either by thought or imprecation, as to shake the air with lightnings and thunder, to cause hail and tempests, to remove green corn or trees to another place, to be carried of her familiar which hath taken upon him the deceitful shape of a goat, swine, calf, etc., into some mountain far distant, in a wonderful short space of time. And sometimes to fly upon a staff or fork, or some other instrument. And to spend all the night after with her sweetheart, in playing, sporting, banqueting, dalliance, and diverse other devilish lusts, and lewd desports, and to show a thousand such monstrous mockeries.'[3]

This description of witchcraft did but follow continental definitions which had been current since a famous papal bull in 1484.

[1] *The Witch-cult*, p. 22.
[2] Ewen, op. cit., pp. 5 f.
[3] Ibid., pp. 23 f., spelling modernized.

Before then on the Continent of Europe witchcraft and sorcery had also long been regarded with abhorrence, but with no very clear line of demarcation between them. All magical practices were diabolical, but the distinction of witchcraft as riding through the night to worship Satan is a late growth.

The first suggestion of this notion, which links up with ancient beliefs in night-fliers, is found in a fragmentary decree attributed to an obscure Council of Ancyra in the ninth century. 'Some wicked women, reverting to Satan, and seduced by the illusions and phantasms of demons, believe and profess that they ride at night with Diana on certain beasts, with an innumerable company of women, passing over immense distances, obeying her commands, as their mistress, and evoked by her on certain nights. . . . Therefore, priests everywhere should preach that they know this to be false, and that such phantasms are sent by the Evil Spirit, who deludes them in dreams. Who is there who is not led out of himself in dreams, seeing much in sleeping that he never saw waking? And who is such a fool that he believes that to happen in the body which is done only in the spirit?'[1]

Whether women really did go out at that time on such night revels is disputed. It should be noted that the Council shows a sturdy scepticism as to the reality of these claims, and attributes them to dreams. The classical goddess Diana is simply a convenient mistress of such meetings, for she was one of the manifestations of the nocturnal Hecate. Minerva, Jezebel, and Herodias were also said to lead such revels, suggestive names of notorious classical and biblical figures.

The decree of Ancyra came to have considerable weight. It was known to theologians as the *Cap. Episcopi,* and it long served the purpose of branding all claims to night-flying as illusory. This became part of the Church's canon law and it was not permissible to believe in the reality of night-meetings. But in the ensuing centuries other beliefs came to be associated with the illusion of night-flying. It was said that some people had secret meetings with the Devil who was in the form of a cat and they kissed him under the tail. Others said that demons carried away women from one place to another, and great debates arose as to whether the Devil could transport

[1] H. C. Lea, *A History of the Inquisition of the Middle Ages,* 1911, iii, pp. 394 f.; *Materials towards a History of Witchcraft,* 1939, pp. 178 f.

human bodies invisibly or make them pass through tiny holes. Some said that when the witch had anointed herself the Devil could take away her soul and return it later. Others rejoined that she went into a transport and imagined all these things. The great doctor Albertus Magnus quoted a case in which a young noblewoman was carried away every night for some hours, and this gave a great impetus to the development of a theory to explain such strange happenings.

Ancient beliefs in werewolves were still active. As late as 1521 the Dominicans in France tried two men, one of whom was said to have taught the other how to become a werewolf by rubbing his body with ointment. The man then became covered with hair, grew claws, and was able to run like the wind and eat children. Both were burnt alive at Besançon. In 1588, in Auvergne, a man asked a hunter to bring him some game. The hunter was attacked by a wolf, but succeeded in cutting off one of its front paws. He showed this to the gentleman, who saw that the paw had a ring on it like that belonging to his wife. When he got home his wife was hiding her arm under her clothing, and when it was drawn out she was seen to have lost the hand. She confessed and was burnt. Similar beliefs, if not penalties, may still be traced. It is said that Neapolitans still believed, until the last century, that men born on Christmas night were accursed and became werewolves.[1]

THE RISE OF THE WITCH-FEAR

It is realized today that the witchcraft persecution needs to be studied in relation to the condition of the society in which it is prevalent. Witch-hunting is an expression of the dis-ease of society and must be related to it in Europe and in Africa. At the same time the beliefs of the Church and populace had decisive effects on the beginning and course of the persecutions.

In the twelfth century movements for the reform of the Church had begun among the poorer classes, which opposed the power of the Church and the ungodly lives of many of its leaders. Soon the Cathari ('pure') and the followers of Waldo (Waldensians) were powerful sects. They were branded as heresies, and one doctor even derived the name Cathari from a practice in which, he alleged, they

[1] Lea, *Inquisition*, ii, p. 145.

kissed Satan in the shape of a cat. The Church took active measures against the reformers and found convenient tools in the new preaching orders, especially the Dominicans. So began the Inquisition in the thirteenth century, with its tribunals, police, spies, informers, and torture.

The Cathari were accused of flying to their assemblies on broomsticks or poles anointed with oil, of singing songs to the Devil who appeared in a monstrous form, of capturing and burning children and drinking potions made from their bodies.[1] 'These popular beliefs formed material for questions put to the Cathari under torture by the Inquisitors.'

In the fourteenth century the great scourge of bubonic plague, called the Black Death, ravaged all Europe. It came from the Crimea, by rats in grain ships in 1346, and spread over the whole of Europe to England by 1350. There was terrible mortality, and it is estimated that one-third of the population of Europe was carried off in the first three years of the plague. But it recurred almost every ten years and this had the effect of greatly reducing the hitherto increasing population of Europe. The ignorant masses looked for scapegoats, and found them in the hated Jews who were accused of causing the plague. The Jews were charged with eating unbaptized children and other victims in their Synagogues and Sabbaths. Most of the Jews in Germany were exterminated (as in the twentieth century when scapegoats were again needed), and the rest fled eastwards to Poland and Russia. After the Jews had been destroyed or expelled other victims were required.[2]

The Inquisition also proved useful in high places, where accusations of diabolical influence could be made against the over-powerful. At the beginning of the fourteenth century Philip IV of France began an attack on the Knights Templar, jealous of their power and privileges and envious of their wealth. The Inquisition got to work and soon produced confessions of blasphemy and idolatry, 'following certain lines suggested to the victims'. They were accused of denying Christian doctrines, giving homage to Satan, and worshipping an idol called Baphomet (Mahomet!). The Templars were said to have renounced Christ, spat upon the Cross, kissed their superiors

[1] *Chambers' Encyclopaedia*, 1950, 14, p. 626; Lea, *Witchcraft*, p. 231.
[2] C. W. Previté-Orton, *The Shorter Cambridge Medieval History*, 1952, ii, p. 847.

in indecent places, worshipped a cat, roasted children and anointed idols with their fat, and all manner of horrors.[1]

After a careful consideration of the trials of the Templars, Lea concludes, 'There is absolutely no external evidence against the Order, and the proof rests entirely upon the confessions extracted by the alternative of pardon or burning, by torture and the threat of torture.'[2] It is pleasant to find that the inquisitors, allowed to come to England for this special cause, could not extract any confessions from the Templars because English law did not permit the use of torture, and so they could not be destroyed. But on the Continent they were 'liquidated'.

Having disposed of Cathari, Jews and Templars, the inquisitors turned their attention to witchcraft. It was in the fifteenth century that witchcraft began to be distinguished from sorcery and black magic, and that the secular courts began to pass the accused to the Inquisition for trial for heresy.

By the thirteenth and fourteenth centuries theologians had had great difficulty in abiding by the rule of the *Cap. Episcopi* which had declared night-riding to be illusory. They had to judge the accusations made of and confessed to by persons brought before them, Cathari and others. But in 1458 an inquisitor, Nicholas Jaquerius, got round the old canon of Ancyra by saying that modern witchcraft was a 'new sect', and that the old heretics denounced by the Council of Ancyra were quite different from the new ones. Jaquerius brought Satan into full conjunction with the night-flying, and he maintained that witches had confessed to him of their flight to a Sabbath, their presentation to Satan in the shape of a goat, and their marking with his stigma, the cloven hoof. He said that even if the night-flying was an illusion yet the witches were still heretics, since they held to Satan in their waking hours.[3]

This opinion did not gain much ground at first, and it was disputed. A jurist, Ponzinibio, wrote a tract in which he maintained that witchcraft was an illusion, following the *Cap. Episcopi*. He rejected the idea that witches were a new sect, argued that their confessions were worthless since they were impossible, and said that their implication of confederates was dangerous and a delusion.

[1] *Chambers' Encyclopaedia*, loc. cit.; and Previté-Orton, op. cit., ii, p. 787.
[2] H. C. Lea, *Inquisition*, iii, pp. 266 and 298 f.
[3] Lea, *Witchcraft*, pp. 276 f.

To this, however, others returned the arguments of Jaquerius. A Dominican general, Mozzolino, affirmed that witches were a new sect which had originated in 1404. He added that to deny the activities of witches at their Sabbaths is to deny the efficacy of the Inquisition and discredit its proceedings. Others took up this point, demanding whether the inquisitors must not abjure their own doctrines. Indeed, the Inquisition was asked to take proceedings against Ponzinibio as a defender of heretics.[1]

Belief in witchcraft as a new sect and a heresy soon became the established rule. The new beliefs had ousted the Church's earlier caution and scepticism. Nearly everybody now believed that witches flew to their Sabbaths, where they indulged in cannibalistic feasts of unbaptized babes. Rare individualists might theorize, at their peril, as to whether witchcraft were true or an illusion. But in both secular and ecclesiastical courts confessions were commonplace which gave more detail than necessary about horrible and impossible orgies. The force of authority and popular frenzy became too great for any but the boldest critics to question. An important pronouncement clinched matters.

In 1484 Pope Innocent VIII, 'a man of scandalous life', as a Catholic historian calls him, promulgated his bull *Summis desiderantes* which marks the open declaration of war by the Church against witches. Some of the inquisitors in Germany had been hindered by critical clerks who questioned their commission to proceed against witches. Innocent gives them full authority and calls upon Church and secular powers to give them every assistance. 'It has indeed lately come to our ears, not without afflicting us with bitter sorrow, that . . . many persons of both sexes, unmindful of their own salvation and straying from the Catholic Faith, have abandoned themselves to devils, incubi and succubi, and by their incantations, spells, conjurations, and other accursed charms and crafts, enormities and horrid offences, have slain infants yet in the mother's womb . . . and at the instigation of the Enemy of Mankind they do not shrink from committing and perpetrating the foulest abominations and filthiest excesses to the deadly peril of their own souls. . . . Our dear sons Henry Kramer and James Sprenger, Professors of

---

[1] J. Bodin, in an influential book, *De la Démonomanie des Sorciers,* 1580, declared that those who denied the existence of witchcraft were almost always witches themselves.

Theology, of the Order of Friars Preachers, have been by letters Apostolic delegated as Inquisitors of these heretical pravities.'[1]

Whether this papal pronouncement is still valid is debated by Catholic writers. The author of the article 'Witchcraft' in the *Catholic Encyclopaedia* says, 'Neither does the form suggest that the Pope wishes to bind anyone to believe more about the reality of witchcraft than is involved in the utterances of Holy Scripture.' But Father Summers calls this interpretation 'a statement which is essentially Protestant in its nature', and he maintains that Innocent's bull 'must at the very least be held to be a document of supreme and absolute authority, of dogmatic force'.[2]

THE INQUISITION

Europeans have, rightly, a bad conscience over the persecution of witches. Yet the large-scale witch-hunts were not the constant policy of the Church or of society. They only arose in the periods of the later Middle Ages and the Renaissance, and under the stimulus of great public unrest.

Before Innocent's bull gave authority and precision to the doctrine of witchcraft, earlier trials had shown but few of the characteristic marks which were displayed in the later witches' confessions. Trampling on the Cross, touching and fascinating children, are early charges. There is a suggestion of a witches' dance at Toulouse in 1353. In 1424 a man in Rome was accused of turning himself into a mouse. In the early years, too, the witch-hunters feared the danger of being bewitched themselves, which served as a check to their activities. Only with the development of theory was it conveniently agreed that the officers of justice were immune to bewitching, and that the witch who had done such powerful deeds lost her potency when apprehended.[3]

In a notorious series of trials at Arras in 1459 the accused witches were burnt under the name of Vaudois, a title that applied to the Waldensian heretics. These trials were plots against rich and highly-placed persons. Under torture they were forced to admit to lurid details of the Sabbath, which they afterwards denied. Eventually the

---

[1] Quoted in *Malleus Maleficarum*, 1484, E. T. by M. Summers, 1928, p. xliii.
[2] Ibid, p. xxvii.
[3] Lea, *Inquisition*, pp. 534 f.

scandal became so great, as a despoiling of the rich by their rivals, that the French Parliament instituted an inquiry which finally annulled the sentences, ordered restitution to be made and masses to be said for the souls of those who had been executed.[1]

The Arras affair gave only a temporary setback to the Inquisition. With the promulgation of Innocent's bull the Church now took witchcraft with deadly seriousness as a heresy. It entered upon a period of intensive persecution, which had the effect of spreading abroad the typical ideas of witchcraft. Witch-hunting thus encouraged the very beliefs that it professed to oppose. Never can it be seen more clearly that persecution defeats its own ends and spreads the error that it seeks to combat by these wrong methods.

Within five years of Innocent's bull the two chief inquisitors for Germany produced the most notorious textbook of procedure for witchcraft trials ever written. It was entitled *Malleus Maleficarum,* which may be translated as 'the Hammer of Witches', said to destroy witches and their heresy as with a two-edged sword. It was published by Fr. Henry Kramer and Fr. James Sprenger, of the Order of Preachers, Inquisitors. Sprenger, who was the principal author, was a dangerous and evil-minded fanatic. He claimed to have gathered disinterested statements from eye-witnesses, confessions of witches maintained even to the stake. He revels in the preposterous and even more in the sensual. Altogether the *Malleus* is one of the wickedest and most obscene books ever written.

Sprenger's work did more than any other single agency to perfect the persecution of those people accused of witchcraft. He gives the method of procedure in trials, insisting on torture which could be continued on successive days. Children could denounce their parents, criminals give evidence, defending lawyers be themselves suspect. Condemned witches were to be handed over to the secular power to be burnt alive.

Armed with the papal recognition of the reality of witchcraft, and with a manual of answers to objections and of judicial procedure, the inquisitors went through much of western Europe spreading blood and fire. How many thousands of people perished nobody knows. A single bishop in Bamberg is said to have burnt six hundred witches. Lea says, 'Christendom seemed to have grown delirious, and Satan might well smile at the tribute to his power in the endless

[1] Ibid., pp. 519 f.

smoke of the holocausts which bore witness to his triumph over the Almighty. . . . Could any Manichean offer more practical evidence that Satan was lord of the visible universe?'[1]

Strangely enough it was in Spain, the home of the Inquisition, that persecution on the Continent was the least active. Spain was at this period rather aside from the rest of European ideas of witch-craft and Sabbaths. The new notions had to struggle against the scepticism of informed theologians and the control exercised by more enlightened officers of the Inquisition. There was a spirit of doubt and inquiry, so different from the frenzy and credulity of central Europe. When the secular authorities stimulated a witch-craze in Navarre in 1526, a congregation of the Inquisition seriously debated the root question of the reality of witchcraft, and the punishment to be applied. They were divided, six against four, over the question whether witches really did commit the crimes to which they confessed. But they agreed that confession was not proof enough, and that in any case the witch should be dealt with by the Inquisition which would impose penance.

The Inquisition in Spain checked the popular and civil efforts to destroy witches and it protected their lives. Its efforts were notably successful in 1611 when the inquisitor Salazar Frias examined 1,800 cases, compiled masses of evidence, and submitted his report to the Suprema. He gave many instances to show that witches were the subjects of delusions and that many confessions had been extracted under torture.

Salazar concluded, 'I have not found even indications from which to infer that a single act of witchcraft has really occurred. . . . This enlightenment has greatly strengthened my former suspicions that the evidence of accomplices, without external proof from other parties, is insufficient to justify even arrest. . . . I also feel certain that, under present conditions, there is no need of fresh edicts or the prolongation of those existing, but rather that, in the diseased state of the public mind, every agitation of the matter is harmful and increases the evil. I deduce the importance of silence and reserve from the experience that there were neither witches nor bewitched until they were talked and written about.'

Salazar gave instances of this creation of a witch-fever and con-fession. 'This impressed me recently at Olague, near Pampeluna,

[1] Lea, *Inquisition of Middle Ages*, p. 549.

where those who confessed stated that the matter started there after Fray Domingo de Sardo came there to preach about these things. . . . So, when I went to Valderro . . . I only sent there the Edict of Grace and, eight days after its publication, I learned that already there were boys confessing.'[1]

Not all Salazar's colleagues agreed with him, but the Suprema followed his counsels. The existence of witchcraft was not denied, but the Inquisition in Spain pressed on with checking the secular authorities, examining the accusations carefully, and protecting the accused unless proof of their complicity in poisoning was clear. Thus Spain was one of the most tolerant countries during the witch-craze and, like England, never saw the mass burnings that ravaged Germany and France.

Over central and western Europe the fever raged and declined little with the Renaissance and the Reformation. Protestant and Roman Catholic vied with each other in their fanatical zeal. The new movements of thought and religion added to the general unrest. Unable to burn each other, often, they found ready scapegoats in the witches. All manner of ills were attributed to witches, and one archbishop is said to have burnt 120 people who confessed that by their spells they had prolonged the winter.

The power of the Inquisition was broken, of course, in Protestant lands. But Calvin was obdurate, and Luther, in his Table Talk, said, 'I would have no pity on these witches; I would burn them all.' Nevertheless, scepticism began to spread and the new thought gradually took effect. One writer complained that many who followed Luther and Melancthon held 'that witches only assist at these assemblies in their imagination'.

PERSECUTION IN BRITAIN

Innocent's bull does not seem to have been acted upon in England and Scotland, and both countries were free from the Inquisition. The Templars had not been tortured or condemned here. Nor did the belief in witchcraft as a new sect obtain much hold in Britain. Indeed the Reformation separated Britain from such Continental thought during much of the witch-craze, which only began here about 1560.

[1] H. C. Lea, *A History of the Inquisition of Spain*, 1907, iv, pp. 233 f.

Not only was there no Inquisition in England, but witches were not burnt here. That penalty had been applied to heretics since the time of the Lollards, but witchcraft was not regarded as a heresy. Further, torture was prohibited in England under common law. So that this land saw little of the violence and cruelty that marred so much of the Continent of Europe. The leniency of the English was regretted even in Scotland: 'There is too much witchery up and down our land; the English be too sparing to try it.'[1] This was under the Commonwealth.

It used to be maintained that the days of the Commonwealth were the worst for witches in England, and Lecky in his rationalist essays did much to popularize the notion that witch-hunting in England was largely due to 'the fanaticism of Puritanism', and that Scotland even more 'cowered with a willing submission before her clergy'. But C. L'Estrange Ewen has now shown, from a most painstaking study of the records of the assizes in the home counties, that there were more witch trials under Elizabeth than during the whole of the seventeenth century. Elizabeth's reign was full of plot scares. We shall come back to this later in more detail.

In the fifteenth century the practice of magic and sorcery was believed to be growing in England and was recognized by Parliament. Continental notions of organized witches' Sabbaths and cannibalism were slow to reach this country, and the general belief awaited the precision of legislation. With the passing of laws the numbers of accusations greatly increased; as elsewhere the legislation defeated its own ends by spreading the ideas which it sought to combat. Continental laws and writings were referred to, and with the accusations came justification in elaborated theory.

The Church had been content with moderate punishments and penances for magic and witchcraft. Late in Henry VIII's reign a vicious statute was passed against the supposedly growing witchcraft and enchantment, the making of images and the pulling down of crosses. This was repealed in the first year of Edward VI. But the apparent ineffectiveness of the procedure against sorcery led to an investigation at the beginning of Elizabeth's reign, witches were brought before the assizes, and a new statute was enacted in 1563.

It was a time of unrest, religious and social, and Elizabeth's own life was not safe. Her act declared: 'Where at this present, there is no

[1] M. A. Murray, *The God of the Witches*, p. 136.

ordinary nor condign punishment provided against the practisers of the wicked offences of conjurations and invocations of evil spirits, and of sorceries, enchantments, charms and witchcrafts. . . . For reforming whereof be it enacted that . . . if any person or persons after the said first day of June shall use, practise or exercise witchcraft, enchantment or sorcery, whereby any person shall happen to be killed or destroyed . . . [they] shall suffer pains of death as a Felon or Felons and shall lose the privilege and benefit of sanctuary and clergy.'[1]

James I in 1604 replaced the Act of Elizabeth by an even more severe statute. This Act of James I was finally repealed by George II in 1736. At this latter date the death penalty, which had long been discontinued, was abolished for witchcraft. But imprisonment for one year without bail was still enacted against those who pretended to use witchcraft, sorcery, conjuration, or even 'to tell fortunes' or to discover lost goods by 'any occult science'.

There was a brave resistance to the spread of witchcraft ideas in England, shown notably by the publication in 1584 of *The Discoverie of Witchcraft* by Reginald Scot. This is a learned work, quoting over two hundred English and foreign authors, and ridiculing especially the *Malleus Maleficarum*. Father Summers has done good service in editing a modern printing of this book, though as he believes in witchcraft himself he calls Scot an atheist. There is no evidence for this charge, except that Scot says that the age of miracles has ceased. On the contrary, Scot's work is full of devout references to the disorders of nature as being due to God rather than to the witches. Scot was supported nine years later by a nonconforming clergyman, George Gifford, who wrote *A Dialogue concerning Witches*. Gifford does not deny the existence of witches, but he doubts the validity of the evidence brought against them and seeks to protect innocent women.

James I, 'the wisest fool in Christendom', published in 1597 his *Daemonologie*, in which he opposed 'the damnable opinions' of Reginald Scot and ordered all copies of his book that could be found to be burnt by the common hangman. (He could not burn Scot himself!). James accepted much of the popular opinion of the witches' meetings: 'As to their consultations thereupon, they use them oftest in their Churches, where they convene for adoring: at

[1] Ewen, op. cit., pp. 15 f., spelling modernized.

which their master enquiring at them what they would be at: every one of them propones unto him what wicked turn they would have done. . . . To some others at these times he teacheth, how to make pictures of wax and clay: That by the roasting thereof, the persons that they hear the name of, may be continually melted or dried away by continual sickness.'

James had the background of Scotland where persecution of witches was fiercer than in England. It must be remembered also that he felt himself to be threatened by plotters and workers in the black arts. When he came to the throne of England he pushed through his new legislation. He took an active part in the examination of witches. But he was acute enough to see that being in league with the Devil did not guarantee omniscience, as when an accused girl could not recognize a verse of the Gospel read in Greek. It is said that later in his reign James, being troubled by impostures, and perhaps feeling safer on his throne, 'receding from what he had written in his *Daemonologie*, grew first diffident of, and then flatly to deny, the workings of witches and devils, as but falsehoods and delusions'.[1] We have this on two authorities, later than James, who suggest that the king recanted to some degree but was withheld by politic reasons from publishing it. Charles I was milder than his father had been.

Authorized by the acts of Elizabeth and James, and primed by the royal book on demonology, the courts and assizes of that time considered many hundreds of accusations of witchcraft. The panic became especially widespread in Essex and Lancashire. The trial of the Lancaster witches in 1612, to which fuller reference will be made later, caused a great stir. It was the most famous case in England, and the playwright Shadwell based a popular but dull play upon it. Other notorious trials were held in Northampton, Leicester, and Huntingdon, the records of which have a suspicious family resemblance.

As there was no Inquisition in Britain, its place was taken for a time by witch-finders. One of the biggest bouts of witch-finding took place under the Long Parliament. This was not due to the Puritanism of the Parliament, but to the activity of the witch-finder, Matthew Hopkins. Samuel Butler in *Hudibras* probably referred to Hopkins when he called him

[1] W. Notestein, *A History of Witchcraft in England*, 1911, pp. 143 f; and see R. T. Davies, *Four Centuries of Witch Beliefs*, 1947.

Persecution in Britain

A leger to the devil sent,
Fully empower'd to treat about
Finding revolted witches out?
And has he not, within a year,
Hang'd threescore of 'em in one shire?

Matthew Hopkins, self-styled 'Witchfinder Generall', began his work in 1644 in Manningtree. In 1647 he published a short treatise '*The Discovery of Witches,* in answer to severall Queries lately Delivered to the Judges of Assize for the County of Norfolk. And now published by Matthew Hopkins, Witch-finder. For the Benefit of the whole Kingdom.'

Hopkins declared that at Manningtree seven or eight witches met near his house and offered sacrifices to the Devil. He searched the accused women for the Devil's mark, and pricked them to find out insensitive spots which were supposed to come from the Devil. In his booklet he defends himself against the charge of using torture, except pricking and sleeplessness, and maintains that he did not his work for love of gain. But some authorities estimate his takings at anything up to a thousand pounds.

Hopkins is said to have sent to the gallows more witches than any other witch-finder in England. He died soon at Manningtree, the legend reported that he himself had been put to the swimming test and had drowned. Butler said of him,

Who after proved himself a witch
And made a rod for his own breech.

The persecutions brought about by Hopkins were a final burst of the witch-fever, lasting two or three years, and thereafter proceedings declined rapidly. As Professor Trevelyan says, 'The government of Charles I and of the Regicide Republic and Protectorate were both honourably marked by a cessation of this foolish atrocity.'[1]

Not only was England a country where torture, at least in its grosser forms, was forbidden, but also the nature of the courts helped to prevent abuses. The educated classes became sceptical of

---

[1] *Illustrated English Social History*, 1950, ii, pp. 90, 117. But R. T. Davies maintains that 'the Calvinists were, as far as evidence survives, invariably believers in the reality of witchcraft, and that the Royalists by the time of the Great Rebellion, were almost without exception, averse from the prosecution of witches'. *Four Centuries of Witch Beliefs*, pp. 201 f.

the charges of witchcraft made by so many foolish and ignorant people, and since the judges had almost as much influence as juries, they tended to question the evidence adduced and dismiss the case when it was doubtful. The people still believed in witchcraft, for another century or two, but they were restrained by the gentry. Trevelyan says again, 'It was lucky for the witches that England was aristocratically governed'.

The last execution for witchcraft in the home counties was in 1660, and the last in England was at Exeter in 1684. In Scotland, and even more on the Continent of Europe, executions continued into the following century.

OUTBURST IN NEW ENGLAND

Emigrants to America took with them beliefs in witchcraft that were current in Europe. The beliefs were not specially due to the Puritanism of the migrants, for they were shared by Anglicans and Roman Catholics in Europe. Belief in the Devil who made pacts with men and women, and through them brought sickness on man and beast, were almost universal.

The laws of New England soon made witchcraft a capital offence. Massachusetts in 1641: 'Witchcraft which is fellowship by covenant with a familiar spirit to be punished with death.' Connecticut in 1642: 'If a man or woman be a witch, that is, hath or consulteth with a familiar spirit, they shall be put to death.' New Haven in 1655: 'If any person be a witch, he or she shall be put to death.'

Yet there were only occasional executions, until the last great flare up at Salem in 1692. J. M. Taylor says that from 1630 onwards 'several cases of witchcraft occurred, but the mania did not set its seal on the minds of men, and inspire them to run amuck in their frenzy, until the days of the swift onset in Massachusetts and Connecticut in 1692. . . . The last great outbreak of epidemic demonopathy among civilized people'.[1]

The first execution for witchcraft in New England seems to have been Alse Youngs who was put to death in Windsor, Connecticut, in 1642. Another woman was hanged at Boston in 1648, and several others from 1651 to 1662, and then only one or two till 1692.

[1] *The Witchcraft Delusion in Colonial Connecticut*, p. 26.

Doubts had begun to arise and were seen in the trial of Katherine Harrison at Hartford in 1669. Katherine was accused of familiarity with Satan, bewitching a jacket and breeches, bewitching cattle, and pinching a man in bed. The jury condemned her but the magistrates asked the opinion of local ministers where a plurality of witnesses was needed, and whether an apparition was a sign of the Devil's power. The ministers thought this argued acquaintance with the Devil. Katherine then appealed, and the magistrates released but banished her. In New York in 1670, after some complaints from neighbours, Katherine was vindicated and given freedom to stay anywhere she wished.

Then came the final eruption at Salem in 1692, when twenty people were killed in six months. The alarm was raised in the family of the minister of Salem, Mr. Paris, and some servants were charged with witchcraft. A new governor, Sir William Phipps, had just arrived from England and he set up a special court to deal with the accusations. At the beginning of June the first trial began and Bridget Bishop was hanged. Governor Phipps then sought the advice of eminent Boston clergy.

Increase Mather was a distinguished theologian and president of Harvard College, and he set out his belief in the reality of witchcraft and pacts with the Devil with care and conviction in *Cases of Conscience concerning Evil Spirits personating Men; Witchcrafts*. But his son, Cotton Mather, was more active. He declared that 'the New Englanders are a People of God settled in those which were once the Devil's Territories; and it may easily be supposed that the Devil was exceedingly disturbed when he perceived such a People here accomplishing the Promise of old'. The religion of the Indians had been diabolical, and when it had gone the Devil revenged himself on the colonists. In 1688 a child at Boston had been seized with fits which were ascribed to the evil influence of an Irish washerwoman called Glover. Cotton Mather investigated the matter and Glover was hanged. The following year Mather published an account of this case which probably helped to spread the fear of witchcraft through the colony. He was hardly the man to damp down the fever at Salem.

After the execution of Bridget Bishop five more people were hanged in Salem on July 19th and another five on August 19th. Among the last batch was a minister named George Burroughs,

33

whose chief crime seems to have been scepticism about the existence of witchcraft. Although Cotton Mather was present on horseback at the execution and accused Burroughs of imposture, many people were now alarmed, and even more when John Willard was hanged for refusing to arrest any more people. Eight persons were hanged on September 22nd, making nineteen in all, and one man was pressed to death with stones for refusing to plead. Two dogs had even been accused of witchcraft and killed.

The magistrates were now very worried and asked Cotton Mather to justify his views, which he did in *The Wonders of the Invisible World*, published in Boston in 1692. Agitation moved from Salem to Andover and nearby towns where many people were accused and imprisoned. The accusers turned on the magistrates and even denounced the wife of Governor Phipps. But some of the accused now took action and brought claims of damages for defamation. The accusers took fright; many people were released from prison or fled. Governor Phipps was recalled to England in 1693, the agitation subsided, and people generally lamented their errors.

Cotton Mather and his father stuck to their opinions. In 1693 Margaret Rule in Boston declared that she saw spectres such as had been seen at Salem and Andover. Cotton Mather agreed with her and there might have been another scare. But a Boston merchant, Robert Calef, exposed the delusion and controverted the opinions of the Mathers. The latter burnt his book but could not burn him. By now most people were disillusioned and even accusers retracted their views. But the Mathers remained obdurate, and even as late as 1723 Cotton Mather repeated his views of the doings of Satan in Salem and showed no remorse for his part in the hangings.

As generally in England, no witch was ever burnt in New England. How many were hanged is not quite sure. But G. L. Kittredge's estimate of about two thousand during the seventeenth century is exaggerated at least twenty times. The Salem persecution was by far the most intense. It has been clearly established that twenty people were killed then, 'fifty-five persons suffered torture, hundreds of innocent men and women were imprisoned, or fled into exile or hiding places, their homes were broken up, their estates were ruined'.[1]

[1] J. M. Taylor, *The Witchcraft Delusion*, p. 26; cp. G. L. Kittredge, *Witchcraft in Old and New England* (1929), p. 331.

NUMBERS OF WITCHES KILLED

There is great variation in the estimates of the number of people executed for witchcraft in Europe during the persecutions. The German church historian Kurtz considered that, following the bull of Innocent VIII in 1484, some 300,000 witches were killed. This figure has been widely repeated, and it is stated again in a one-volume *Encyclopaedia of Religions*.[1] It is very difficult to check such figures. The persecution was worst in Germany, and one writer thinks that 100,000 witches were burnt in Germany alone in the seventeenth century. But these numbers are probably much exaggerated.

For England, one estimate gave 70,000 hanged under James I, while another made the total for all time in Great Britain to be 30,000. Clearly these are guesses and err on the side of generosity. The only serious effort that has been made to check the assize records gives a far smaller figure.

Ewen, who goes into the matter most carefully, with constant reference to the original records, comes to the considered conclusion that 'the number of executions for witchcraft in England from 1542–1736 may be guessed at less than 1,000'. This is allowing for the activities of Hopkins and the independent courts as well as the assizes.[2]

It must be remembered that while there were many accusations of witchcraft, not all the accused were convicted or suffered the death penalty. The percentage of hangings to accusations never passed 42 per cent in England, and was usually about half that figure. That is to say that about one in five accused witches were hanged.

Some of the accused escaped before imprisonment or broke out of the rough prisons of those days. Some asked to be submitted to the swimming ordeal to prove their innocence. Witches could be reprieved in England, even after conviction, upon extenuating circumstances, such as pregnancy, at the discretion of the judge. Imprisonment, whipping, or the pillory could be ordered for the first offence.

Certain people accused of witchcraft, especially if educated or

[1] E. R. Pike, 1951, p. 397.
[2] Ewen, op. cit., pp. 112 f. His final date, 1736, refers of course not to executions in the eighteenth century but to the repeal of James I's Act on that date.

wealthy, took action for slander against their defamers and succeeded at times in obtaining damages or having their detractors bound over. Great or rich people could often bribe their way out of prison, though it is noticeable that many of the accused were poor or old people. Far from witchcraft being a plot against society, by discontented Papists or politicians or leaders of secret cults, the accused people were mostly from the poor and uneducated classes. Ewen abstracts the indictments of 590 persons accused of witchcraft in the records of the home counties, and of these all but *four* are described as tradesmen or labourers or, usually, the wives of such.[1]

[1] Ewen, p. 39.

CHAPTER 3

Witches' Meetings

NOCTURNAL GATHERINGS

From the records of the persecution of witches in Europe, from 1484 onwards, there can be assembled details of the wicked deeds of which the accused people were supposed to be guilty. With the emergence of clear doctrines about witchcraft come the indications of the wrongs witches were thought to be doing to society.

It is apparent at once that the accusers agree on the social character of witchcraft. On the Continent, from the time of the Council of Ancyra in the ninth century, the idea had been current that witches 'ride at night with Diana on certain beasts, with an innumerable company of women'. And in England the Lancaster witches, for example, were typical in that they were said to meet at Malking Tower in Pendle Forest to eat mutton and bacon on Good Friday.

Witchcraft was thought of as a social affair. The modern idea of the witch as a lonely crone, of the Walt Disney type, is not the whole picture. It is true that many lonely old women were suspected of witchcraft, and some of them were wise women who were experts at making herbal remedies which, sought after in time of sickness, might be held against them as witchcraft if the patient died. Nevertheless, such solitary people were supposed to go off at night to join their fellows in midnight orgies.

Witches, however separately they lived, were believed to form assemblies, covens and Sabbaths. Whether or not they actually physically went to such meetings, and this was debated, yet they were supposed to be conscious of these meetings and to recognize those whom they met there. Witches who confessed were obliged to divulge the names of their confederates. Some of the people executed in the Lancaster trials were indicted on the sole evidence of one of the chief accused that they had been seen at a witches' gathering. They maintained their innocence to the very end, but were hanged.

The assemblies were believed to be held always at night, in wild places whither the witches were transported immediately. Any place might do, but there were said to be favourite resorts, in Germany the Brocken mountains, in Italy a certain oak tree near Benevento, and more vaguely a wild region beyond the river Jordan.

It is important to note that these meetings were held at night, because some modern writers suggest that the witches' assemblies and rites were relics of pagan customs. We still have traces of some of these practices, for example in the Helston Furry Dance, the Mummer's Play of Marshfield, and Lady Godiva's ride at Coventry, not to mention innumerable Morris dances and maypoles. But these latter rites, pagan though their origin may be, take place in the day-time and with public approval. Whereas witchcraft is essentially nocturnal and anti-social.

'Men loved the darkness rather than the light; for their works were evil.' The Middle Ages knew well that the night was the proper time for nefarious activities, and thought it suitable for witches to meet then. In one of the most amazing inquisitor's manuals, combining gross credulity with apparent attempts at honesty, we read thus of a confession forced from a poor girl. 'Françoise Secretain added that she used always to go to the Sabbath at about midnight. . . . But always it is a condition of these devilish assemblies at night, that as soon as the cock crows everything disappears. . . . Some have said that the sound of the cock is deadly to Satan, just as it is feared by lions.'[1]

The nocturnal assembly is also a feature of African belief in witchcraft. Here again the solitary witch is an anomaly. Witchcraft is not something that the witch does with her solitariness. She is essentially a social being, at least at night, and with her own kind. So witches are believed, and confess, to have met at night. Together they pursue their evil tasks and only return to their homes at cockcrow.

COVENS AND SABBATHS

The witchcraft belief of Europe had special characteristics of its

[1] H. Boguet, *An Examen of Witches*, 1590, E.T. 1929, pp. 51 f.

own, in addition to those which it shared with other continents. This is but to be expected, since witchcraft like other beliefs takes local colour from the country and age in which it is found. The witchcraft of Europe is seen in the midst of the Christian era, and therefore the descriptions of it take Christian forms. The Devil is a Christian figure, if one may put it so, for he is prominent in Jewish and Christian theology. The Black Mass, which some witches were said to celebrate, is but a reversal of the true Mass of the Christian liturgy.

Some of the European witches were said to be organized into covens. The word 'coven' dates from about 1500 and is a variation of the word convent. It means simply an assembly of people, but it came to be applied especially to the organization of the witches' society.

Murray quotes a Scottish witch as saying 'there are thirteen persons in each Coven', and she goes on from there to affirm 'the number in a coven never varied, there were always thirteen, i.e. twelve members and the god'.[1] She interprets this as of universal occurrence and stresses the recurrence of the number thirteen and its multiples.

It must be said, however, that there are many covens mentioned with more or less than thirteen members. Murray herself admits that many records are defective, but where the full account is available, as at Lancaster, the numbers vary. There were eight witches of Salmesbury in the Lancaster trials. Sometimes there were said to be fifteen, as in Spain, or thirty elsewhere. It requires considerable ingenuity to stretch the number thirteen to fit members of all covens that are mentioned.[2]

Whether the attribution of the number thirteen to the covens is a distortion of the number of the Christian apostles with Christ cannot be determined. It might rest upon a suggestion of deliberate anti-Christian practice. Our unlucky number thirteen may come from here.

The coven is said to have been the nucleus of the witches' organization. The main assemblies themselves were often called Sabbaths. Murray declares that this word 'clearly is not connected with the Jewish ceremonial'. She would derive it from the French *s'esbattre*, 'to frolic', as a suitable description of the witches' revels.[3]

---

[1] *The Witch-cult*, p. 193; *The God of the Witches*, p. 64.
[2] Lea, *Inquisition of Spain*, 4, p. 224.
[3] *The Witch-cult*, p. 97.

But the word Sabbath need not have anything to do with Jewish ceremonial to be derived from the Jewish sacred day. The Jews had often been persecuted in medieval Europe for practices similar to those of which the witches were accused. Witches' Synagogues were also mentioned, and the inquisitor Boguet refers to witches going 'to the Sabbat' and 'being assembled in their Synagogue'.[1] It is notable that in England where there were no Jews until the Commonwealth, the Continental notion of a witches' Sabbath does not appear until 1620. The Oxford English Dictionary gives the Hebrew word Sabbath as the origin of the witches' Sabbath.

The Sabbath was said to be held always at night, but opinions differed as to the day of the week. Hopkins says it was always on a Friday night, and as a feast took place that would be contrary to the Church's teaching of a Friday fast. The Lancaster witches were said to have had a big meeting on Good Friday, feasting on 'beef, bacon and roasted mutton'. Boguet said that formerly he thought the Sabbath was held on Thursday night, but later heard confessions that it met sometimes on Monday or Friday, Wednesday or Sunday, or whenever commanded by Satan.[2]

It is said that the important Sabbaths were celebrated at great feasts of the year, Christmas, Easter, and Corpus Christi. Murray collects evidence to show that there were Sabbaths on ancient pastoral festivals on May Eve (Roodmas) and November Eve (Hallowmas), two others being added on Candlemas (February 2nd) and Lammas (August 1st). Midsummer (Beltane) and Midwinter (Yule), the real pagan festivals, seem to have been of less importance. But the whole question is one of interpretation, since there is such variation in the accounts.

Some of these days became great occasions for chasing out the witches. On the Continent May Eve, *Walpurgisnacht*, was the favourite time for 'burning out the witches', till the present century. Even after burnings at the stake had been stopped in the eighteenth century, bells were rung on May Eve, dogs were unchained, bundles of twigs were lit and incense burnt. Men and women ran seven times round their houses and villages (as Joshua round Jericho) to chase away the witches, shouting as they went, 'Witch flee, flee from here,

[1] Boguet, p. 55. Witches' Sabbaths are first mentioned by the Inquisition. Lea, *Witchcraft*, p. 203.
[2] Boguet, p. 53.

or it will go ill with thee'. In Bavaria young men met at the cross-roads, cracked whips, and wound horns to ban the witches.[1]

DREAMS AND WANDERING SOULS

The nocturnal Sabbaths took place while ordinary folk were asleep. According to ancient beliefs this would be explained by the dream activity of the witch herself. The common notion was that the sleeper's soul had wandered away to other places, enabling her to see distant people and even to hold converse with the dead. In modern Africa the witch is believed to go out at night, in spirit only, and to leave her body behind asleep. Yet on waking she will confess to having made the most extraordinary journeys.

Classical Greek and Indian, Egyptian and Hebrew, beliefs turned away from this notion of a wandering soul. Clearly Christian theologians could hardly give such an interpretation to statements about witches' meetings. And the Council of Ancyra had declared these assemblies to be delusions.

When the reality of the Sabbaths came to be widely accepted, the problems of the dreaming soul had to be faced. It is clear from the confessions that witches did sometimes confuse their dreams with reality. This is admitted by all writers, and there are statements which show that a witch was observed sleeping all night, yet on waking she declared that she had been to the Sabbath. Hence one writer, Sinistrari, declared, 'There is no question that sometimes young women, deceived by the Demon, imagine they are actually taking part, in their flesh and blood, in the sabbats of Witches, and all this is merest fantasy. . . . But this is not always the case; on the contrary, it more often happens that witches are bodily present at sabbats and have an actual carnal and corporeal connexion with the Demon.'[2]

James Sprenger seriously considered the question whether the soul can leave the body. Some inquisitors, he said, held that the Devil had no power to transport the witches' bodies away, but that they attended the Sabbath in their sleep by a vaporous substance coming from their mouths. 'They lie down to sleep on their left side, and then a sort of bluish vapour comes from their mouth, through

---

[1] J. G. Frazer, *The Golden Bough*, abridged edn., 1949, pp. 560 f.
[2] *Demoniality*, c. 1700, tr. M. Summers, 1927, p. 6.

which they can see clearly what is happening.'[1] Sprenger himself, however, rejected the notion of a wandering soul, and held that normally the witches went to the Sabbaths both in body and soul.

The question now to be decided is whether all witchcraft was the product of the dream state, of the imagination, or whether the witch met her god at an actual Sabbath and also dreamt of him on other nights. The inquisitors freely admitted that there could be no external witnesses to the Sabbath. 'In order to prove conclusively that a person is a Wizard or a Witch, the actual confession of such person is requisite: for there can be no witnesses to the fact, unless perhaps other Sorcerers giving evidence at the trial against their accomplices.'[2] One is tempted to conclude that when a witch was watched she spent the night on her bed and only dreamt of her god; when she was not watched she went physically to the Sabbath.

However, Murray counters this point of the witch dreaming of the Sabbath and the Devil only, by saying that 'such visions are known in other religions; Christians have met their Lord in dreams of the night and have been accounted saints for that very reason'.[3] This is true, but Christians would not claim that the dream meeting with their Lord implied also a physical meeting. On the contrary, they believe in Him without ever having seen Him, 'Whom not having seen ye love'.

Nevertheless, it is a fact that it is hard to think that the whole extensive system of belief in witches' meetings was pure delusion— until one hears modern African witches confessing freely and with detail to the most impossible things.

NIGHT-FLYING

The belief in flying was one of the oldest strands of witchcraft belief, and strangely enough one of the most enduring. In many cases in seventeenth-century England, we find the plea or the verdict solemnly recorded, 'Not guilty, no flying'.

The witches were believed to go to the Sabbath by abnormal means, though there is often no mention of their means of locomotion. The Devil might be thought to whisk them through the air,

[1] *Malleus*, p. 108.
[2] L. M. Sinistrari, *Demoniality*, p. 94.
[3] *The Witch-cult*, p. 15.

or make them arrive instantaneously at their destination. The old writers affirm their flying most seriously. 'They go there sometimes on a goat, sometimes on a horse, and sometimes on a broom, and generally leave their house by the chimney.'[1]

Flying to the meetings was by no means the only method spoken of in the confessions of the witches. Often they were said simply to go to some wild place outside the town, which could easily have been reached on foot. Sometimes they rode on horses. James Device at Lancaster impressed the court when he described the witches going to their meeting in Pendle Forest. 'That all the witches went out of the said house in their own shapes and likenesses. And they all, by that they were forth out of the doors, gotten on horseback, like unto foals, some of one colour, some of another.'[2]

Even then there was a tendency to add a supernatural touch to the riding. Some witches were said to ride on goats, rams, or dogs. At other times the steed was a demon. Some witches declared that they rode on human beings, either in their own form or changed into animal shape by enchantment. One said that she kept a little horse and would invoke the Devil's name to make it fly: 'Horse and Hattock, in the Devil's name.'[3] In Sweden witches were said to ride on human beings which were shod like horses, but when the bridle was taken off the people got up in their own shape again. One witch confessed to having ridden on a pole, but the pole broke and she fell down, and hence came the lameness from which she still suffered at her trial. In New England one witch was said to fly over a bridge and another jumped in a window in the likeness of a cat and nearly strangled a man in bed.

Murray says that there is 'a certain amount of firsthand testimony' that the witches declared that they had actually passed through the air above the ground. But her principal reference is from the inquisitor Boguet, who gives in his own words what purported to come from the accused women, and who admits that they confessed only after they had been harshly treated and were in despair. He says, 'I will come to what I have learned of this matter. Françoise Secretain said that, to go to the Sabbat, she placed a white wand between

---

[1] Boguet, p. 44.
[2] T. Potts, *The Wonderful Discovery of Witches in the Countie of Lancaster*, 1613, ed. G. B. Harrison, 1929, p. 62.
[3] *The Witch-cult*, p. 100.

her legs and uttered certain words, and that she was then conveyed through the air. . . . Thievenne Paget said that the first time the Devil appeared to her, it was in full daylight in the form of a big black man, and that when she had given herself to him he embraced her and raised her in the air and conveyed her to the house in the field of Longchamois.'[1]

This flying belief is very ancient and widespread. The magic flight is one of the ancient folklore themes found throughout the world, it is a rapid and generally horizontal flight which does not reach the sky. Often it is a hero or man flying before death or some monstrous presence like a witch.[2] In Hindu superstitions witches used spells to enable themselves to fly through the night to places of meeting or to cemeteries where they fed on corpses. Medieval Jewish belief spoke of women flying with unbound hair to nocturnal assemblies. In Africa it is still believed that witches fly to their meetings as nightjars, bats, owls, and fireflies.

In popular European belief the witch flew to her Sabbath riding on a broomstick. Nursery rhymes, such as Mother Goose riding on her gander, reflect the old notions. Some witches are certainly said to have claimed to fly up the chimney or out of the window. Possibly there was a superstition against passing through the doorway, or they were thought to go invisibly. But since many houses of poor people had no chimneys and small windows, this belief may be a later variant.

The Church, we know, had at first condemned this belief in night-flying as erroneous and commanded its priests everywhere to preach against the error. But later doctors declared that flying was possible through the liberty that God allows to demons. Sprenger asserts that witches' flying was 'proved by their own confessions'. Such proof would not pass unquestioned today. He continues, 'Among such there was the woman in the town of Briesach whom we asked whether they could be transported only in imagination, or actually in the body; and she answered that it was possible in both ways'.[3]

Some witches claimed to have a magical ointment with which they anointed their bodies all over, and so were able to fly through the air. Hence they stripped naked before setting out on their flight, a

[1] *The Witch-cult*, p. 101, and Boguet, p. 41.
[2] M. Éliade, 'Symbolisme du "vol magique" ', *Numen*, vol. iii, 1, p. 7.
[3] *Malleus*, p. 108.

sight depicted in many books. 'Some rub themselves first with a certain ointment, and others use none. There are also some who are not witches, but after anointing themselves do not fail to fly up through the chimney and to be carried away as if they were witches.'[1]

The ointment was sometimes said to have been made from the flesh of unbaptized children, a reflection of the belief in the cannibalism of witches. The French writer Bodin said that witches use 'the fat of young children, and seethe it with water in a brasen vessel, reserving the thickest of that which remaineth boiled in the bottom, which they lay up and keep, until occasion serveth to use it'.[2]

The blood of a child, or the powdered bones of a man who had been hanged, with certain herbs, were supposed to be rubbed by the witch on her palms, wrists, and joints of fingers and toes. Thus magically prepared she would take off and be airborne. This ointment might come from a magician or direct from the Devil. Sometimes the ointment might be rubbed on the witch's stick to make it come alive.

Murray gives various formulas for flying ointment, particularly stressing one which contained aconite and belladonna. She produces a medical opinion to state that these two drugs would produce excitement and irregular action of the heart. 'Irregular action of the heart in a person falling asleep produces the well-known sensation of suddenly falling through space, and it seems quite possible that the combination of a delirifacient like belladonna with a drug producing irregular action of the heart like aconite might produce the sensation of flying.'[3]

This is all right, if witchcraft is confined to sleep. Francis Bacon declared more roundly, 'the great wonders which they tell of, carrying in the air, transporting themselves into other bodies, etc., are still reported to be wrought, not by incantations, or ceremonies, but by ointments, and anointing themselves all over. This may justly move a man to think that these fables are the effects of the imagination'.[4]

Flying dreams are very common, without the h~l~
Modern psychology has its own interpretation of

[1] Boguet, p. 44.
[2] Cp. Scot, *The Discoverie of Witchcraft*, p. 105.
[3] *The Witch-cult*, p. 280.
[4] *Works*, 1857 edn., ii, p. 643.

flying dreams and the phallic symbolism of broomsticks. The relevance of dreams to this interpretation will be dealt with later.

ANIMAL FAMILIARS

Witches are commonly associated with animal familiars. The traditional picture of the witch shows her with a black cat. We call black cats lucky today, probably by a reversal of the older taboo on black, just as the superstitious Greeks euphemistically called the unlucky left side the 'well-named' side.

The witch's familiar was regarded as essential to her practice. Michael Dalton lists this first in his *Discovery of Witches* for the guidance of juries. 'These witches have ordinarily a familiar or spirit, which appeareth unto them; sometimes in one shape, sometimes in another, as in the shape of a man, woman, boy, dog, cat, foal, fowl, hare, rat, toad, etc. And to these their spirits they give names, and they meet together to christen them (as they speak).'[1]

In drawings of 1621, now in the British Museum, witches are depicted with their familiars or imps: all manner of dogs, pigs, goats, fishes, lizards, ducks, other birds, and dragons. There are also fanciful combinations of these, monsters with wings, bears walking like men, and animals with fishes' tails. The witches shown are old and 'strange women', bending over their imps in an attitude of invocation.

Two main types of animal have been distinguished as associated with witchcraft. One was a domestic animal. Black cats abound, as might be expected. Also white cats and spotted, dogs, rats, birds, toads, beetles and snails. Many of them were supposed to be abnormal or compounded of several creatures. A witch at Northampton who was watched was said to have an appearance of a 'little thing about the bigness of a cat'. Somewhat suspiciously a 'white thing about the bigness of a cat' had also appeared at Chelmsford. These records often have a close family likeness.[2]

It should be remarked that keeping domestic animals in the house was not the common practice that it is in Europe today. Hence an old woman who had cats or other small animals for company would easily be suspected of having familiar imps. These imps were said to have

Ewen, p. 267.
testein, p. 378.

been obtained from fellow-witches or from the Devil. They were thought to be fed on milk and blood. Sometimes it was reported that they sucked the witch's blood, or some supernumerary teat that she had (see later, page 69 f.). A Chelmsford witch said that the Devil came to her in the likeness of a white spotted cat which required some of her blood from time to time.[1] In America Cotton Mather said that imps sucked some of the witches 'and rendered them venomous to a prodigy'.

Matthew Hopkins, the notorious witch-finder, said that at Manningtree he had found a witch who had several imps. The woman was seized and watch kept for several nights till her imps came. Hopkins says 'there being ten of us in the room' the woman announced the imps as they came; each had its peculiar name. They were: *Holt*, like a white kitling; *Jarmara*, like a fat spaniel 'without any legs at all', she said 'he sucked good blood from her body'; *Vinegar Tom*, like a long-legged greyhound, with a head like an ox; *Sack and Sugar*, like a black rabbit; *Newes*, like a polecat.[2]

Allowing for a certain amount of exaggeration these might all be tame animals with fancy names. Other names of familiars given by the witch were: Elemanzer, Pyewacket, Peckin the Crown, Grizzel, and Greedigut. Hopkins ingenuously says that 'no mortal could invent' such names. The modern reader may not be so sure.

What makes Hopkins's firsthand account so questionable is his declaration that Vinegar Tom changed his shape before him: 'who when this discoverer spoke to, and bade him go to that place provided for him and his Angels, immediately transformed himself into the shape of a child of four years old without a head, and gave half a dozen turns about the house, and vanished at the door.' Whatever explanation may be given of this extraordinary statement it will hardly be the one that Hopkins hoped to evoke in his readers. Rather one wonders at the value of his account, despite the ten witnesses.

Murray says that these small domestic animals were only found in witch trials in England. She suggests that they were used for magical purposes. But it may well be that Hopkins and his fellow witch-finders made a special point of the connexion of these domestic animals with witchcraft. They would add weight to the rather

[1] *The Witch-cult*, p. 209.
[2] *The Discovery of Witches*, pp. 50 f.

flimsy evidence available for the conviction of the accused.

Witches were thought also to change into animal forms, as they are believed to do in Africa today. Cats and hares were the favourites, hence to see a hare was long thought to be unlucky, as it might be a transformed witch. Yet although the hare was the commonest transformation of the witches, the Devil never appeared as a hare. The toad also has a long history in legend as an instrument of evil, 'ugly and venomous'.

The witch-transformations were usually into small animals which go about silently at night and were regarded as unlucky. The widespread belief in werewolves and vampires which sucked human blood belongs to the same class of ideas. Some of Boguet's witches confessed that they had changed themselves into wolves. He solemnly quotes the example of Circe, who 'changed the companions of Ulysses into swine', as a proof that such transformations were indeed possible.[1]

The second main type of animal connected with witchcraft is bigger than the domestic familiar—a goat, dog, or horse. Murray points out that goats and sheep are absent from descriptions of witchcraft in Britain but were French specialities. The principal witch in European assemblies was often spoken of as if he were an animal. One witch said that at her introduction to the Sabbath the Devil welcomed her by taking her hands in his paws; he was like a dog with great horns. Sometimes he was said to be like a great horse, or riding on a horse. Some of the familiars were said to be human beings, of the sex opposite to that of the witch.[2]

The descriptions of these larger familiar animals is taken by defenders of the witch-cult theory as evidence that there were real assemblies, at which some of the people dressed in animal skins. At Lyons one witch said that there were other witches who joined in the dances in goat or sheep form, and they danced with them, holding their hairy feet in their hands.

The question of these devils and masked figures will be discussed later. Here it may be remarked that it would not be difficult for the accused witches to describe dances of masked people, because material lay close at hand in the old traditional masquerades. Dances of people dressed in animal skins are known to have continued for

[1] Boguet, pp. 137 f.
[2] *The Witch-cult*, pp. 67 f.

long in Europe, in the Mummers and play actors. There were fewer of these in England than on the Continent. But there were the Deer Dancers at Abbot's Bromley, the Padstow Hobby-Horse, and at Southam the black Godiva festival in which a mask of a bull's head with horns was worn. But, whatever their origin, these dances were public and performed in daylight. The dancers were generally men, whereas most accused witches were women.

Similarly in African society there are secret organizations whose members wear costumes, often with horns or animal skins. But these masquerades are quite different from the female witches, who have their small familiar animals. The masked dancers are men, and they often have as one main function that of hunting out the witches.

CHAPTER 4

Cannibalism and the Black Mass

CANNIBALISM

In their Sabbaths the witches were supposed to kill and eat new-born and unbaptized children. This was the worst thing with which the medieval populace charged them. Jews also had been accused of committing this horrible crime in their Synagogues and Sabbaths, and of course they were supposed to have an interest in stealing children before they had been protected with the water of baptism. Children were believed to be kidnapped and taken away to be devoured, or to have magical preparations made from their corpses.

African witches today are accused of similar deeds. It is commonly believed that a new witch must bring one of her own relatives to the assembly. There the company feasts on the body, and when they reach the heart or liver the victim dies. The connexion of witches with vampires is clear, for both are believed to suck the blood or spiritual substance of the victims on which they batten.

Dr. Murray, who shows considerable sympathy with the witches as representing an old religion persecuted by the Church, thinks that child sacrifice was not uncommon, if the records are to be believed and the common charge of cannibalism accepted. She says that there is no record of this in England.[1] On the other hand, many of the English indictments were for bewitching people until they died, though there is no suggestion of sacrifice or cannibalism.

Murray's principal theory is that there was a god of the witches (see next chapter), who was himself sacrificed by his worshippers at a quarterly festival. She says that it was thought to be essential for the

[1] *The God of Witches*, pp. 130 f.

god to be burnt. But once again this never happened in England, since witches were not burnt in this country.

On the Continent the inquisitors firmly believed the stories of child murder and cannibalism. Sprenger records these words from the confession of a Swiss witch: 'We set our snares chiefly for unbaptized children, and even for those that have been baptized, especially when they have not been protected by the sign of the Cross and prayers . . . and with our spells we kill them in their cradles or even when they are sleeping by their parents' side, in such a way that they afterwards are thought to have been overlain or to have died some other natural death. Then we secretly take them from their graves and cook them in a cauldron, until the whole flesh comes away from the bones to make a soup which may easily be drunk. Of the more solid matter we make an unguent which is of virtue to help us in our arts and pleasures and our transportations.'[1]

Witches were thought to enter houses at night, through the windows or even the cracks of the doors by the aid of magical potions. They would sprinkle powder on the parents to stupefy them, and then touch the children with poisonous hands so that they died in a few days. Some were said to tear children to pieces, eat their souls, and then return their bodies to their cradles.

Boguet goes into this thoroughly. His witches 'confessed that in the year 1597 . . . they killed a girl and a boy saved himself by running away. They confessed also that they had eaten part of the children which we have mentioned, but that they never touched the right side.' Others, particularly 'those midwives and wise women who are witches are in the habit of offering to Satan the little children which they deliver, and then of killing them, before they have been baptised, by thrusting a large pin into their brains. There have been those who have confessed to having killed more than forty children in this way. They do even worse; for they kill them while they are in their mother's wombs.'[2]

Sacrifices of blood are said to have been demanded of the witch as the price of her admission to the coven. With the blood of the sacrifice, or sometimes with the witch's own blood, a contract might be written to bind the witch faithfully to the society. Sometimes dead babies were said to be dug up from churchyards to serve this pur-

---

[1] *Malleus*, pp. 100 f.
[2] Boguet, pp. 88, 137.

pose. 'At Douzy, on the 1st October 1586, Anna Ruffa confessed that she helped a witch named Lolla to dig up in this way a corpse which had recently been buried, and from its burned ashes they compounded a potion that they afterwards used for killing those whom they would.'[1]

Confusion was made between the work of witches and that of evil magicians. Gilles de Rais was burnt as a sorcerer and child-murderer in 1440. H. C. Lea is convinced of his guilt, 'attentive examination of the evidence brings conviction that amid manifest exaggeration there was a substantial foundation of fact'. Dr. Murray doubts this and prefers to regard him as a divine victim of the old religion. She admits that 'according to his own confession he killed at least eight hundred children', but she maintains that the whole trial was an arranged affair and that the records give only the evidence for the prosecution. This may be so. The same judgement would apply to many of the witch trials.[2]

It is said that Madame de Montespan took part in child murders in order to retain the love of Louis XIV. The Paris women are said to have celebrated Mass over a woman's naked body, with a child's blood in the chalice. We shall see more of this under the Black Mass. But clearly there were notions of child-murder current apart from witchcraft.

In face of these horrible accusations of murder and cannibalism the Continental inquisitors felt justified not merely in burning witches alive, but also in tearing their flesh with hot pincers or roasting them over a slow fire. Some modern writers believe that these murders actually took place. Montague Summers affirms that 'there is ample and continuous evidence that children, usually tender babes who were as yet unbaptized, were sacrificed at the Sabbat. . . . Sometimes they ate the tender flesh of little children, who had been slain and roasted at some Synagogue, and sometimes babes were brought there, yet alive, whom the witches had kidnapped from their homes if opportunity offered.'[3]

Yet this terrible indictment for child-murder is hard to credit, despite the mass of testimony, some of it apparently coming from the

[1] F. M. Guazzo, *Compendium Maleficarum*, 1608, ed. M. Summers, 1929, p. 89.
[2] Lea, *Inquisition of the Middle Ages*, 3, 468 ff; Murray, *The God of the Witches*, pp. 191 f.
[3] *The History of Witchcraft and Demonology*, pp. 144 f.

witches themselves. That witches killed children, often their own babies, for consumption at a midnight feast, seems such an unnatural act that the records must be more closely examined. The facts are not established from 'confessions', unless there are supporting testimonies from outside. We must exercise the same scepticism as Miss Murray does over the trial of Gilles de Rais.

One begins to hesitate to give credence to these stories when one finds African women today making just the same sort of confession, without clear proof that they have actually done these wicked things. Evidence from other parts of the world tends to weaken rather than strengthen these accusations of cannibalism.

To understand the situation both in medieval Europe and modern Africa, it must be remembered that for all practical purposes medicine scarcely existed. Hence child mortality was high. Ignorant mothers might well imagine that they had been responsible for the mysterious deaths of their children. Angry fathers might accuse them of murder. The fact that old women would often be midwives, and liable to suspicion if children died at birth, must also be noted and will be considered later.

THE BLACK MASS

The Black Mass, said to have been celebrated by some witches, has seized the popular imagination. Writers such as Huysmans did much to spread the belief that this ritual was common in France. Some modern dabblers, like Aleister Crowley, with more taste for the morbid than sense of humour, have tried to revive these ceremonies. Yet the performance of the Black Mass was far from being the invariable accusation made against the witches, except for vague statements that they had their own rites.

An American writer, Cotton Mather, said that witches in New England had their Diabolical Sacraments, imitating 'the Baptism and the Supper of our Lord'. It seems obvious, though this is disputed, that stories of a Black Mass were attempts at describing an unknown witches' rite, by simply reversing the ceremonial of the true Mass. Increase Mather reported that witches had a Sacrament and 'they had *Red Bread* and *Red Drink*'. Thus witchcraft was branded as not only pagan but blasphemous and heretical, with added touches of filth or cannibalism to make the description more horrific.

Part of the origins of the idea of the Black Mass may have come from the superstitious regard in which the elements of the sacrament were held. In the First Prayer Book of Edward VI it is said that before the time of the Reformation people tried to take away holy bread from the church for their own uses, magical or protective, but not necessarily for witchcraft.

The first witch recorded as having been accused in Ireland, Lady Alice Kyteler, was said to have a sacramental wafer hidden in a closet, and the wafer had the Devil's name stamped on it in place of that of Christ. One of the Lancaster witches was said to have been told to 'go to the church to receive the Communion (the next day after being Good Friday) and then not to eat the Bread the Minister gave him, but to bring it and deliver it to such a thing as should meet him on his way homewards'.[1]

Sprenger said that witches commonly performed their spells through the sacrament of the church and gives the following example: 'When a certain witch received the Body of Our Lord, she suddenly lowered her head, as is the detestable habit of women, placed her garment near her mouth, and taking the Body of the Lord out of her mouth, wrapped it in a handkerchief; and afterwards, at the suggestion of the Devil, placed it in a pot in which there was a toad.'[2]

All this may well refer to superstitious practices done for magical purposes. But some writers insist that there was a Black Mass at the Sabbath in which everything was done opposite to the Christian rite. 'Sometimes, again, they say Mass at the Sabbat. But I cannot write without horror of the manner in which it is celebrated; for he who is to say the office is clothed in a black cope with no cross upon it, and after putting the water in the chalice he turns his back to the altar, and then elevates, in place of the Host, a round of turnip coloured black, and then all the witches cry aloud: "Master, help us."'[3]

Summers makes much of the Satanic masses which were said to have been celebrated in Paris in 1680 for Madame de Montespan in order to secure her the supreme power. The royal mistress was said to have laid herself perfectly nude upon a black altar, black candles

---

[1] Potts, p. 67.
[2] *Malleus*, pp. 116 f.
[3] Boguet, p. 60.

were lit, the celebrant wore a chasuble bearing esoteric characters, the chalice was placed on the woman's belly, a child had its throat cut over the chalice and then the corpse was flung into an oven. In her confession Madame de Montespan's assistant declared that 2,500 babies had been killed in this way. The priest confessed that he had invoked Ashtaroth and Asmodeus, suggestive names from Biblical demonology.[1]

In Scotland, of course, the Presbyterian rite was supposed to be performed in reverse. There too, as we might expect, long sermons by the witches' leaders were commoner than elsewhere. In America, 'witches do say that they form themselves much after the manner of Congregational churches, and that they have a Baptism and a Supper, and Officers among them, abominably resembling those of our Lord'.[2]

However, much less is said about the Black Mass in the medieval confessions than about sacrifice in general. There were said to be blood sacrifices, for pricking or marking newly admitted witches. An animal was sacrificed, usually a dog, cat, or fowl. These had to be black else they were not liked, thought some writers. 'Such offering was not acceptable unless it was entirely black.'[3]

Murray says that the witches' feasts were joyful and pleasant. But this was not the opinion of all people at the time. 'All who have been honoured at his table confess that the banquets are so foul either in appearance or smell that they would easily cause nausea in the hungriest and greediest stomach . . . for drink he gives them in a dirty little cup wine like clots of black blood.'[4]

Shakespeare's description of the witches' brew in *Macbeth* is deliberately horrific, but it reflects the popular ideas:

> *Liver of blaspheming Jew,*
> *Gall of goat and slips of yew*
> *Sliver'd in the moon's eclipse,*
> *Nose of Turk and Tartar's lips,*
> *Finger of birth-strangled babe,*
> *Make the gruel thick and slab.*

Murray makes much of the sacrifice of the chief or god of the witches himself, linking it with ancient cults in which the god was

[1] *The Geography of Witchcraft*, 1927, pp. 432 f.
[2] C. Mather, *Wonders of the Invisible World*, 1862 edn., p. 160 f.
[3] N. Remy, *Demonolatry*, 1595, E.T. 1930, p. 40.
[4] Ibid., p. 57; *The God of the Witches*, pp. 120 f.

said to be killed ritually every year. She says that the rite was decadent when the records of witchcraft were made in the sixteenth and seventeenth centuries, and that a goat was substituted for the witch, but that the sacrifice was still made by fire.

In her book *The God of the Witches* she maintains that William Rufus, Thomas Becket, Joan of Arc, and Gilles de Rais were all divine victims, sacrificed by the adherents of the old religion, and hence they suffered mysterious deaths to which they were freely abandoned by the populace. And in *The Divine King in England* (1954) she makes the much more stupendous claim that all the kings of England down to 1648 were divine priest-kings who were either sacrificed themselves or preserved by the substitution of another victim. I believe that no professional historian has accepted such a radical re-writing of the lives of these historical personages.

OTHER ACTIVITIES

When the witch-fever increases almost any mischance can be attributed to the maleficence of witches. In modern Africa if children die, if men are impotent, if the harvests fail, if cattle do not bring forth, if the fowls do not lay, if the rains are late in coming, in short, if the times are out of joint then that is laid at the door of the nearest scapegoat, usually the witches.

In medieval and Renaissance Europe witches were not only thought to kill and eat children, or devote themselves to the worship of the Devil, but also to cause barrenness, abortion in pregnancy, and dryness in nursing mothers. Sprenger goes into coarse discussions as to whether witches can make men impotent and hebetate the powers of generation. Boguet says that they dry up the milk of nurses and cause all manner of ill 'of the stomach and the head and the feet, with colic, paralysis, apoplexy, leprosy, epilepsy, dropsy, strangury, etc'.[1]

Making wax images of their enemies was supposed to be a speciality of witches. Dalton said, 'They have often pictures of clay or wax (like a man, etc., made of such as they would bewitch) found in their house, or which they roast, or bury in the earth, that as the picture consumes, so may the parties bewitched consume.'[2] Old Demdike, the chief witch at Lancaster, said, 'the speediest way to take a man's

[1] Boguet, pp. 89 f.
[2] Ewen, p. 267.

life away by Witchcraft, is to make a Picture of Clay, like unto the shape of the person whom they mean to kill, and dry it thoroughly: and when they would have them to be ill in any one place more than another; then take a Thorn or Pin, and prick it in that part of the Picture you would so have to be ill.'[1] Murray regards this as the communal work of covens, but it is a worldwide practice of black magic and is often done by individuals.

Witches were believed to make horses go mad under their riders, to bring plagues of locusts and caterpillars, and to be responsible for as many evils of man and beast as there were plagues of Egypt. 'Alexia Violaea bore witness that, after running here and there like the Bacchantes with her companions, she used to scatter in the air a fine powder given to her by the Demon for that purpose; and that from this were generated caterpillars, bruchuses, locusts, and such pests of the crops in such numbers that the fields on all sides were at once covered with them.'[2]

Even the control of the weather was thought to be within their grasp, and the seasons were delayed at their word. Murray suggests that the witches were professional rain-makers. But their works were regarded as evil, not as good. The witch would moisten her broom in some dark liquid and twirl it round over the fields or towards the sky. Then would come those storms and showers of local rain and hailstones which can ruin the crops of particular districts.

Remy, an inquisitor who boasted of having burnt nine hundred people in fifteen years, insists that when trees and houses are struck by lightning they often bear the marks of demon's claws, and also there is frequently 'a most foul smell of sulphur'. He gives a naïve account of a magistrate who saw a storm brewing, 'there was a sudden flash of lightning, and he saw six oak trees near him torn up by the roots, while a seventh which still stood was all rent and torn as if by claws. . . . There came another crack of thunder, and he saw in the top of an oak near by a woman resting, who (as is probable) had been set down there from a cloud.' The magistrate accused the woman of being a witch, and of course she confessed.[3]

It was a mild thing for a witch to have familiar imps. She could cause sickness to men or cure it at will. She could bring love and

---

[1] Potts, p. 20.
[2] N. Remy, *Demonolatry*, p. 67.
[3] Ibid., p. 84.

hatred into the lives of her enemies, in much the same way as Puck did in *A Midsummer Night's Dream*. She could strike men with lightning, turn them into animals, or wither them up by a simple look. Pope Innocent VIII in his bull in 1484 declared that witches 'have slain infants yet in the mother's womb, as also the offspring of cattle, have blasted the produce of the earth, the grapes of the vine, the fruits of trees, nay, men and women, beasts of burden, herd-beasts, as well as animals of other kinds, vineyards, orchards, meadows, pastureland, corn, wheat, and all other cereals'.[1]

If men wanted an explanation of the ills of nature they found it in the diabolical activities of witches. They provided a scapegoat for the troubles of society, as the Jews had done at certain periods, and as they were to become again to the German Nazis in the twentieth century. Reginald Scot, who lived in the midst of the witch-fear and wrote so bravely against the whole superstition, gives the same picture. 'For if any adversity, grief, sickness, loss of children, corn, cattle, or liberty happen unto them; by and by they exclaim upon witches. As if there were no God in Israel that ordereth all things according to his will . . . but that certain old women here on earth, called witches, must needs be the contrivers of all men's calamities. . . . Insomuch as a clap of thunder, or a gale of wind is no sooner heard, but either they run to bells, or cry out to burn the witches.'[2]

CHARMS AGAINST WITCHCRAFT

Men and women in Europe used all manner of charms to preserve themselves from witchcraft, or to cure themselves when bewitched. Some of these were plainly pagan relics: eating a haggister or pie, using the smoke or a tooth of a corpse, anointing with the gall of a crow, sitting on a quill filled with quicksilver, spitting into your own bosom, and many less mentionable nostrums.

Then there were the Christian charms, of which a favourite was the Agnus Dei. This was a small cake, with a picture of a lamb and a flag on one side and Christ's head on the other. It had a hollow cavity in which was placed St. John's Gospel written on very fine paper. Another was a proof waistcoat, spun on Christmas night by a virgin, in the name of the Devil. There were incantations in the

---

[1] *Malleus,* p. xliii.
[2] Scot, p. 1.

many names of Christ, the four evangelists, and the three

More simple were the sign of the cross, holy water, Aves Paters, blessed oil, palms, candles, wax, and salt. Boguet decla. that 'salt is held in bitter abhorrence by the Devil, for salt is a symbol of immortality'. Water is also a great scourge of devils, 'demons whine and bark like dogs when we sprinkle the bodies of those whom they possess'.[1]

Anna Whittle, accused of witchcraft at Lancaster, gave this very Christian charm which would be used to cure bewitching:

> *Three Biters hast thou bitten,*
> *The Heart, ill Eye, ill Tongue;*
> *Three bitter shall be thy Boot,*
> *Father, Son, and Holy Ghost*
> *a God's name.*
> *Five Pater-nosters, five Aves, and a Creed,*
> *In worship of five wounds of our Lord.*[2]

Anna however was hanged. The Church seemed to have no completely infallible remedy against witchcraft. Some witches said that they had been deterred in their rounds by encountering houses where there were palms or blessed bread. Others said that the victims having protected themselves with the sign of the Cross they were only able to harm part of their harvest. But the more charms were multiplied the more were needed. And once the spell had been cast the victim could find no relief from men or saints unless the witch withdrew her power.

Some people had resort to curative sorcery, trying to cast out Satan by Satan. The doctors solemnly debated whether it was legitimate to use demonic power against the Devil. But the Church at length decided that this was unlawful, since 'there is war declared between man and the devils', and making a pact with the Father of Lies could only lead to more evil than ever. The conclusion was that the best way to deal with a witch was to beat her and make her release her prey. 'Threatening or beating witches is the best method of removing the spells cast by them,' declared the inhuman inquisitors.[3]

---

[1] Boguet, p. 58.
[2] Potts, pp. 42 f., spelling modernized.
[3] Guazzo, p. 124; Remy, p. 143.

CHAPTER 5

Witches and Devils

THE PEOPLE SAID TO BE WITCHES

Most of the people accused of being witches in Europe were women. Murray gives a list of some 700 accused witches in Britain from 1556 to 1718, of whom the great majority were women. The significance of their Christian names will be referred to later. Similarly, Ewen in his study of the witch trials in the English home circuit shows that of 200 convicted witches only fifteen were men. This corresponds to the records of Continental witches.[1]

This predominance of accused women is significant in view of the place of women in society. The emancipation of women in Europe would hardly have been possible while the Continent was still dominated by the fear of female witches. In many African societies today witchcraft is believed to be hereditary in the female line; a woman may pass on witchcraft to her daughters but not to her sons. There are to this day numerous African secret societies which seek to keep women in subjection to the males, and the witchcraft belief serves the same end. The women may be thought to find some escape from male domination in witch associations, and witch-hunts put them back in their place.

One might have thought that witches would have been people of wide influence and deep knowledge, perhaps engaged in some widespread plot to overthrow the order of society, as the fevered imagination of Summers suggests. One finds, on the contrary, that many of the accused were old women, ignorant peasants, whose physical powers were obviously far below the possibility of performing the

[1] *The Witch-cult*, pp. 255 ff.; Ewen, pp. 102 ff.

evil deeds ascribed to them. That great opponent of witchcraft, Reginald Scot, said, 'One sort of such as are said to be witches, are women which are commonly old, lame, blear-eyed, pale, foul, and full of wrinkles. . . . These miserable wretches are so odious unto all their neighbours, and so feared, as few dare offend them.'[1]

Of the two chief accused witches in the Lancaster trials one was 'a very old woman, about the age of fourscore years'. She was blind. The other was 'a very old withered and decrepit creature, her sight almost gone'.[2] The chief witch denounced by Matthew Hopkins at Manningtree was a one-legged old woman whose principal offence seems to have been that she kept pet animals.

In her first book Murray welcomed this evidence of witchcraft among the ignorant and women as a sign that they still held to the ancient pagan religion. 'The so-called conversion of Britain meant the conversion of the rulers only: the mass of the people continued to follow their ancient customs and beliefs with a veneer of Christian rites.'[3] In her later works, however, this writer has rather spoilt her case, in this and other directions, by maintaining now that the organization of witches which functioned for peasants influenced also the proceedings of the highest in the land, leading to the ritual sacrifice of the kings, despite the Church. Miss Murray cannot have it both ways.

It was a difficult thing for the persecutors to explain why many of the arrested women were so feeble, whereas they had been accused of the most diabolical and potent actions. The explanation was given that their evil deeds had been performed by the help of the Devil, but that, like the deceiver he is, he had abandoned his disciples in their moment of need. One of the inquisitors quotes this explanation. 'There are those who believe that, once witches are made prisoners and are fallen into the hands of Justice, the Devil deserts them and assists them no more.'[4] This was very convenient for the inquisitors, for it meant that they could handle these dangerous women without risk to themselves.

All demonologists agree that far more women than men had become caught in the toils of Satan and were his tools. The worst of the

---

[1] *The Discoverie of Witchcraft*, p. 4, spelling modernized.
[2] Potts, pp. 16, 33.
[3] *The Witch-cult*, p. 19; *The Divine King in England*, 1954, passim.
[4] Boguet, p. 132.

inquisitors, James Sprenger, gives pious thanks to God for saving the male sex from these sins and utters a most violent tirade against women. It is not pleasant to find his modern editor saying of these misogynic passages, 'I am not altogether certain that they will not prove a wholesome and needful antidote in this feministic age, when the sexes seem confounded'.[1]

Sprenger's reasons why women are chiefly seduced by witchcraft are ludicrous. 'They are more credulous . . . more impressionable . . . they have slippery tongues . . . she is more carnal than a man . . . they are more prone to abjure their faith . . . women also have weak memories. . . . As she is a liar by nature, so in her speech she stings while she delights us. . . . There was a defect in the formation of the first woman, since she was formed from a bent rib, that is, a rib of the breast, which is bent in a contrary direction to a man. And since through this defect she is an imperfect animal, she always deceives. . . . And all this is indicated by the etymology of the word; for *Femina* comes from *Fe* and *Minus*, since she is ever weaker to hold and preserve the faith.'[2] The ridiculous etymology has often been criticized, and it is matched by the intelligence that could put forth such arguments.

No doubt there were women who practised magic, in culling simples and mingling herbalism with incantations. The wise old women, with a store of knowledge of remedies, inextricably blended with superstition, are to be found in every land. But they have nothing to do with witchcraft or devil-worship. Only after the notions of the Devil and evil magic had been applied to all kinds of superstitious and semi-pagan practices were these women likely to suffer the accusation of witchcraft. Then the fact that they perhaps lived alone, lived longer than most men, and may have been jealous of young mothers (the mother-in-law problem), would render them liable to suspicion in the fever of witch-panic.

But were they not lusty young women, seeking the satisfaction of repressed desires? Sprenger suggests this, saying that 'a woman is more carnal than a man', and quoting Delilah and other wayward women from the Scriptures in support of his argument. He does not mention David or Solomon and many other men, with their poly-

[1] Introduction to the 1928 edition of the *Malleus Maleficarum,* p. xxxix.
[2] *Malleus,* pp. 43 f. Richard Bernard repeated these anti-feminine arguments in his *Guide to Grand Jurymen with respect to Witches,* London, 1627.

gamous and extra-marital adventures. But Ewen's detailed abstracts of indictments shows that many of the accused were widows. Others were married women, but we do not know whether they had children. Others were spinsters, of unrecorded ages. Since the fear of the jealousy of childless women is a potent factor in witchcraft accusations in Africa, it may have been so in Europe also.

THE DEVIL

Some of the accused were men, a small minority. In the witchcraft assemblies the chief figure was often said to be a man, a devil, or a male animal. In European witch trials the Devil played a prominent part, and this addition of Hebrew-Christian demonology distinguishes witchcraft in the Christian era from that of other lands, and makes its interpretation more complex.

While most of the witches were women they were supposed to have a male leader, called the Devil or Satan, who was Grand Master of the covens, in the manner of a masonic official. They 'first worship Satan, who appears to them now in the shape of a big black man and now as a goat; and to do him greater homage they offer him candles, which burn with a blue flame; then they kiss him on the shameful parts behind'.[1] Everything was supposed to be opposite to normal and decent worship.

The witches were believed to have sold their souls to the Devil, giving him their allegiance and becoming his factors for evil works. So Elizabeth Sowtherns at Lancaster declared that a spirit or devil had appeared to her and demanded her soul in return for giving her anything she wished. James Device confessed to the same court 'that the said Spirit did appear unto him sundry times, in the likeness of a Dog, and at every time most earnestly persuaded him to give him his soul absolutely . . . when he could not prevail with him to have his soul absolutely, as aforesaid, the said Spirit departed from him, then giving a most fearful cry and yell, and withall caused a great flash of fire to shew about him: which said Spirit did never after trouble this examinate'.[2]

An Essex woman, accused of witchcraft in Elizabeth's day, confessed that she had learnt the art of witchcraft from her grand-

[1] Boguet, p. 55.
[2] Potts, p. 79, spelling modernized.

mother Eve. 'When she taught it her, she counselled her to re-
nounce GOD and his word and to give of her blood to Satan (as she
termed it) which she delivered her in the likeness of a white spotted
Cat, and taught her to feed the said Cat with bread and milk, and
she did so, also she taught her to call it by the name of Satan and to
keep it in a basket. When this mother Eve had given her the Cat
Satan, then this Elizabeth desired first of the said Cat (calling it
Satan) that she might be rich and have goods, and he promised her
she should—asking her what she would have, and she said sheep
(for this Cat spoke unto her as she confessed in a strange hollow
voice, but such as she understood by use) and this Cat forthwith
brought sheep into her pasture.'[1]

The Continental inquisitors went into much more elaborate
detail over the supposed allegiance given by witches to the Devil.
Guazzo claimed that there were eleven ceremonials of profession of
witchcraft to be followed by the witches when they joined the Devil's
company, and other writers follow these suggestions. First the
witches deny the Christian faith and baptism and insult the Virgin
Mary. Then the Devil bathes them in a new mock baptism. Next
they forswear their old name and are given a new name. They deny
their godparents and are given new ones. They give the Devil a
piece of their clothing as a sign that they belong to him. They swear
allegiance to the Devil within a circle traced on the ground. Their
names are struck voluntarily out of the book of life and written in a
black book of death. They promise to sacrifice to the Devil, and
some vow to strangle a child for him every month. They must at
least make a gift to him every year, of a black colour. The Devil
places his mark on their body, especially on the private parts. They
make many vows, e.g. to insult the Eucharist, and to fly to the
Sabbath.[2]

Dr. Murray places practically the whole of her theory of witchcraft as an ancient cult upon the place of the Devil as god of the cult.
Her principal book begins with a discussion of the Devil as God.
She says, 'It is impossible to understand the witch-cult without
first understanding the position of the chief personage of that cult.
He was known to contemporary judges and recorders as the Devil,
and was called by them Satan, Lucifer, Beelzebub, the Foul Fiend,

[1] Ewen, p. 317, spelling modernized.
[2] *Compendium Maleficarum*, pp. 13 ff.

the Enemy of Salvation, and similar names appropriate to the Principle of Evil, the Devil of the Scriptures, with whom they identified him.'[1]

Murray continues by asserting that this view of the Devil as evil was far from the opinion of the witches themselves. 'To them this so-called Devil was God, manifest and incarnate; they adored him on their knees, they addressed their prayers to him, they offered thanks to him as the giver of food and the necessities of life, they dedicated their children to him, and there are indications that, like many another god, he was sacrificed for the good of his people.'

It seems unlikely, to say the least, that people should have confessed, as Murray admits that they are supposed to have done, to using such an opprobrious name as the Devil for their spiritual leader, unless this name were suggested to them by the inquisitors under the power of the confessional and the torture chamber. Are there no instances of other, more honourable, titles being used? Apparently not. All these names and prayers are from the evidence of the confessions recorded by the inquisitors. It is strange that the confessions should so distort the names of the leaders of the witches and yet still be considered reliable.

Further, if the witch-cult was a relic of ancient paganism, it is surprising that we have no mention of ancient European gods given to devils or deities in the confessions. All the names of the personages recorded are Biblical, ecclesiastical, or fanciful: Devil, Satan, Lucifer, Belial, Beelzebub, Mammon (Mamillion), Serpent, Asmodeus, Ashtaroth, Christsonday, Antecessor, Queen of Sabbath, Queen of Elfhame, Queen of Heb, Fancy, Tibb, Pretty. But we never find the old pagan gods Thor or Woden, Loki or Grendel, or the trolls. Nor are there to be found traces of Druidic or Celtic gods, or those of prehistoric fertility cults.

Similarly, it is curious that the names of the witches themselves are most frequently Biblical and saints' names. Murray recognizes this, and admits that in her list of some 700 British witches there is an 'entire absence of Saxon names', and also that 'Scandinavian names are not found'. She classifies the commonest under eight heads: Ann, Alice, Christian, Elizabeth, Ellen, Joan, Margaret, Mary. About the same proportions are found in Ewen's list of 200

[1] *The Witch-cult*, pp. 28 f.

convicted witches. Murray suggests that Mary should have been the commonest name. It does occur some forty times. But her list (with one exception) only begins in the sixteenth century, and in this post-Reformation era it was not to be expected that Mary would be very common.[1]

Murray also diligently lists names given to familiar imps, but they are either fanciful, such as Dainty, Filly, Greedigut, Lightfoot, Littleman, Makeshift, Mounsier, Robin, Tissy, Tiffin, and the like, or else they are consciously horrific, e.g. Jezebel, Satan, Christ, Thief of Hell, Roaring Lion.[2]

To return to the Devil, the confessions record words such as these from the witches: 'the said Devil or spirit bade her call him by the name of Mamillion'; 'we recognize you for our Master, our God, our Creator'; 'he asked me of whom I prayed, and I answered him to Jesus Christ, and he charged me then to pray no more to Jesus Christ, but to him the Devil.'[3]

We have seen that the Devil was said to come in various disguises to meet his followers, as a dog, a cat, or a goat. It has been suggested that perhaps the witches' leaders dressed themselves in animal skins. There may be a link here with the Mummers' dances. But there is also great play for the imagination, and many of these stories used the materials found in popular myth about animals or devils to compose a narrative of bewitching.

This may be illustrated from a pamphlet of 1613 entitled *Strange News out of Somersetshire*, where an account is given of a devil in the guise of a tiny headless bear. The bewitched woman's husband 'espied a thing come to the bed much like unto a Bear, but it had no head nor tail, half a yard in length, and half a yard in height: her husband seeing it come to the bed rose up, and took a joined stool and struck at the said thing, the stroke sounded as though he had struck upon a featherbed. . . . At last this Monster, which we suppose to be the Devil, did thrust the woman's head between her legs and so rolled her in a round compass like a hoop through three other chambers.' Eventually the Devil went away and then there was an angelic vision. 'She then thought she saw a child. So at the last they all looked out at the window: and lo they espied a thing like unto a

---

[1] *The Witch-cult*, pp. 255 f.
[2] Ibid., pp. 297 f.
[3] Ibid., pp. 29 etc.

Child, with a very brightshining countenance.' The woman recovered. Six people appended their names as witnesses to the
account, declaring that 'it is most true'.[1]

The Devil was said frequently to appear as a black man or black
animal. 'Satan appears to them now in the shape of a big black man
and now as a goat.'[2] He may be described as a tall black man, with a
black beard, at times with cloven feet, or riding on a black horse.
Black has been the colour of the Devil in Christian art. But the fear
of black people may also be expressed here, as occasionally devils
were described as Ethiopian or 'like two Indians'.[3] The superstition
still lingers in parts of England that if one meets a black man one
must turn right round, to shake off the bad luck.

In New England one bewitched person testified that in her sickness a little black-haired man came to her, telling her to set her hand
to a book which he showed her. 'She should be well and need fear
nobody if she would but sign it', and she was tormented with pains
when she refused to do so. Another said that he was told to sign a
book with ink like blood. The witches were supposed to call the
Devil a Black Man and said he resembled an Indian.

INCUBI AND SUCCUBI

Some of the confessions, and the role played therein by the Devil,
read like sexual orgies. The gross character of the records is in
strong contrast to the ascetic teaching of the Church at that time.
The inquisitors write blandly of women who 'had carnal relations
with Satan. . . . The Devil uses them so because he knows that
women love carnal pleasures.'[4] The Church's strictness may well
have brought about reactions, but not necessarily in witchcraft.
Some of the writings of the inquisitors are lurid examples of porno-
graphy, and their authors clearly have 'the fascination of their
repressions'.

From some of the accounts of witchcraft, and the role played
therein by the Devil, one would assume that communal sexual
orgies took place at the Sabbaths. One writer asserts that this is the

[1] P. Simpson, *Studies in Elizabethan Drama*, chapter on 'The Headless
Bear'.
[2] Boguet, p. 55.
[3] *The Witch-cult*, pp. 42 f.
[4] Boguet, p. 29.

very object of the witches' meetings. 'The purpose, both of witches and wizards, in the midnight sabbaths that take place, is none other but that infamous intercourse . . . connexion with the Demon, whether Incubus or Succubus (which is, properly speaking, Demoniality).'[1] This writer gives obscene details of debauches between demons and witches. But he naïvely says that none of these can ever be witnessed by outsiders, since the Devil is invisible to all but the witch herself.

Some of the chief figures that appear in these lascivious accounts are the incubi and succubi who were ancient European mythological figures. A succubus was believed to be a female demon who had relations with sleeping men, by which certain physical phenomena were accounted for. The incubus was a male demon who preyed upon sleeping women; the name was later given to nightmares. 'Almost all the Theologians and learned Philosophers are agreed, and it has been the experience of all times and all nations, that witches practise coition with demons, the men with Succubus devils and the women with Incubus devils.'[2]

The existence of these creatures was recognized by law in the Middle Ages. Later Milton acknowledged their diabolical character when he wrote of

> *Belial, the dissolutest Spirit that fell,*
> *The sensualest, and, after Asmodai,*
> *The fleshliest Incubus.*[3]

The celibate inquisitors take a morbid interest in these sexual questions. Sprenger and Boguet debate whether children can be generated by incubi and succubi, whether witches copulate with devils, and whether witches can obstruct the venereal act or deprive men of their virile organ. Others seem much concerned with the lechery of the incubi and the types of people most afflicted by them; celibate nuns appear much troubled.

Murray maintains that all this adds weight to her theory of witch-craft as a fertility cult. But much was in European mythology already, indeed some of the fantasies are worldwide. Modern psychology would have a great deal to say about the causes of these

---

[1] Sinistrari, pp. 2, 93.
[2] Guazzo, p. 30.
[3] *Paradise Regained*, ii, ll. 150-2.

fantasies without the necessity of postulating a cult. Boguet goes into crude detail to explain the difference of the relations of women with men and that with devils. But the further he plunges the less probable it seems. The Devil may use the corpse of a man that has been hanged in order to have relations with a witch. Or he may appear in the form of a dog, a cat, or even a fowl. And he solemnly quotes the case of a dog found in a convent who was obviously a devil in disguise.[1]

WITCHES' MARKS

The demon was supposed to give a Devil's Mark or Witch's Stigma to his followers, as a sign that they belonged to his fraternity. Some African witches today are believed to have a witchcraft-substance in their bodies, which is discoverable by autopsy.

So it was authoritatively laid down, 'all witches have a mark some on the shoulder, some on the eyelid, some on the tongue or the lip, and others on the shameful parts; in short it is said that there is no witch who is not marked in some part of her body.'[2] Hare marks and any bodily patches were taken as clear signs of witchcraft. Any marks that looked like teeth-marks were said to be the Devil's own imprinted in the flesh. So Boguet stripped Françoise Secretain naked to find her mark. He did not find anything, but as soon as her hair had all been shaved off the poor woman trembled violently and began to confess.

In England Michael Dalton laid down that for purposes of suckling their familiar the witches had 'some big or little teat upon their body, and in some secret place, where he sucketh them. And besides their sucking, the Devil leaveth other marks upon their body, sometimes like a blue or red spot, like a flea biting; sometimes the flesh sunk in and hollow. . . . And these Devil's marks be insensible and being pricked will not bleed, and be often in their secretest parts, and therefore require diligent and careful search.'[3]

The 'little teat' was believed to be a supernumerary nipple for which bodies were searched. Matthew Hopkins was a great seeker for this. He 'bid them go to another Witch, who was thereupon appre-

---

[1] Boguet, pp. 31 ff.
[2] Boguet, p. 128.
[3] Ewen, p. 267.

hended, and searched by women who had for years known the Devil's marks, and found to have three teats about her, which honest women have not'.[1] From these teats the witches were supposed to nourish their familiar imps with milk or blood. At Leicester we read, 'Searching the old witch publicly before a great number of good women in their town, they deposed there were found in her secret parts two white pieces of flesh like paps, and some swore they were like the teats of an ewe, and some like the paps of a cat.'[2]

Cotton Mather said that at the trial of Bridget Bishop in Salem 'a jury of women found a preternatural teat upon her body; but upon a second search, within three or four hours, there was no such thing to be seen'. But other ministers in Connecticut declared that bodily marks 'ought not to be allowed as evidence against them without the approbation of some able physician'.[3]

Dr. Murray thinks that the devil's marks may have been some sort of tattoo, but of course she rejects the idea of extra teats being due to the Devil. She quotes medical evidence to show that seven or eight per cent of people have some kind of extra teat growth.[4]

The Devil was also supposed to give his followers a mark or spot which was insensible to pain, and finding this anaesthetized place was to find a sure sign of guilt. In Scotland, especially, witch-prickers prodded, scratched, and blooded many people, not uncommonly with fatal results. Scottish experts were also employed in the north of England to prick suspected women. One such, 'in sight of all the people, laid her body naked to the waist, with her clothes over her head, by which fright and shame, all her blood contracted into one part of her body, and then he ran a pin into her thigh, and then suddenly let her coats fall, and then demanded whether she had nothing of his in her body but did not bleed, but she being amazed replied but little, then he put his hand up her coats, and pulled out the pin and set her aside as a guilty person, and child of the Devil'.[5]

People who had boils, pustules, warts, or other growths, as many people had in those days, were obvious prey. One woman clearly

[1] *The Discovery of Witches*, p. 50.
[2] Ewen, p. 316.
[3] J. M. Taylor, *The Witchcraft Delusion in Colonial Connecticut*, p. 74 f.; C. Mather, *Wonders of the Invisible World*, p. 137 f.
[4] *The Witch-cult*, p. 90.
[5] Ewen, p. 63.

had a rupture which she said came from carrying water, but the searchers found a little hole in it 'as if it had lately been sucked, and upon the straining of it there issued out white milky matter'.[1] The conclusion was drawn that she had been suckling imps.

Hopkins had to face the criticism that the marks he found were warts, natural excrescences, piles, or scars from child-bearing. He defended himself by saying that they were far distant from any usual place where such growths are to be found (though it is plain from the cases quoted above that this was not so), and in any case he said that such spots were commonly insensible and felt no pain when a pin or an awl were thrust into them. The conclusion was that the Devil had made these marks.

Other signs of witchcraft given seriously by Boguet are that a witch is unable to shed tears in the presence of a judge, and that her eyes are continually bent on the ground before him. His chief accused woman used a rosary and was most devout in her prayers (not a devotee of a pagan god). But Boguet declared that the cross on her rosary was imperfect, and so she was really opposed to Christianity despite her fervent and orthodox prayers.

PACTS WITH THE DEVIL

Admission ceremonies into the covens of witches were said to be the opposite of those into the Christian Church. They were supposed to comprise an introduction to the society, taking of vows, renunciation of past faith, a covenant, a baptism, and reception of the Devil's mark. Often these are not mentioned in the records, but it was believed that the witch had abandoned Christ for the service of the Devil. 'Satan forms a league with his followers against Heaven, and plots the ruin of the human race. He makes these wretched creatures repeat their renunciation of God, Christ, and Baptism, and renew the solemn oath they have taken never to speak of God, the Virgin Mary, or the Saints except in the way of mockery and derision.'[2]

Sprenger also gives a most dogmatic description of the diabolical covenant. 'The devil asks whether she will abjure the Faith, and forsake the holy Christian religion and the worship of the Anomalous

---

[1] Ewen, p. 62.
[2] Boguet, p. 59.

Woman (for so they call the Most Blessed Virgin MARY), and never venerate the Sacraments; and if he finds the novice or disciple willing, then the devil stretches out his hand, and so does the novice, and she swears with upraised hand to keep that covenant.'[1]

The notion of denial of baptism was present later in Protestant countries where the cult of the Virgin Mary had disappeared. King James I in his *Daemonologie* said, 'It is a certain rule Witches deny their Baptism when they make Covenant with the Devil, water being the sole element thereof, and when they are heaved into the water it refuseth to receive them but suffers them to float.' The rejection of witches by pure water, because they had abjured their baptism, was the theory behind the duckings to which many of them were subjected.

It was unlucky for women in Protestant countries, too, that saying prayers in the forbidden Latin could also be regarded as due to a pact with the Devil. Mother Waterhouse (who had given her granddaughter the cat called Satan, and who was hanged in Elizabeth's reign) was asked what prayers she said. 'She answered the Lord's Prayer, the Ave Maria, and the belief, and then they demanded whether in Latin or in English, and she said in Latin, and they demanded why she said it was not in English but in Latin, seeing that it was set out by public authority and according to God's word that all men should pray in English and mother tongue that they best understand, and she said that Satan would at no time suffer her to say it in English, but at all times in Latin.'[2]

Miss Murray declares that the devils had made written pacts with the witches, some of which pacts are supposed to have fallen into the hands of the Continental inquisitors. But she admits that 'unfortunately the exact wording is never given in the records', while in Britain 'there is no record of such a contract having been brought into court as evidence against an accused person'.[3] She supposed that the Devil always managed to destroy these contracts. But it is strange that there is absolutely no written material of any kind originating from these diabolical rites and pacts. Clearly the devils were not illiterate, if they wrote out their pacts. But just as the Sabbaths could never be witnessed, nor could the pacts ever be seen by a non-witch. The

---

[1] *Malleus*, pp. 99 ff.
[2] Ewen, p. 324.
[3] *The God of the Witches*, pp. 106 f.

literature of witchcraft is wholly the product of the persecutors. So there is no material or objective evidence whatever of the witches' meetings or contracts with the Devil.

Murray stresses the mentions in the records of some witches dying impenitent and apparently unashamed of the Devil's service. Some were said to die very stubborn and refractory without remorse, others were never heard to pray or to ask pardon of God for their offences. Two in Northampton 'being desired to say their Prayers, they both set up a very loud Laughter, calling for the Devil to come and help them in such a Blasphemous manner as is not fit to mention'. The sheriff was properly shocked and had them executed without further delay.[1]

One cannot rely on the records for these statements, for they clearly show the wish to prove that the accused either were guilty and stubborn, or else were converted to the true faith at the end. Mother Waterhouse is said to have 'asked mercy of God, and all the world forgiveness and thus she yielded up her soul, trusting to be in joy with Christ her Saviour, which dearly had bought her with his most precious blood'.[2]

WITCHES AND FAIRIES

The European belief in witches was comparable with that in fairies. The Sabbath dances were similar to the fairy revels in the popular mind. 'Then no planets strike, no fairy takes, nor witch hath power to charm.'

The modern notion of fairies as wholly good and pleasant little creatures is not the whole picture. They could do good, it was thought, and the fairy godmother stands in contrast to the wicked old witch. Some of them had pet names, Puck and Robin Goodfellow being among the most popular. But fairies were often mischievous too. They could turn the milk sour, deceive people with fairy gold, and were not above stealing human babies and taking them away to live with them in fairyland.

One opinion is that the belief in fairies in Europe may be derived from the memory of smaller races which inhabited Europe in prehistoric times and who were gradually driven to the less accessible

[1] *The Witch-cult*, pp. 26 f.
[2] Ewen, p. 324.

parts of the Continent. Murray suggests that the witches practised the fairy cult which had survived down the ages.

On the other hand the family likeness between fairies and pixies and the elves, dwarfs, and trolls of earlier European mythology can hardly be denied. Popular imagination filled the world with all manner of invisible beings, indeed they helped to explain many of the curious happenings of life. Still today in Africa and many other lands people believe firmly in small beings who live inside trees, or underground, who fly like birds and whistle like the wind, and play all manner of pranks or more serious tricks on unsuspecting men. But they are nothing to do with witches.

Whatever the origins of the European beliefs, there is undoubtedly much similarity between the activities ascribed to fairies and witches. Both witches and fairies were believed to travel through the air, headed by a Hecate or a Queen of Sabbath. Both must end their revels by cockcrow. They were supposed to kill cattle by uncanny means (perhaps our more prosaic foot and mouth disease), steal the substance of milk and corn, and ride horses so furiously in the night that in the morning the poor beasts had the shivers and perhaps died. Child-stealing is associated with both, but the fairies were not cannibalistic. Both groups might be linked with the wise women who appear at the births of important people.

The medieval church and later Protestants included witches and fairies under the same ban. Some witches under trial were accused of resorting to the Fairy Queen, or the Queen of Elfhame, and of using elf-arrows. Shakespeare artificially devotes one play to witches and another to fairies, and a third to a magician, but it is clear that he did not know much about them.

CHAPTER 6

The Confessions

The evidence for the activities of European witches in past ages rests mainly upon the accusations made against them, and the confessions supposed to have been extracted from them. Those modern writers who think that witchcraft in Europe was a survival of an ancient cult, rely upon the witches' confessions for the details of the Sabbaths and the orgies held with devils or animals.

That many women were convicted solely upon their own admissions, made under pressure, is quite indubitable, though scarcely an ideal method of judicial procedure. That the witches' ideas were derived from the prevailing current beliefs seems likely, though this point is disputed. But the inquisitors were most anxious to obtain confession from the witch's own mouth. 'Common justice demands that a witch should not be condemned to death unless she is convicted of her own confession.'[1] Confession proved that the inquisitors were right and were doing a noble work in saving society from this spiritual evil.

It is true that the witch-hunters adduced other lines of evidence in addition to confessions. But it was not thought possible to get independent outside testimony to the witches' orgies, since they were secret and could only be described by members of their society. So Sir James Altham told the jury at York, 'against these people you may not expect such direct evidence, since all their works are works of darkness, no witnesses are present to accuse them'. And sceptical Reginald Scot declared, 'I believe never an honest man in England

---

[1] *Malleus*, pp. 222 f.

nor in France, will affirm that he hath seen any of these persons, that are said to be witches, do so' (i.e. eat human flesh).[1]

On the Continent Sinistrari maintained that 'there can be no witness of that crime, since the Devil, visible to the witch, escapes the sight of all beside'. And Boguet admits that 'witches work at night and in secret, and a clear proof of such deeds is, as the Jurisconsult [Bodin] somewhere says, impossible'.[2] Without external evidence then, the judges proceeded to conjecture, 'In the crime of witchcraft it is lawful at times to proceed on the strength of those indubitable indications and conjectures, neither more nor less, which are applicable to other atrocious crimes committed in secret'.

The sickness or death of the witches' victims whose vital powers had been devoured at the Sabbaths was formerly supposed to constitute a proof of their activity. The advocates of the witch-cult today do not take this line of evidence very seriously, preferring to believe, contrary to the opinion of past ages, that the Sabbaths were pleasant feasts and not cannibalistic orgies. But that witches bewitched their victims who languished and died, used to be taken as the strongest external proof of their evil ways.

Boguet gives other lines of procedure in addition to obtaining a confession. The confession itself should be followed by torture, to prevent the witch recanting. Then association with a known witch is a sign of witchcraft. So is possession of 'certain powders and unguents'. Common rumour is sufficient ground for accusation; lying and discrepancies in the defence are signs of guilt. Then there are the 'light indications' which are warrant for torture, such as keeping the eyes turned to the ground, inability to shed tears, bearing a devil's mark, falling easily into a rage, having no cross on her rosary or a defective one, asking to be re-baptized since the witch had renounced her baptism to join the Devil's gang, being a child of a witch. The scrupulous Boguet, who was a Chief Justice, says that if the accused persists in denial, even after torture, he must be released. But he should not be let go completely lest he fall into the Devil's clutches again, but only 'subject to being again called for trial'.[3] Really there was no point in denial, one was never likely to be free again.

---

[1] Potts, p. 185; Scot, pp. 18 f.
[2] *Demoniality*, pp. 93 f.; Boguet, pp. 228, 236.
[3] Boguet, pp. 220 ff.

THE MATTER OF THE CONFESSIONS

The inquisitors were determined that the accused should confess and thereby prove their guilt. 'If the Judge can draw no confession from the accused he must confine him in a very narrow and dark cell; for it has been proved that the hardship of prison very often impels witches to confess, especially when they are young.'[1] When one thinks of the state of prisons in those days, it is not surprising that so many did confess, but rather that a minority did not. Even in England, where there was no Inquisition and no burning, Ewen says that the accused had to plead and must not remain silent, for fear of punishment by death by the *peine forte et dure* reserved for the worst criminals.[2] Increase Mather in New England said that 'a free and voluntary confession . . . is a sufficient ground of conviction'.

To the unwarned reader the confessions of the witches would be most startling. Some are plainly impossible, such as flying through the air or changing into animal form. Others read like accounts of real events: the Sabbaths, organization, devils, and so on. But how far were these details suggested to the witches, or put out by them as a means of escape from torture? And so how valuable are the records that have come down to us?

The *Malleus Maleficarum* contains many accounts purporting to have come verbatim from the lips of witches, from which one can choose at random. One is said to have declared: 'The following is the manner in which I was seduced. It is first necessary that, on a Sunday before the consecration of Holy Water, the novice should enter the church with the masters, and there in their presence deny Christ, his Faith, baptism, and the whole Church. And then he must pay homage to the Little Master, for so and not otherwise do they call the devil.' Another reported, 'In the diocese of Basel, at the town of Dann, a witch who was burned confessed that she had killed more than forty children, by sticking a needle through the crown of their heads into their brains, as they came out from the womb.' Again a woman professed, 'When the devil has come, we sacrifice to him a black cock at two cross-roads, throwing it up into the air; and when

[1] Boguet, p. 217.
[2] Ewen, p. 28.

the devil has received this, he performs our wish and stirs up the air.'
Again, 'Saying that for more than eighteen years she had given her
body to an Incubus devil.' And again, 'I was in my house, and at
midday a familiar came to me and told me to go with a little water on
to the field.'[1]

The most detailed account of the testimony given at a witch trial in
England is that of the Lancaster witches in 1612. It was supposed to
be based upon the witches' 'Own Examinations, Confessions, and
Evidence at the Bar'. Yet no sign is given as to how the confessions
were obtained, what questions were asked the accused, and in short
no verbatim account of the interrogation. Professor Notestein points
out that despite the apparent weight of the evidence, most of it echoes
the first narrative, and the various testimonies lack the characteristic
differences which would mark out their independence. The most
impressive story is that of secret meetings at Malking Tower, where
feasts were held and plots made against society. This begins to look
like treasonable deeds and diabolical orgies, but Notestein comments,
'The concurring evidence in the Malking Tower story is of no more
compelling character than that to be found in a multitude of Continental stories of witch gatherings which have been shown to be the
outcome of physical and mental pressure'.[2] This trial will be examined in more detail in the next chapter.

Other English trials were sometimes handicapped through lack of
confessions. These were difficult to obtain since torture, in the main,
was forbidden. At Northampton in 1612 a certain Master Avery
was 'possessed' and even succeeded in reproducing his convulsions in court. After considerable flurry and search fourteen people
were accused; some endured the water ordeal and most of them
were hanged, but they protested their innocence up to the very
end.[3]

One might multiply examples of confessions, of flying witches in
Somerset, or meetings with the devil at Rocquaine Castle in Guern-
sey where witchcraft was believed in particularly strongly, and so on.
There is no need here to accumulate stories, they have been carefully
amassed by Murray in her *Witch-cult*. Not the material, but the
interpretation to be placed upon it, is the matter at issue.

---

[1] *Malleus*, pp. 148, 149, 166, ect.
[2] *A History of Witchcraft in England*, p. 124.
[3] Ibid., pp. 130 ff.

EXAMINATION AND LEADING QUESTIONS

Many of the methods used in the examination of witches would not be admissible in modern courts of law, at least in the western world. Guilt was assumed from the outset in the majority of cases. The witches had been arrested upon accusation, public or private; they were often taken by a hostile crowd to the inquisitors or magistrates, as likely as not being ducked or manhandled on the way.

Normally the accused was not allowed to know the names of witnesses, 'because such a person has many evil accomplices'. If the names were given the order was arranged so as to mislead. The witch might be disabled in his defence, by being enticed into saying that he knew the accusers or even that they were his friends. Proof of their malice would then be revealed and upheld.[1]

The accused was constantly plied with questions; these were shuffled and repeated so that he might 'be very easily trapped into contradicting himself'.[2] His countenance was closely watched, and any mutterings observed. He could be examined in public or in private. He could be stripped and shaved, to discover spells and reveal the Devil's mark.

Witches were often not allowed counsel, or if one was permitted then it must be one chosen by the inquisitors and not by the witch. It can have been little comfort to be defended by the nominee of an inquisitor, for such an advocate had been known to extract a confession in confidence and then he 'revealed it to the Judge'. The counsel's task was usually confined to advising the witch to confess in his own interest, or possibly warning him how to disable the witnesses. The *Malleus* discusses what the advocate is to do 'when the names of the witnesses are withheld both from himself and his client'. He could but exercise patience. The advocate might himself become liable to excommunication if he made undue difficulties in the trial, for aiding and abetting a witch was even more serious than being a witch, and he was warned of these dangers when undertaking the defence.[3]

Appeals were refused if at all possible, as 'frivolous and worthless'.

---

[1] *Malleus*, p. 217.
[2] Boguet, p. 214. Many questions were prepared and demanded a single 'yes'. Lea, *Witchcraft*, p. 1169.
[3] Boguet, p. 218; *Malleus*, p. 218.

One could appeal to Rome against improper procedure, but the inquisitor could refuse this, or avoid it by getting someone else to sit in his place when the appeal was made.

The testimony of one witness was sufficient to bring condemnation. A judge at Leicester hanged nine women on the testimony of a boy who declared that they had bewitched him, and a further group would have been executed but for the intervention of the king. It appears that there were professional witnesses, as well as witch-finders and prickers.[1]

Clearly leading questions were often put to the witches, so that many of their apparently free confessions were made in a set and expected form. This helps to explain the remarkable similarity of many of the confessions. Hopkins was accused of putting this type of question: 'You have four Imps, have you not? She answers affirmatively, Yes. . . . Are not their names so and so? Yes, saith she. Did you not send an Imp to kill my child? Yes, saith she.' Hopkins denies that he used this method, but he suggests that the magistrates did not question the accused sufficiently about their supposed confessions.[2]

In the *Malleus* we read this sort of interrogation. 'I went out at the town gate, and found the devil standing under a tree. The judge asked her, under which tree; and she said, Under that one opposite that tower, pointing it out. Asked what she did under the tree, she said, The devil told me to dig a little hole and pour water into it. Asked whether they sat down together, she said, I sat down but the devil stood up. Then she was asked with what words and in what manner she had stirred the water.'[3]

Witches were asked if they had denied their baptism, if they had a meeting with the Devil, how many were there, what were their names. Sprenger gives some of the questions that a judge must ask: 'Let her be asked why the common people fear her. . . . Let her be asked what harm that person had done her, that she should have used such words to threaten him with injury. . . . Asked why she was seen in the fields or in the stable with the cattle, and touching them. . . . Asked why she touched a child, and afterwards it fell sick. . . . Also she was asked what she did in the fields at the times of a tempest. . . . Why having

[1] Notestein, p. 140.
[2] *The Discovery of Witches*, p. 58.
[3] *Malleus*, p. 149.

one or two cows, she had more milk than her neighbours. . . . Why she persists in a state of adultery or concubinage; for although this is beside the point, yet such questions engender more suspicion than would be the case with a chaste and honest woman.'[1]

Witches were often forced to declare themselves as such, even against their will, so that the victims of bewitching might be released from their pains. At trials in Huntingdonshire in 1593, the accused was forced to repeat, 'As I am a witch and consenting to the death of Lady Cromwell, I charge thee, come out of her'. At these words the sick person is said to have recovered from her fits, a cure that had not been effected as long as the accused denied the bewitching. The witch's father was also constrained to use the same words. At first he refused, but the judge warned him that in refusing he was endangering his own life. He confessed.[2]

Witnesses were also primed with suitable names for accusation. At Northampton, Mistress Belcher having been ill for a long time was told that her malady was due to witchcraft. It was not known who was responsible and so a list of names of supposed witches was reeled off to her. She seemed to be impressed by the name of Joan Brown. 'Hath she done it?' she asked. The name was repeated, and from then on she believed Joan to be guilty. Joan was hanged.[3]

CONFESSION UNDER TORTURE

That many of the confessions were fabrications becomes clearer than ever in the many cases of torture. Some witches indeed confessed freely, even too anxiously. We shall refer to their psychology later. Many others were obdurate. Their very stubbornness in refusing to confess was taken as a mark of the Devil, who is known to be taciturn. They needed the softening influence of the rack and the boot, or at least of pricking and ducking.

Although Boguet says that the judge must avoid torture where possible, yet this is because witches were supposed to carry charms which prevent them from feeling pain. But he gives a number of counts in which torture should be used. And Sprenger solemnly dis-

[1] *Malleus*, pp. 212 f.
[2] Notestein, pp. 49 f.
[3] *Ibid.*, p. 130.

cusses the method of sentencing a witch to torture and how long it is to be continued.[1]

By far the worst tortures were perpetrated by the Inquisition on the Continent. A burgomaster at Bamberg was racked and screwed so cruelly that the very executioner implored him, 'Sir, I beg you for God's sake confess something, whether it be true or not, for you cannot endure the torture which you will be put to, and even if you bear it all, yet you will not escape.' The poor wretch followed this advice and asked for a day's respite to prepare his confession. He produced a story of a witches' meeting, in the classic form, and when threatened with further torture he added the names of his supposed accomplices.

Writing to his daughter Veronica the burgomaster told her the true story. 'Now, dear child, here you have all my confession, for which I must die. And they are sheer lies and made-up things, so help me God. For all this I was forced to say through fear of the torture which was threatened beyond what I had already endured. For they never leave off with the torture till one confesses something; be he never so good, he must be a witch.' In the margin he wrote that others had confessed under the same pressure. 'Six have confessed against me at once . . . all false, through compulsion, as they have told me, and begged my forgiveness in God's name before they were executed.'[2]

Very often these confessions were extorted with the promise of deliverance from death. The judge could promise mercy, and make a mental reservation that he meant mercy to society and not to the witch.

In 1460 there was the notorious case at Arras in which eminent people were accused of witchcraft. Eventually they confessed and were in due course brought out to the scaffold, and hats put on their heads showing them worshipping the Devil. After a sermon, the inquisitor read out their confessed descriptions of the Sabbath and asked them if these were correct, and they all individually assented. They were then handed over to the secular power for death, their goods going part to the seigneur and part to the bishop. Immediately they shrieked out that they had been cruelly deceived, that they had been promised a light pilgrimage if they would confess, and burning

[1] Boguet, pp. 218 f.; *Malleus*, pp. 223–7.
[2] Lea, *Witchcraft*, pp. 1175 f.

if they persisted in denial. Especially they loaded with reviling the advocate who had lured them on by false promises of freedom. They cried that they had never been to the Sabbath, and kept up their protestations of innocence and appeals to the people to pray for them until the flames had silenced their voices for ever.[1]

Some brave spirits resisted even torture, and refused to admit any of the crimes with which they were charged. One of the Arras men, having resisted all forms of torture, the rack, mock-hanging and mock-drowning, should have been released. But he was then told that he had broken jail and so would be confined to prison for twenty years on a diet of bread and water. This broke his spirit at last, and he begged and wept for mercy. He was the only one who survived, to be restored finally as innocent and his rights maintained by the Parlement.

The accused were often only too anxious to conform to all the requirements of the judge. They knew that if they persisted tortures would be endless, and so they clung to the confessions once they had been made. When the confession was read over at the formal tribunal or the gallows they usually adhered to it. For the accused persons were anxious to put themselves right with the Church, in time and in eternity. The last sacraments could be administered to them if they were repentant (though Boguet disputes this). But refusal to confess might bring them complete excommunication. Thenceforth their lot would be deemed to be everlasting damnation.

Belief in the truth of the confessions was obligatory on the laity. They were clear proof of the guilt of the accused and of the Church's doctrine. To doubt the confessions laid one open to strong suspicion, if not to charges of heresy. Sprenger insists on this. An accused person is to be asked, 'Whether he believes that there are such things as witches. . . . If they deny it, they must be questioned as follows: Then are they innocently condemned when they are burned? And he or she must answer.'[2]

The confessions proved that the Church was right, and so exculpated her from charges of cruelty. She was but defending the faithful from the most insidious spiritual dangers. The Communist confessions today appear to have a similar purpose.

[1] Lea, *Middle Ages*, pp. 522 ff. Yet Murray seriously quotes one of these 'confessions' as evidence of Satanic practices.
[2] *Malleus*, p. 212.

Torture was used in Scotland in the early years of James VI. Ropes were tightened round the witch's head, finger-nails pulled off, needles inserted, and application made of 'the most severe and cruel pain in the world, called the bootes'. But many withdrew their confessions after the torture was removed.[1]

Torture was against common law in England, although it was occasionally used for workers in the magic arts. It was not applied to witchcraft, and there is no record of a woman suffering from it. Yet threats were made to produce confessions, and we have seen what an ordeal the witch-pricking might be. The swimming test, a survival of the ancient water ordeal, was long in use. The royal demonologist, James I of England, advocated this because 'the water shall refuse to receive them in her bosom, that have shaken off them the sacred waters of Baptism'. The accused witch was stripped and hands and feet tied crosswise, often to a ducking-stool.

The agonies of sleeplessness were as well understood in those days as in these enlightened times. Some witches were made to walk about for days and nights and kept from food. Hopkins was expert at this. 'Having taken the suspected witch, she is placed in the middle of a room upon a stool or table, cross-legged, or in some other uneasy posture, to which if she submits not, she is then bound with cords; there she is watched and kept without meat or sleep for the space of 24 hours for within that time they shall see her imp come and suck.'[2]

At Framlingham Hopkins arrested an old vicar, over eighty years of age, and it was later reported of his treatment, 'that they kept him awake several nights together, and ran him backwards and forwards about the room, until he was out of breath; then they rested him a little and then ran him again: and thus they did for several days and nights together, till he was weary of his life, and was scarce sensible of what he said or did'.[3]

The witches, then, confessed to all manner of horrible, disgusting, and impossible things. If all society said that these things were true, who were they to deny them? Many of them were so deranged by prolonged torture that they half-believed the truth of what was said about them, by so many witnesses and doctors of theology. Others might think that they had bad dreams about their neighbours. Per-

[1] Ewen, p. 65.
[2] Ibid., p. 66; Hopkins, p. 55
[3] Notestein, p. 176.

haps their souls had been away from their bodies when they we̲ṟ̲
asleep and had got them into mischief. Perhaps they had jealous and
spiteful thoughts about their enemies, even if they had not actually
used poisons or eaten their children.

It is worth noting what was said by Thomas Ady in *A Candle in
the Dark* (1655, p. 126): 'Let any man that is wise, and free from
prejudice, go and hear but the Confessions that are so commonly
alleged, and he may see with what catching, and cavelling, what
thwarting and lying, what flat and plain knavery, these confessions
are wrung from poor innocent people, and what monstrous additions and multiplications are afterwards invented to make the matter
seem true, which yet is most damnably false.'

DID WITCHES REALLY ATTEND SABBATHS?

The confessions declare that witches met in Sabbaths, during the
night, and caroused and danced till dawn. Nevertheless it was early
recognized that some, at least, of the witches were deluded in their
accounts of nocturnal journeys. In the life of St. Germain it was
written that 'several women declared that they had been present at
a banquet, and all the time they slumbered and slept, as several
persons attested'.[1]

In the *Compendium Maleficarum*, published in 1608, dislike is expressed of the new scepticism that was coming in with the Reformation. 'Many of the followers of Luther and Melancthon maintained
that witches went to their Sabbats in imagination only, and that
there was some diabolical illusion in the matter, alleging that their
bodies had often been found lying at home in their beds and have
never moved from them.'[2]

Another account from the inquisitors themselves tells of a woman
who voluntarily surrendered herself for examination, and said that
bolts and bars could not keep her from flying to the Sabbath. She
was locked in a cell and watched through a secret hole all night.
She at once threw herself on the bed and stretched out rigid, becoming completely insensible and remaining so all night. The inquisitors entered and tried to wake her, gently at first and then
roughly. She was pulled and pinched but remained insensible. A

[1] Lea, *Middle Ages*, iii, 495 n.
[2] Guazzo, p. 33.

lighted candle was placed near her naked foot until the flesh was scorched, but she never moved. In the morning she came back to her senses and told the inquisitors in detail of all that she had done at the Sabbath, the place, the people present, the ritual, and all that had been said and done. Then she complained of a hurt on her foot.[1]

The inquisitors were bound to recognize that in some cases, at least, the accused person had never been to a Sabbath when she declared that she had done so. This raised a theological problem of the wandering soul. 'The question of the soul's wandering from the body, and its subsequent return to it as if to its home, is one of great difficulty and quite beyond the understanding of any man. . . . Now if witches, after being aroused from the profoundest sleep, tell of things they have seen in places so far distant, as compared with the short period of their sleep, the only conclusion is that there has been some unsubstantial journey like that of the soul.'[2]

The conclusion would seem to be that when the witch was watched and did not go away, then her soul or some 'bluish substance' had gone off to the Sabbath. And when she was not watched and also said she had been to the Sabbath, then she really had been physically absent. It is not surprising that a robust sceptic like Reginald Scot declared: 'Therefore S. Augustine saith well, that he is too much a fool and a blockhead, that supposeth those things to be done indeed, and corporally, which are by such persons fantastically imagined.'[3]

If the confessions were untrue, and the Sabbaths imaginary, why were people suspected of witchcraft? Scot gives us his reasons for the persecution of old women. Another writer of the same period, George Gifford, a non-conforming minister, sets out similar views. 'Some woman doth fall out bitterly with her neighbour: there followeth some great hurt. . . . There is a suspicion conceived. Within a few years after she is in some jar with another. He is also plagued. This is noted of all. Great fame is spread of the matter. Mother W. is a witch. . . . Well, Mother W. doth begin to be very odious and terrible unto many, her neighbours dare say nothing but yet in their hearts they wish she were hanged. Shortly after another falleth sick and doth pine. . . . The neighbours come to visit him. Well neighbour, saith one, do you not suspect some naughty dealing, did ye never

---

[1] M. Summers, *History of Witchcraft*, pp. 129 f.
[2] Remy, p. 52.
[3] Scot, op. cit., pp. 38 f.

anger Mother W.? Truly neighbour (saith he) I have not liked the woman a long time, I cannot tell how I should displease her, unless it were this other day, my wife prayed her, and so did I, that she would keep her hens out of my garden. We spake as fair as we could for our lives. I think verily she hath bewitched me. Everybody now saith that Mother W. is a witch in deed. . . . It is out of all doubt, for there were which saw a weasel run from her houseward into his yard even a little before he fell sick. The sick man dieth, and taketh it upon his death that he is bewitched: then is Mother W. apprehended, and sent to prison, she is arraigned and condemned, and being at the gallows, taketh it upon her death that she is not guilty.'[1]

Such was the opinion of some clear-sighted men who lived in the midst of the witch-fear. Today such argument seems fair and convincing. It did not convince those who believed themselves bewitched, or troubled with strange diseases, and still less the inquisitors and prickers who made a fair living out of the persecutions. James I was enraged at such arguments. Matthew Hopkins was indignant. But many people suffered upon such slender evidence.

One argument advanced by believers in witchcraft, and which I have heard in Africa today, is that the existence of such words as 'witch', and the laws against witchcraft, prove that witches really do exist. But Reginald Scot said, 'The witch laws, with the executions and judicials thereupon, and the witches' confessions, have beguiled almost the whole world.'

[1] Notestein, p. 71 n.

CHAPTER 7

Witchcraft Trials in Britain and America

LADY ALICE KYTELER

A short examination of some of the more notable trials for witchcraft held in the British Isles may help to show both the nature of the offences with which people were charged, and the procedure of the prosecution.

One of the first cases recorded was in Ireland in 1325. Indeed this is an isolated instance, and the main trials did not begin until two centuries later, mainly from Elizabeth's time onwards. But as it is often quoted as a fair instance of a witch-cult, the case needs brief mention here.

Lady Alice Kyteler was accused of witchcraft and sorcery, and was fiercely pursued by a zealous Franciscan, the bishop of Ossory. Her trial illustrates the mixture of magic and witchcraft beliefs current at the time, before distinctive definitions of witchcraft were made.

Dr. Murray sees Lady Alice as persecuted for worshipping a heathen deity, 'which the lady apparently did not deny'.[1] She was said to have met a man, as black as an Ethiopian, and to have had a demon lover. A staff was taken from her room on which, it was alleged, 'she ambled and galloped through thick and thin, when and in what manner she listed, after having greased it with ointment which was found in her possession'.[2]

The background of these accusations, however, is important. Lady Alice had had four husbands, and, not agreeing with her children over the testamentary dispositions, they accused her of having

---

[1] *The God of the Witches*, p. 91.
[2] See Camden Society, *Proceedings against Dame Alice Kyteler*, 1843.

killed her husbands by sorcery after bewitching them to make unjust wills. This would provide an interesting murder case today, but not an accusation of witchcraft.

The bishop of Ossory took up the case with vigour, but he met many obstacles on account of the state of the law. The canons against heresy were unknown in Ireland, torture was prohibited under British common law, and the bishop seemed likely to be checked. However, quite illegally, he took to whipping Petronilla, one of Lady Alice's women, and after she had been scourged six times she furnished all that was required.

Petronilla then confessed that both she and her mistress were sorceresses. She had sacrificed cocks at the crossroads to a demon called Robert Artisson (*Artis filium*); they had made love charms with the brains of an unbaptized child in the skull of a beheaded robber. She had been at erotic orgies with the demon and two Ethiopians in her lady's chamber. To this was added the evidence of the anointed staff, and a wafer of sacramental bread which was said to be stamped with the Devil's name and found in the lady's closet.

Petronilla having confessed under this ill-treatment stuck to her story and was burnt at the stake. Some others who were implicated suffered in the same manner, while some abjured and were punished with crosses—a unique instance of this penance in the British Isles. Lady Alice escaped to England out of the bishop's way. Her family seized their rights.[1] It is pleasant to find that the bishop himself was later accused of witchcraft and fled for sanctuary to Rome.

TRIALS IN THE HOME CIRCUIT

The records which give evidence of witchcraft proceedings in England start in 1559 and continue until the end of the following century. England had long been divided into six circuits for the administration of justice, these were: Home, Midland, Norfolk, Northern, Oxford, and Western. C. L'Estrange Ewen has made a most careful and valuable study of the documents and trials in the Home Circuit, that is the five counties: Essex, Hertford, Kent, Surrey, and Sussex. These were selected because the records are the oldest and best preserved. They give the best series of Elizabethan indictments, and include Hopkins's work in Essex.

[1] Lea, *Inquisition of the Middle Ages*, iii, 456 f.

In the Home Circuit during these 150 years there were 790 indictments for witchcraft brought to the assizes. Possibly about an equal number were brought before independent courts by municipal authorities. Essex was by far the most superstitious county, and indeed it knew more indictments than the other four home counties put together, 473 out of 790. These 790 bills refer to 513 persons, of whom only 112 were hanged, about 20 per cent of the total.[1]

The trials were much more numerous under Elizabeth than at any other time, even taking into account the last spurt of activity with Hopkins during the Civil War. There were 455 indictments (nearly 300 of them in Essex) in the Home Circuit in the forty-five years of the reign of Elizabeth; 103 in the twenty years of James I; 108 (over 70 in Essex) in the twenty years of Charles I; 72 (41 in Kent) in the ten years of the Commonwealth; 44 in the twenty-four years of Charles II; 1 in the three years of James II; 7 in the twelve years of William; none in the succeeding reigns.

The charges made against the witches varied considerably. By far the commonest accusation was that someone had been bewitched and had died. Bewitching a person to death was practically the only offence for which convicted witches were hanged, until Hopkins came on the scene. The sole exceptions were two men who were hanged for consulting evil spirits. Bewitching animals was also a common charge, but even where convicted the normal punishment was one year in prison. The same penalty was laid upon a spinster who had bewitched a neighbour's unborn infant so that it died.

Witches were not indicted or executed in England normally for attending Sabbaths or witches' meetings (except at Lancaster), but for bewitching men or beasts. The Devil is mentioned only formally, e.g. 'The said John, not having God before his eyes, but being moved and seduced by the instigation of the devil . . . did bewitch and enchant, etc.' Familiars, spirits, or imps are rarely mentioned before Hopkins appeared. At St. Osyth, always a centre of superstition, in 1583, Margery Barnes was charged with having in her possession 'three imps otherwise called spirits named or called by the name or names: Pygine, resembling a mole; Russoll resembling a grey cat; and the other called Dunsott resembling a dun dog with

[1] *Witch Hunting and Witch Trials,* pp. 98 ff.

intent that she might enchant and bewitch as well men as beasts and other things, to the grievous damage of the entire people of the said lady the Queen Elizabeth'.[1]

With the coming of Hopkins this sort of charge became common. At the Essex assizes in 1645 nineteen persons, all of them women, were condemned to be hanged for witchcraft, and of these six were convicted for 'entertaining evil spirits'. There was Elizabeth Clarke whom Hopkins charged with entertaining Vinegar Tom and company. Other poor women suffered for having 'an evil spirit in the likeness of a bird called a jay', or 'a grey cat called "Germany" ', or 'the likeness of a mole', or mice, rats, squirrels, and birds. Truly it was a hard time for pet lovers.[2]

This sort of thing lingered on in popular superstition. In 1652 Elizabeth Hynes was charged 'for that she hath confessed of herself that she entertains two imps or evil spirits in the shape or likeness of kitlings, and that the said kitlings each night come to her and suck of her body'. But the jury rejected this accusation: 'We do not find this to be a true bill.' There were no hangings in the Home Circuit after 1660 (possibly 1657). But even under William III three women were accused at the Kent summer sessions for covenanting with 'evil spirits in the likeness of mice'.[3]

Even in 1717 depositions were made at Leicester against an old woman and her son and daughter for witchcraft. They had been ducked by the populace: 'all the supposed witches had severally their thumbs and great toes tied together and that they swam like a cork, a piece of paper, or an empty barrel, though they strove all they could to sink.' They were supposed to have bewitched sick people. 'Several of the informants deposed that they themselves had been bewitched and afflicted after this manner and besides had seen and felt great black bees to come out of their own and other peoples noses and mouths, which bees could not be struck down or taken but would make a terrible humming and then fly up the chimney.' The old woman had been searched publicly and was said to have pieces of flesh on her body like supernumerary teats. But the bill was not granted, and the trial did not come on.[4]

[1] Ibid., pp. 78, 84.
[2] pp. 223 ff.
[3] pp. 238, 263.
[4] pp. 314 f.

THE LANCASTER TRIALS

The trials of eighteen people accused of witchcraft in Lancashire in 1612 was the most famous trial for witchcraft in England. It made a great stir all over the country. Thomas Potts, a lawyer, made a careful abstract of the official documents, which were revised by one of the presiding judges, Sir Edward Bromley. It is the most detailed account of a witchcraft trial in the English language, including confessions purporting to have been taken direct from some of the accused, and it deserves attention.

As background to the story it is worth noting the religious struggles of the times. Strong efforts had been made to suppress Roman Catholicism for the past twenty years, and searches were made for Jesuit priests and recusants. Lancashire was then, as now, a stronghold of the old religion, and the commissioners had failed in their efforts at exterminating it. Churches were empty, and secret rites were celebrated by Jesuit priests. There was official suspicion of the underground activities of these priests. During the witch trials the eight so-called 'witches of Salmesbury' were acquitted because it was held that their accuser had been primed by a Jesuit. 'She went to learn with one Thompson a Seminary Priest, who had instructed and taught her this accusation against them, because they were once obstinate Papists, and now came to Church.'[1]

Nothing of the sort is suggested about the main body of the Lancashire witches. But the atmosphere of the time was favourable to beliefs in secret societies, and plots against the public safety. These witches were said to meet at Malking Tower in Pendle Forest, for secret feasts, and finally to have plotted to blow up Lancaster Castle.

The story centres round two families who lived in a wood in the east Lancashire hills. Each was led by an ugly old woman; one, Elizabeth Sowtherns or Old Demdike, was a blind beggar eighty years old; the other, Anne Whittle or Chattox, was a withered old wool-carder. Though both were believed to be witches and to meet together, yet they were always at cross purposes with each other. They and their families were feared by all they met. Their supposed deeds in the forest, and bewitching of their enemies, were the root of the matter. When one Robert Nutter had died, with whom Chattox

---

[1] *The Wonderful Discovery of Witches in the Countie of Lancaster*, p. 101.

had quarrelled and bewitched, four of these women were arrested and put in Lancaster Castle.

Now come the confessions and statements of these women. How they were extracted is not known, nor what questions were put to them. But they seem to have stuck to their words, and later to have embroidered them further. Old Demdike said that twenty years before in the forest she had met a spirit or devil in the shape of a boy, wearing a black and brown coat, who demanded her soul and promised in return that she could have anything she wished. His name was Tibb, and as she agreed he appeared to her for the next five or six years at intervals. At the end he appeared as a brown dog, and sucked the blood under her left arm. At this time she had a child on her lap, and cried out 'Jesus save my child', which was strange if she was a pagan. Later, being threatened as a witch by a certain Richard Baldwin, she saw Tibb and asked him to revenge her on Baldwin. He did this, and she never saw Tibb again. She then gave details of how to prepare a clay image against her enemy.

Chattox then said that she had been seduced by Demdike into witchcraft, and that the Devil had appeared to her as a man at midnight at Demdike's house and had demanded her soul. He sucked a place near her right ribs. A spotted bitch came and offered her wealth. They held a meal of meat, butter, cheese, bread, and drink with two spirits, called Fancie and Tibb, but they were no better for this food. She said they were she-spirits, although Demdike had said Tibb was male. Chattox said Demdike had bewitched to death Robert Nutter, a widow Lomshaw and Richard Ashton.

Alizon Device, granddaughter to Demdike, said that her grandmother had tried to seduce her to witchcraft. Demdike had cursed a neighbour's cow, she had fallen out with Richard Baldwin, cursed him several times and bewitched his child to death.

These three women and a fourth, Anne Redferne, Chattox's daughter, were arrested and put in Lancaster jail. Then it is said that there was a special meeting of their friends and witches at the house of Demdike's daughter, Elizabeth Device, a place called Malking Tower. They had a great feast, and decided that Lancaster Castle should be blown up and its keeper killed. But news of this reached the magistrate and he arrested Elizabeth and James Device and six others, and eight so-called witches of Salmesbury.

Old Demdike died in prison before she came for trial, and the proceedings centred round the Device family and Chattox. Chattox had a reputation for bewitching or curing the bewitched, and she made public a charm she had used for curing bewitched milk; a very Christian charm, though rather Popish, 'Five Paternosters, five Aves, and a Creed'. James Device added that Chattox had taken eight teeth from skulls cast out of graves and had given four to his grandmother Demdike, and they had now been found by him buried in her house with a clay image. He had previously seen a brown dog at his grandmother's house, and a hare or cat lay heavily on his bed at night when he was there.

Clearly Demdike and Chattox were nasty old women, who knew little of the Reformation, and had a reputation for black magic from living in a wood. Their familiars, brown dogs, a spotted bitch, cat, hare, 'likeness of a bear', may have been fierce animals that they kept. But according to the ideas of the time they were familiars which they suckled, and with whom they made diabolical pacts.

Not much else was added in this formal trial at the assizes, until James Device and his younger sister Jennet, a girl of nine, added new touches. James accused his mother Elizabeth of killing Henry Mitton by witchcraft. With the help of a brown dog called Ball, and with a clay image, she had also killed James Robinson. He had told his mother to arrange the meeting at her house to deliver Demdike and the others from prison. Particularly important was it that James named a number of other people as having been present at this meeting.

Jennet Device then witnessed against her brother, as having been a witch for three years and owning a black dog familiar called Dandy, which killed and injured various people for him. She also confirmed the meeting at her mother's house, where twenty people feasted on a sheep they had stolen. Her mother cursed Jennet in court, whereupon she was removed and the girl was set on a table to give her evidence. A feeble attempt to check her story, by identification of one of the accused, seemed to show her truthfulness, but the trap was transparent. All this child's evidence was illegal, for by law only persons of fourteen years and over could be witnesses.

After the eight 'witches of Salmesbury' had been acquitted, as accused on a priest's trumped-up charge, the six other accused Lancaster witches were tried. They all protested their innocence. But James Device testified to their presence at Malking Tower. They were held to be guilty of bewitching people to death (note the double charge all the time), and were condemned to death on this flimsy evidence. The sole exception was Margaret Pearson who, having only bewitched a horse, was sent to be pilloried each quarter and imprisoned for a year without bail.

An instructive footnote is found in the trial of Jennet Preston shortly before at York. She was accused of bewitching a neighbour, Thomas Lister. To this was added the accusation of James Device that she had come to Malking Tower to get the other witches to agree to Lister's death. When Lister was sick he called out 'that Jennet Preston was in the house, look where she is, take hold of her: for God's sake shut the doors, and take her, she cannot escape away . . . and so cried very often in his great pains'. When he was dying, 'He cried out in great extremity: Jennet Preston lies heavy upon me; help me, help me.' When the corpse was laid out, 'the said Jennet Preston coming to touch the dead corpse, they bled fresh blood presently, in the presence of all that were there present.'[1]

In his summary to the jury Sir James Altham, who was also chief judge at Lancaster, stressed these points: of Jennet's attendance at Malking Tower, of Master Lister's complaints that he saw her, and especially 'the conclusion is of more consequence than all the rest, that Jennet Preston being brought to the dead corpse, they bled freshly'. He admitted freely that there was no external evidence of the witches' meetings, 'since all their works are works of darkness, no witnesses are present to accuse them'.

Jennet was hanged. She had protested her innocence throughout. Her husband and family maintained that she was maliciously persecuted by Lister's son, and that 'she died an innocent woman, because she would confess nothing'.

This space has been given to the trial of the Lancaster witches because it was and still is often held up as a model trial, giving careful first-hand evidence and the confessions of the accused. But the more one looks at it, the more uneasy one becomes over such procedure under English law. It has been stressed that England was more humane and lenient than most European countries during the witch-fever. Even in Lancashire, with its troubled religious situation, the judges professed to have given the accused every chance and a completely fair trial.

[1] Potts, pp. 180 ff.

The Demdike-Device and Chattox families were probably a bad lot, rough people living in the woods. They were the only ones that confessed. They were also the chief accusers and took five others to the scaffold with them. Whether Elizabeth Device's house, Malking Tower, was a haunt for the witch-cult, where they had feasts of mutton; whether the dogs and animals with their fanciful names (not at all diabolical or pagan) were fierce beasts, devils or spirits; whether the women really bewitched men and children, cows and horses to death; these are matters for debate. A modern judge and jury would not be so easily convinced by such a motley array of evidence, some possible, much absurd.

Lancashire was to have several other bursts of witch persecution. It is worth mentioning that twenty years later, in 1633, an eleven-year-old boy, Edmund Robinson, said that he saw near Pendle Forest two dogs, a black one that turned into a woman, and a brown one that turned into a boy. The woman offered him money, and when he refused she turned the other boy into a horse, seized Robinson, and rode away with him to a house where people were feasting on meat and bread. When he got home Robinson named eighteen people as witches who were there. The magistrates got busy and made a number of arrests.

Robinson was taken round Lancashire as a boy-wonder and witch-detector. But when the trials came on the Privy Council in London sent the bishop of Chester to make an inquiry, as a result of which he reported his doubt of the whole matter. Four women accused of having devil's marks were brought to London, and Charles I ordered his physician (the great Harvey who later discovered the circulation of the blood) to examine them. He proved that the charges were baseless. Edmund Robinson and his father were then summoned to London, and the boy confessed that the whole story was an invention. He knew of the old yarns of feasts at Malking Tower, and admitted that those he had named as witches were the sort of people who were already suspected by their neighbours. Both he and his father were imprisoned.[1]

An interesting story is told of William Harvey, the physician, who had long been sceptical about witchcraft. It is said that when he was at Newmarket with King Charles, he heard of a lonely witch nearby and went to see her. He professed to be a witch himself and asked to

[1] Notestein, pp. 136 f.; Davies, pp. 79 f., 87 f.

see her familiar. She brought out a dish of milk and made a chuck
noise, whereupon a toad came out from under a chest and dra.
some of the milk. Harvey then got rid of the woman by sending her
out for ale. In her absence he seized the toad and cut it open, the
milk coming out. He examined it, and found it no different from
other toads. The woman was furious on her return, but Harvey
quietened her by threatening to denounce her if she were indeed a
witch, and revealing himself as the king's physician come to discover
frauds. This story dates from 1685, but it is in character with Harvey
and the inquiring spirit of educated men of the time.[1]

HOPKINS AND THE LAST PANIC

Matthew Hopkins was the chief instigator of some of the most
groundless executions for witchcraft in England, and he deserves
the place suggested for him as one of the wickedest men of this
country. When both king and Parliament were becoming sceptical
of the whole thing, Hopkins so played on the superstitions of the
people that there was a flare-up of witch trials such as had not been
seen in Essex and East Anglia since the days of Elizabeth.

Hopkins was a Suffolk lawyer 'of but little note', an energetic
man and apparently not unduly religious. When he moved from
Ipswich to Manningtree he found scope for his energy, and set
about revealing witches in such earnest that he took to himself the
title, 'Witch Finder Generall'.

In 1645, having heard that witches met near his house and called
up their imps, Hopkins had lame Elizabeth Clarke arrested. He
could not use Continental methods of torture, but he justified his
ways of pricking and keeping his victims awake all through the
night by saying that in this way the witches would be quicker in
calling up their imps. After three days and nights of 'watching',
Elizabeth Clarke confessed many things and called up her imps in
the sight of Hopkins and his companions, as we described it in an
earlier chapter.

Upon these confessions five other women were arrested, some of
whom had been suspected of witchcraft before, and one old beldame,
Anne West, had previously been imprisoned. Neighbours gave
evidence against them, that they had heard noises in the night 'like

[1] Notestein, pp. 161 f.

the shrieking of a polecat', that they had lost cattle, that children had died unaccountably. All but one of the accused confessed to these dark deeds. Hopkins extracted a confession from one of them that she had been married to the Devil.

Twenty or more women were further implicated. One simply because a hare had been found in front of her house. Five others completely denied their guilt. Others added new confessions. The trial was held at Chelmsford, and nineteen women were hanged. Arthur Wilson, a historian who was present at the trial at Chelmsford, said that he saw nothing more in the accused women than 'ill-dieted atrabilious constitutions, whose fancies working by gross fumes and vapours might make the imagination ready to take any impression'.[1]

Hopkins went on to Suffolk and so spread the witch craze that four searchers were appointed for the county, charged to 'take the party or parties so suspected into a room and strip him, her, or them, stark naked'. The accused would then be searched for teats and pricked for insensible spots. Fasting and sleeplessness were imposed, and often they were made to walk 'till their feet were blistered, and so forced through that cruelty to confess'. Eighteen people were hanged at Bury St. Edmunds.[2]

Hopkins proceeded to Norfolk, where twenty witches were executed, then on to Suffolk again. We trace him next in Cambridgeshire, where only one woman was hanged, and at Northampton where ghostly apparitions also played a part in the evidence against witches. Thence he went to Huntingdon and Bedford.

It was unfortunate for the accused people that the Civil War was raging. Even so the Long Parliament was disturbed and sent a commission down to Bury. They put an end to the swimming ordeal, but did not prevent the executions. There was local opposition too. In Huntingdon a clergyman, John Gaule, preached and wrote against Hopkins. While he did not doubt that there were witches, yet he suspected many of the stories about witchcraft, flying on broomsticks and the like. He was sceptical of the value of confessions, believing them to be forced or diabolically inspired. He said that witch-seeking was 'a trade never taken up in England till this'.

Opposition had grown against the witch-finding in Essex. Stearne,

[1] Notestein, p. 173.
[2] Ibid., p. 175.

Hopkins's colleague, and some forty others were themselves charged with conspiracy and forced to leave the county. But it was in Norfolk that there was the greatest antagonism. Hopkins was charged not only with cruelty and torture of women, but also with enriching himself at the expense of the country.

Hopkins and Stearne went into retirement and tried to clear their names. Within a year, in 1647, Hopkins had died of consumption. The rumour that he was put to the swimming test and drowned is probably untrue, but it was current shortly after his death and shows how he was detested.

After this there was a lull in the proceedings for witchcraft in England. There was an epidemic in the north of England in 1650, and one in Kent. But after that there was a rapid falling off. The death penalty was not applied in the Home Circuit after 1660, and even accusations became increasingly rare.

THE SALEM TRIALS

The Salem trials in 1692 were held under a special court of justices, not one of them a lawyer, appointed by governor Phipps. Cotton Mather gives a record of the trial of Bridget Bishop and several others. Significantly he prefaces these with a version of an English trial several years before, which set the pattern for the Salem accusations: children vomiting pins, fits, bewitching animals and carts, possessing extra teats and suckling imps. But a good deal was made of the spectral appearances of the witches to their victims.

Bridget Bishop was indicted for 'bewitching several persons in the neighbourhood. . . . There was little occasion to prove the Witchcraft, it being evident and notorious to all beholders.' However, several people testified that 'the shape' of the prisoner often bit, choked and afflicted them, and urged them 'to write their names in a book'. Another had been threatened with drowning unless the book was signed. At the examination of the prisoner before the magistrates the bewitched people were greatly tormented; if she cast her eyes on them they were struck down at once, but if she laid her hand upon them they revived immediately. Deliverance Hobbs confessed to having been a witch and testified against Bridget that she had been at a general witches' meeting and there partook of a diabolical sacrament of bread and wine. Others testified that 'the shape' of

Bridget had appeared to them in their bedrooms, knocked apples out of a man's hand, assaulted a child in a cradle, bewitched a sow, bruised a child by an invisible hand, appeared as a black pig or monkey jumping in at a window, making a cart sink in a hole in the road, and having rag dolls with pins in them in her possession. William Stacey suspected Bridget of having caused his daughter's death, 'of which suspicion pregnant reasons were assigned'. Finally, as Bridget, under guard, was led past the Salem meeting-house, 'she gave a look towards the house, and immediately a demon invisibly entering the meeting-house tore down a part of it'. This wicked act seems only to have consisted in moving 'a board with nails' from one part of the house to another.[1]

Such a motley collection of accusations was bound to include some items that would convince those who believed diabolical power to be on the warpath. Yet most of them were so patently ridiculous that once the excitement had abated they would not pass critical examination. But by then Bridget had been hanged.

Falling into fits was regarded as proof of diabolical attacks, and children who suffered from fits or vomited nails and pins were thought to be possessed by the Devil. Fits in court seemed clear evidence against the witches. 'There was an extraordinary endeavour by witchcrafts', says Mather, 'with cruel and frequent fits, to hinder the poor sufferers from giving in their complaints, which the Court was forced with much patience to obtain, by much waiting and watching for it.'

The chief magistrate questioned Susanna Martin, another accused person, about these fits in court:

Magistrate: Don't you think they are bewitch'd?
Martin: No, I do not think they are.
Magistrate: Tell us your Thoughts about them.
Martin: No, my Thoughts are my own, when they are in, but when they are out they are another's. Their Master——
Magistrate: Their Master? Who do you think is their Master?
Martin: If they be dealing in the Black Art, you may know as well as I.
Magistrate: Well, what have you done towards this?

[1] *Wonders of the Invisible World,* p. 138.

Martin: Nothing at all.
Magistrate: Why, 'tis you or your Appearance.[1]

Susanna was accused of being one of the most wicked creatures in the world, 'impudent' and 'scurrilous'. But her chief plea was 'that she had led a most virtuous and holy life'.

So the trials went on, in much the same pattern. Children testified as well, and were regarded as having been particularly subject to fits. Some of the accused were reprieved. Mercy Disborough was a typical case at Fairfield; accused of bewitching a roast pig, a canoe, and a horse, of blotting out words of scripture, and of causing numbness to a sick man. She was searched for witch's marks but none were found that were unusual. She and another, Elizabeth Clauson, were ducked, 'bound hand and foot, and put into the water, and they swam upon the water like a cork'. After some hesitation the jury found them guilty and sentence of death was passed. But a number of ministers and laymen appealed for mercy. They said that the swimming ordeal was 'unlawful and sinful and therefore it cannot afford any evidence'. They wanted medical opinion on witch's marks. They doubted the evidence of witnesses and declared the bewitching of cattle 'to be upon very slender and uncertain grounds'. So the women were released.[2]

Finally, after twenty executions at Salem, the fever died down. Most of the jurors signed a paper expressing their repentance and pleading that they had laboured under a delusion. One of the most zealous, Samuel Sewall, 'made a public confession of his errors before the congregation', in 1697. 'He observed annually in private a day of humiliation and prayer, during the remainder of his life, to keep fresh in his mind a sense of repentance and sorrow for the part he bore in the trials.'[3]

This short sketch of witch trials may have served to give some notion of the kind of charges that were made against those accused of witchcraft. Bewitching was the stock charge. It was thought to be possible through the help of the Devil. Under Hopkins, in particular, the possession of tame animals and birds was taken as proof of demonic presence. Mention of a witches' Sabbath does not occur in

---

[1] *Wonders of the Invisible World*, p. 139.
[2] *The Witchcraft Delusion in Colonial Connecticut*, pp. 62 f., 74 f.
[3] Ibid., pp. 27 f.

England till 1620, though we have seen that in Lancashire there were rumours of strange meetings at Elizabeth Device's forest home.

Whatever there may have been under the accusations for witch-craft, if anything more than superstition, it is clear that mysterious death was explained by this notion. 'Wasting', 'languishing', and 'consumed', are common complaints in the indictments. It must surely be clear that many of the charges of witchcraft were utterly baseless, and that many people suffered in entire innocence.

If this is so, and it can hardly be disputed, then it is a pity that defenders of the witch-cult theory include the names of those accused of witchcraft regardless of their accusations. Murray, in her list of 700 'Names of Witches', includes a number of names over which we might well hesitate. And if all the other names were carefully weighed, with the charges and circumstances of trial fully considered, many others might be eliminated. Lady Alice Kyteler is in this list (but why not Petronilla?). The Lancashire witches are here in force, not only the Devices and Anne Chattox, but also Margaret Pearson who had only bewitched a horse, and Jennet Preston in whose presence a corpse bled. It is true that Murray regards the latter as members of a coven, but they denied it constantly. She even includes (bad luck for them) the eight from Salmesbury whom the Lancaster jury had dis-charged as not guilty. Hopkins's witches are fully represented, not only the lame Elizabeth Clarke and Anne West, but others whose chief crime was that they kept tame jays or mice. Whatever may be the case for the existence of a witch-cult, that argument is not strengthened by the inclusion of the names of many people who obviously had nothing to do with it.

CHAPTER 8

The Interpretation of European Witchcraft

CRITICS OF THE BELIEF

As it has been said, our knowledge of European witchcraft is almost entirely derived from the writings of the persecutors, or from the records of confessions said to have been given by or extorted from the people accused of witchcraft.

It has often been assumed in modern times that the records of the confessions of witches are largely fabrications or, at best, products of the witches' imaginations. Many anthropologists hold that 'witchcraft is an imaginary offence because it is impossible'. But a serious challenge was made to this assumption by the proposition that witchcraft in Europe, at least, was the remains of old pagan fertility cults which were only finally suppressed by the Church in the witch-hunts of the fifteenth to the eighteenth centuries. Some writers have gone on to assume that witchcraft in Africa and other lands was also an ancient cult.

Dr. Margaret Murray, in *The Witch-cult in Western Europe*, says that in the interpretation of witchcraft there have been and still are two main schools of thought. One class accepted all the evidence and placed upon it 'the unwarranted construction' that the witches' activities were due to supernatural power. The other class, 'taking the evidence on hearsay', comes to 'deny the facts *in toto*'.[1]

Miss Murray claims to occupy an intermediate position, after making a new examination of the records of ancient European witchcraft. She believes that the witches actually performed many of the deeds which were ascribed to them, but not by supernatural power.

It is possible also, however, to examine the evidence and decide

[1] P. 9.

that it is false. We all, Murray and everybody else, must now take the evidence on hearsay. But we can maintain that the inquisitors and witch-finders were wrong, though contemporary, and that they put into their victims' mouths false statements. The artificially created diabolical 'possession' of the nuns of Loudun, as described by Aldous Huxley, is a comparable case. But it is to prejudge the matter to speak of 'the facts' before examining the evidence critically.

Murray, in an *argumentum ad hominem*, says that it is interesting to compare the class of mind of those who believed in witchcraft with those who doubted. 'The most brilliant minds . . . were among the believers.' Men like Francis Bacon, Raleigh, Boyle, Henry More, and Thomas Browne. But there were degrees of belief. Bacon, for example, while assuming the belief and no doubt deferring to the credulity of James I, is often critical: 'The witches themselves are imaginative and believe oft-times they do that which they do not; and people are credulous in that point, and ready to impute accidents and natural operations to witchcraft.'[1]

On the other hand the sceptics, says Murray, were not infrequently fanatics and bigots. This is an attempt to turn the tables on the rationalists with a vengeance, for there never were such bigots as the witch-finders, such as Hopkins and Stearne in England, and inquisitors like Sprenger, Boguet, Remy, and Guazzo on the Continent. Whereas some of the sceptics were men of great intellect: Montaigne, Malebranche, and Charron in France; Thomas Hobbes, William Harvey, Reginald Scot, and Bishop Hutchinson in England. It was Hobbes who said, 'I think not that their witchcraft is any real power; but yet that they are justly punished for the false belief they have that they can do such mischief, joined with their purpose to do it if they can'.[2] While in Spain it was the inquisitor Salazar who did so much to check persecutions in that country by his careful and first-hand investigations of charges against witches, and after examining hundreds of cases he concluded that 'there were neither witches nor bewitched until they were talked and written about'.[3]

Belief in witchcraft gradually declined during the seventeenth and eighteenth centuries. The social conditions which had favoured its rise, the disorders of European wars, the epidemics, the high child

[1] *Works of Bacon*, 1857 edn., ii, 642 f.
[2] *Leviathan*, 7.
[3] Lea, *Inquisition of Spain*, 4, pp. 233 f.

mortality, the general unsettlement of religion and society, gave way to better conditions and higher education. Later disorders were attributed to other scapegoats. Practically nobody in western Europe now believes in witchcraft.

The importance of belief can scarcely be over-emphasized. The Church's declaration of witchcraft as a heresy unleashed the Inquisition. This belief remained until the coming of better education. There is no doubt that the persecutions helped to spread the very beliefs that they professed to combat. But in the end they defeated their own purpose in another way. So many impossible things were attributed to the witches that at length reason revolted and the persecutions were stopped.

If the Church had been responsible for much shortsighted action, particularly on the Continent, it should be noted that some of the clergy helped to end the superstition. Salazar was a member of the Spanish Inquisition. George Gifford, who supported Scot, was a non-conforming minister. Hutchinson, who in 1718 published his *Historical Essay concerning Witchcraft*, was an Anglican bishop. Professor Notestein says, 'It was an Anglican clergyman who administered the last great blow to the superstition.'[1]

A WITCH-CULT?

But was it superstition? Margaret Murray's theory, put forward since 1921, is that European witchcraft was the remains of ancient pagan cults which survived in Europe long after the adoption of Christianity. Her theory attracted so many people that she was asked to write the article 'Witchcraft' in the fourteenth edition of the *Encyclopaedia Britannica*. It is worth quoting this article.

She says: 'When dealing with the records of the medieval witches, we are dealing with the remains of a pagan religion which survived, in England at least, till the eighteenth century, 1,200 years after the introduction of Christianity. . . . The number of witches put to death in the sixteenth and seventeenth centuries is a proof of the obstinate paganism of Europe. Whole villages followed the beliefs of their ancestors; and in many cases the priests, drawn from the peasant class, were only outwardly Christian and carried on the

[1] Op. cit., p. 342; and see R. T. Davies, *Four Centuries of Witch Beliefs,* on the restraining influence of the bishops appointed under Charles I.

ancient rites; even the bishops and other high ecclesiastics took part. As civilization increased and Christianity became more firmly rooted, the old religion retreated to the less frequented parts of the country and was practised by the more ignorant members of the community. . . . It was only when the new religion had gained sufficient strength that it ventured to try conclusions with the old. Backed by the civil law, it overcame the old religion, not only by persuasion but by the use of force.'

Parts, at least, of this argument sound plausible at first sight, and it is supported by such a weight of quotations from confessions in her other books that it has gained considerable following. G. B. Harrison in the modern edition of the Lancaster trials, Aldous Huxley in the story of the Loudun possessions, Lewis Spence in his study of myth and ritual, Robert Graves in his interpretation of Greek myths, Montague Summers in his many books on witchcraft and demonology, and Pennethorne Hughes in one of the popular studies of witchcraft, all follow Miss Murray's lead. Royston Pike in his one-volume *Encyclopaedia of Religion and Religions*, writing of witchcraft and its explanations says, 'A more understanding approach is Margaret Murray's who not long since advanced the theory that witchcraft was the survival of classical paganism.'[1]

Murray's first book on the *Witch-cult*, especially, is a monument of industry and research. She quotes verbatim from innumerable records of confessions of witches to prove her theory. That her later books, *The God of the Witches*, and even more *The Divine King in England*, have seemed to become more extreme and fantastic, involving far too radical and dubious a re-writing of history, need not detract from the value of her earlier work. Some reviewers have been at pains to point this out. Thus one writes, 'It seems to the present reviewer that Dr. Murray has tried to press her case much too hard. . . . This is the greater pity since it may obscure the lasting value of her earlier works.'[2]

Yet when one begins to examine closely the case argued in the *Witch-cult* it seems to throw its net far too widely, accepting any and all confessions, ignoring the manner in which they were obtained, or the credulity of those by whom they were related (e.g. Boguet), ignoring or dismissing the sceptics (Salazar, Scot, etc.). The whole

---

[1] P. 397.
[2] *The Listener*, 4/2/1954.

account begins with the assumption that the Devil or god of the witches was a real pagan person, despite his very Christian names. And as one works through the evidence, as we have tried to do to some extent above, doubts constantly grow.

There is no question that the conversion of Europe was superficial at first, and that it took the Church centuries to establish itself in the lives of the people. Yet, as we have seen, it was not until 1484 that the organized persecution of witches began, with the authority of Innocent VIII. It did not begin in England till about 1560, and the persecutions lasted just about a century and killed about a thousand people of the poorer uneducated classes. It is true that witchcraft, magic, spells, idolatry, and the like were condemned from time to time over the centuries by the Church. But witchcraft did not come alive until it was made a heresy, the conjunction of night-riding delusions with Satan, and so was persecuted by the Inquisition.

The supporters of the theory that witchcraft was ancient paganism fail to show effectively why it should not receive serious attention from the Church for a thousand years and more. Christianity was not a 'new religion' in the fifteenth century. Is it true that the Church had only gained sufficient strength to combat paganism by the fifteenth to eighteenth centuries? This assertion ignores the vast hold that the Church had gained during the early Middle Ages, the centuries of the building of great monasteries, cathedrals, and universities, the ages of the preaching friars and of the domination of the Church over the empire. Never was the Church more powerful, yet it undertook no large-scale action against witchcraft.

Chaucer, who gives such an extensive picture of English life in the fourteenth century, with its pilgrims drawn from all walks of life and with all manner of opinions, has in all his voluminous works only two mere mentions of the name 'witch' among other evils, and he gives no details about witches, which is strange if they were a vast anti-Christian society. Dante nearly a hundred years earlier never mentions witchcraft.

Not until Shakespeare do we come across witchcraft clearly, in the one play that he dedicates to the subject. In *Macbeth* Hecate is the chief to whom the three witches report. We know that Hecate was a classical figure. Shakespeare's witches are conventional and deliberately horrific, but perhaps not very seriously believed. His Graymalkin was the name for a cat, Paddock a toad, and Harpier a bat or harpy in woman's form but with wings and claws. Shakespeare lived in the midst of the Elizabethan and Jacobean witch persecutions, and so he has more about witchcraft than had Chaucer two centuries before, being sure that his audience would appreciate the references.

It is noteworthy that Sprenger, in the *Malleus Maleficarum,* had to argue his case strongly against those who maintained that witches did not exist, and who held that it was not a part of the catholic faith to believe in witches. Other writers do the same. We have seen that Jaquerius had taught that witchcraft was a 'new sect'. To justify his persecutions Sprenger had to show that 'the practice of witchcraft hath so notably increased'. In Spain the inquisitors seriously debated the existence both of witches and of witchcraft.

It is true that the ancient paganism took a long time to die, especially in its magical beliefs. But the druidic and sun cults were not the same as night-riding witchcraft. Ancient superstitions and dances long remained, but they were performed publicly, tolerated by the Church in many places, and not in the secrets of the night.

It is a well-known fact that when a new religion spreads rapidly, the old pagan gods tend to disappear. But the lower sort of superstitions can linger on and are often taken up into the semi-magical practices of the new religion. This phenomenon was seen in Europe in the conversion to Christianity, and in much of Africa and Asia in the conversion to Islam. The same phenomenon is observable today in Africa, where both these missionary religions are ousting successfully the old gods, but many superstitions remain, with them the belief in witchcraft. Belief in witchcraft, indeed, is akin to magical belief, and it is tenacious because it is vague and not a cult, but a convenient explanation of the ills of life.

We have seen that many of the names of witches and devils from the confessions are but too consciously horrific: Devil, Satan, Apollyon, Mammon, Lucifer, Asmodeus, Jezebel, Herodias, Diana, Hecate. Miss Murray does not quote a single pagan name. It is hard to think that the witches would all confess to such evil names if they were indeed followers of a non-Christian cult. And if they did not, but the records were distorted by the inquisitors, then what is the value of those records?

If 'the old religion retreated to the less frequented parts of the country', it is strange that many so-called witches were caught in

A Witch-cult?

East Anglia, the home counties, Arras, Paris, and Rome.[1] Perhaps some priests were not so educated and such good theologians as was desirable, but the accusations made against them were liable to the same distortion as those made against others. John Lowes, an Anglican parson who was hanged for witchcraft in Suffolk, seems to have had as chief fault that he had fallen out with his parishioners who could not get rid of him by any other means after he had spent fifty years in the same parish. At first he denied all charges, but after Hopkins had kept him awake for several nights and run the old man about till he was weary, Lowes confessed to having sunk a ship with the loss of fourteen souls, by the help of his imps.[2]

The great majority of witches, we have seen, were women. Mostly they were old women, and not likely to be active in riding about the country at night or seeking the sensual delights which their accusers imagined for them. This was admitted at the time. 'Certainly I remember to have heard of far more cases of women than men: and it is not unreasonable that this scum of humanity should be chiefly drawn from the feminine sex . . . since that sex is the more susceptible to evil counsels.'[3] On the other hand, old women would be mid-wives, mothers-in-law, often living alone and suspected of killing children.

To fill up, a little, the long gap of over a thousand years between the coming of Christianity to western Europe and the beginning of the witch persecutions, the supporters of the cult theory adduce certain prominent individuals as leading witches in the early centuries. Lady Godiva's naked ride through Coventry by day is said to be analogous to the rides of witches at night. Robin Hood has been called a pagan woodland figure like Jack-in-the-Green.[4] This may, or may not, be so but it does not thereby make him a witch. But when Miss Murray would include William Rufus, Thomas Becket, Joan of Arc, and now every king of England down to Charles I as pagan victims sacrificed to make a witches' holiday, the mind revolts against such a reading of history.

Clearly some of the accusations were false. The Arras trials were

---

[1] R. T. Davies says that south-east England, being most highly developed and nearest the Continent, had become infected with the witchcraft beliefs of returning Continental refugees during Elizabeth's reign (op. cit., p. 19).

[2] Notestein, pp. 175 ff.

[3] Remy, p. 56.

[4] But see 'The Final Truth about Robin Hood?', in *Folk-lore*, June, 1956.

demonstrably so, although Murray quotes these people as witches. Many of the Essex and East Anglian accusations were solely due to the malevolent activity of professional finders like Hopkins. Yet one finds these also being used in evidence, and the defenders of the cult theory include these falsely traduced people in their lists of the distribution of witchcraft.

Moreover, many of the witches were charged and hanged or burnt not for going to Sabbaths with Satan, but for such crimes as bewitching cows, causing hailstorms, making the milk go sour, keeping pet animals, or causing children to have convulsions. These can hardly be claimed as proof of a witch-cult, even though in those days people believed these works to be done with the help of the Devil. William Drage, a doctor of Hitchin, in his book *Daimono-mageia* in 1665, declared that fits, convulsions, unnatural voiding or vomiting, are signs of witchcraft. If the sick person voids 'knives, scissors, whole eggs or dogs' tails, conclude he is bewitched'. Witch-craft was simply an explanation of the abnormal, concludes the same author: 'If there were ever such diseases in man that were impossible to be effected by natural causes, they must be made supernatural; and if so, by diabolical; and if so, by Agents; but it is clear there have been such; Ergo we conclude the Devil hath done these, and that by agents, which we call witches.' Even the learned Sir Thomas Browne, being asked to give his medical opinion on swooning fits, declared that they might be natural but were 'heightened to a great excess' by demonic co-operation through the agency of witches. However, in his *Commonplace Book*, he seems to be keeping an open mind: 'We are no ways doubtful that there are witches, but have not always been satisfied in the application of their witchcraft.'

Even when devils are specifically mentioned there was often clearly no Sabbath involved. The modern reader will be doubtful if there was any witchcraft or witch-cult at all in many of these cases. In one of the most notorious instances, on which Boguet bases his writing and which is often quoted in evidence for witch-craft, the imagination has clearly taken a large part. Françoise Secretain was charged with having cast a spell on a girl, who was convulsed until 'devils came out of her mouth in the shape of balls as big as the fist and red as fire . . . they danced three or four times round the fire and then vanished'. Françoise was accused, but prayed hard and told her rosary (with a defective cross!), until she was stripped naked and had all her hair cut off. Only then did she tremble and begin to confess, 'adding to her first confessions from day to day', and starting with saying that 'she had wished five devils on the girl'.[1] Is comment necessary?

Aldous Huxley, in his study of *The Devils of Loudun,* has shown most clearly how the whole scandalous business of possession, exorcism, confession, and burning at the stake, was artificially begun and stimulated by exorcizers such as M. Barré. 'He saw the print of cloven hoofs in everything, he recognized Satan's work in all the odd, all the disastrous, all the too pleasurable events of human life. Enjoying nothing so much as a good tussle with Belial or Beelzebub, he was for ever fabricating and exorcizing demoniacs. Thanks to his efforts, Chinon was full of raving girls, bewitched cows, husbands unable, because of some sorcerer's malignant spells, to perform their conjugal duties.'[2]

It is all the more pity, then, that Huxley seems to accept the cult-theory of witchcraft, by saying, 'At all high Sabbaths the devil himself was invariably present . . . the witches' organization was a secret society.'[3] It is true that Huxley only discusses witchcraft incidentally and in a few pages, and one feels that if he had studied it as closely as he did the possessions of Loudun he might have come to the conclusion that both were equally illusory.

It seems likely that Ewen's conclusion is correct. 'Delusions fostered by the Church, became the beliefs of the people. If the Devil existed, it was a small step to the supposition that personal acquaintance was possible and that agreements and liaisons could be made.'[4] And Professor E. O. James has said that, 'Miss Murray has over-stated her case . . . it is difficult to believe that an organized secret society of the kind she describes ever existed.'[5]

Much more might be said, if every example of Murray's were to be answered point by point. It is admitted that pagan superstitions survived in many minds, though it is likely that, as in Africa today, the pagan gods disappeared first while the magical charms subsisted for generations. But that the superstitions formed a cult, which only appears as organized as late as the fifteenth century, is highly

---

[1] Boguet, pp. 2 f.
[2] Huxley, p. 128.
[3] Ibid., p. 157.
[4] *Witch Hunting,* p. 11.
[5] *The Concept of Deity,* 1950, p. 126.

questionable. All but one of Murray's numerous examples of witches are from the sixteenth century onwards.

Murray's *Witch-cult* is called in the sub-title *A Study in Anthropology*. The same sub-title appears in her *Divine King in England*, perhaps as a defence against the historians. Most anthropologists who have worked in lands where witchcraft is still believed in would hesitate to accept her conclusions. It is, indeed, when one turns to African witchcraft, to find there today such similarity and such delusions, that one comes finally to a halt in belief in a witch-cult. Before going on, however, there are further qualifications which need to be made that affect the interpretation of the evidence in Europe.

THE PSYCHOLOGY OF WITCHCRAFT

We have mentioned something of the mythology of ancient Europe, and lingering ideas that gave substance to witchcraft beliefs. Not only was there much external material for the belief in witchcraft, but the witches themselves often freely provided matter that sounded convincing to their interlocutors. Some witches confessed without pressure. One in France was said to have 'confessed freely without torture and continued constant in it in the midst of the flames in which she was burnt'.

Until the rise of the modern study of psychology one might well have been excused for refusing to credit the witches with the invention of the catalogues of their horrible deeds. But we now know so much more of the strange complexities of the human mind, that one would hesitate to assert that the confessions cannot have been invented. Some people like confessing, even what is impossible. Confession is said to be good for the soul. For every murder committed today there are several false confessions. What seemed in olden days to be unnatural desires now appear but too human.

The connexion of witches' assemblies with dreams has been noted. The witches believed that they went to the Sabbaths flying or riding through the air. Often they were proved to be at home on their beds. But this is one of the commonest delusions of dream life. One of the most universal dreams is that of flying or jumping through space. Various explanations are given of it, but it seems to be a dream of well-being, buoyant feeling, and physical urges.

In dream life, too, the most strange thoughts come to the surface.

With the censorship of the conscious mind removed, friends and enemies alike may be attacked. Sigmund Freud has described this in a notable passage: 'Hate, too, rages, unrestrainedly; wishes for revenge, and death-wishes, against those who in life are nearest and dearest—parents, brothers, sisters, husband or wife, the dreamer's own children—are by no means uncommon. These censored wishes seem to rise up from a veritable hell; when we know their meaning, it seems to us in our waking moments as if no censorship of them could be severe enough. Dreams themselves, however, are not to blame for this evil content: you surely have not forgotten that their harmless, nay, useful function is to protect sleep from disturbance.'[1]

From our enlightened point of view we can look with tolerance at the repressed wishes that come out in dreams. But in an age when dreams were thought to be grim reality, and given a belief in a soul which wandered about like a vampire, or a 'bluish vapour', no wonder people confessed to evil deeds. Such confession would give relief to the tormented mind, and who knew if it was not actually true?

Even in waking life, the obsessional neuroses, described by Freud, would torture sufferers from nervous complaints. 'Mostly they consist of something terrifying, such as temptations to commit serious crimes, so that the patient not only repudiates them as alien, but flees from them in horror, and guards himself by prohibitions, precautions, and restrictions from the possibility of carrying them out.'

Such obsessions, once hinted at, would ensure the accusation of the subject for witchcraft. Many of the accused were women whose position in society was uncertain, who had outlived their husbands, and lived themselves in poverty and were suspect by their very isolation. Their minds would naturally harbour (or be suspected of harbouring) jealous thoughts against those more fortunate than themselves, who had children and security. The very suggestion of an old woman approaching a child, in affection or for sympathy, would send a shudder through the breasts of the well-off.

Old and ugly women would be particularly suspect, however unfairly. We still think of the witch as an ugly skinny old crone. Of two of the chief Lancaster witches we read that one 'was a very withered, spent and decrepit old creature, her sight almost gone. . . . Her lips ever chattering and talking: but no man knew what.' Of the other it was said, 'This odious witch was branded with a pre-

[1] *Introductory Lectures on Psycho-analysis*, E.T. 1922, pp. 119–120.

posterous mark in Nature, even from her birth, which was her left eye, standing lower than the other; the one looking down, the other looking up, so strangely deformed, as the best that were present in that Honourable assembly, and great Audience, did affirm, they had not often seen the like.'[1]

Many of the women accused as witches would be midwives. Sprenger declares, 'No one does more harm to the Catholic Faith than midwives.'[2] Infant mortality was very high in those days, and clearly midwives could be accused if the children died. If the unhappy babe were unbaptized he would be lost to salvation, according to the ideas of the time, and eventually the Church had to make provision for this and to recognize the validity of baptism *in extremis* by laymen, provided the trinitarian formula was uttered.

Mothers themselves must have wondered why their children died, sometimes one after another. Had they been responsible for taking the child's soul-substance, in dream if not by day? With the terrible ravages of the Black Death, and later plagues and epidemics, let alone the casualties from the general insanitary conditions of confinements, society had to find some scapegoats. It purged itself by their blood, and the witches were veritable martyrs to the easing of social conscience.

It is quite credible that accused witches sometimes imagined seeing figures of devils at Sabbaths. To realize this one only has to turn to records of dreams and of paranormal psychology. I myself have seen strange people in medieval dress, and witches riding on thunderclouds, most vividly in that brief interval between waking and sleeping, generally before dropping into a profound sleep. And Madame David-Neel, a Buddhist writer, claims to have been able to conjure up imaginary figures before her waking sight; but she dismisses them as creations of the imagination.[3] Yet imagination, said William Blake, 'is the only true reality'.

THE END OF IT ALL

There was clearly a rich field for the development of witchcraft belief. The superstitions of ancient Europe provided a background.

---

[1] Potts, pp. 33, 55.
[2] *Malleus*, p. 66.
[3] See *With Mystics and Magicians in Tibet*.

To these the Church added its demonology. The wars and diseases of the time demanded scapegoats. The imaginations of inquisitors and of witches themselves, added to confessions produced under torture and prickings, supplied the material.

The witchcraft belief was not killed by inquisition and persecution. Penal severity does not easily destroy beliefs. Indeed the persecution served to spread abroad the very ideas that it sought to oppose. But it was the enlightenment brought by modern education and a reformed religion that finally scotched the superstition in Europe.

This did not happen all at once. The Renaissance, the new birth of European learning, was at first no better than the preceding age for the persecution of witches. Professor Butterfield says, 'It would appear to be the case that astrology, like witch-burning, was considerably on the increase in the sixteenth and seventeenth centuries, in spite of what we say about the beginning of modern times.'[1]

But slowly the new knowledge and the spirit of inquiry and criticism spread. Medical men became reluctant, despite exceptions, to ascribe sicknesses to diabolical influence. The Swiss Paracelsus (1490–1541) said, 'mental diseases have nothing to do with evil spirits or devils . . . one should not study how to exorcise the devil but how to cure the insane'. Johann Weyer of Holland wrote an attack on witchcraft in 1563, which was condemned by James I along with Reginald Scot's work. Weyer said, 'The uninformed and unskilful physicians relegate all the incurable diseases, or all the diseases the remedy for which they overlook, to witchcraft. When they do this, they are talking about disease as a blind man talks about colour.'[2]

As the seventeenth century came on the Church itself produced its thinkers who recognized natural causes and effects for phenomena that hitherto had often been ascribed to witches and devils. There were some like Joseph Glanvill in his *Sadducismus Triumphatus* (Unbelief Conquered), who tried to combine belief in witches with the new spirit of science: Glanvill was a member of the Royal Society. But he was answered in 1677 by John Webster, a non-conforming clergyman turned doctor, who declared that the 'impious and Popish

[1] *The Origin of Modern Science*, 1949, p. 21.
[2] Quoted by S. R. Burstein, 'Demonology and Medicine', in *Folk-lore*, lxvii, 25 f.

opinions of the too much magnified powers of Demons and Witches, in this Nation were pretty well quashed and silenced'.[1]

Bishops of the Church in England commended the 'learned and inquisitive age' of the seventeenth century. So says Trevelyan, 'While the episcopal blessing was thus enthusiastically given to the questioning spirit of science, it is not surprising that in the later years of the Century, the reaction of educated minds to charges of witchcraft was very different from what it had been a short time before. Evidence of these "odd stories" was now critically and sometimes contemptuously examined by the magistrates. Popular superstition on this subject was almost as gross as ever, but the gentry were now predisposed to be sceptical. . . . In 1736, greatly to the indignation of many simple folk, Parliament repealed the already obsolete law that condemned a witch to die.'[2]

[1] Notestein, p. 299.
[2] *Illustrated English Social History*, ii, 117.

CHAPTER 9

Witchcraft in the Bible and the Near East

BIBLICAL WITCHES?

'Thou shalt not suffer a witch to live' (Exodus xxii, 18) was an oft-quoted verse used in justification of the persecution of witches in Europe. It is printed on the title-page of Hopkins's *Discovery of Witches*. Biblical verses that mentioned witchcraft were seized upon by the persecutors, and it was assumed that witchcraft was rife in Palestine in Biblical times and was the work of the Devil. This chapter seeks to show how mistaken these interpreters were, and how neither they nor modern witch-hunters in Africa are justified in using the Bible for their purposes.

King James I in his *Daemonologie* based his belief in witchcraft, as against the scepticism of Reginald Scot, on arguments from Scripture. 'As first in the law of God, it is plainly prohibited: But certain it is that the law of God speaks nothing in vain, neither doth it lay curses or injoin punishments upon shadows, condemning that to be ill, which is not in essence or being as we call it. Secondly, it is plain where wicked Pharaoh's wise man imitated one number of Moses' miracles, to harden the tyrant's heart thereby. Thirdly, said not Samuel to Saul, that disobedience is as the sin of Witchcraft? To compare a thing that were not, it were too too absurd. Fourthly, was not Simon Magus a man of that craft? and fifthly, what was she that spake of Python? beside innumerable other places that were irksome to recite?'

After this from the learned king it is not surprising that other men justified their belief in witchcraft from the Bible. Even after the modification of the English laws we find John Wesley writing in 1768: 'It is true likewise that the English in general, and indeed most men of learning in Europe, have given up all accounts of witches and apparitions as mere old wives' fables. I am sorry for it, and I willingly take this opportunity of entering my solemn protest against this violent compliment which so many that believe the Bible pay those who do not believe it.'

The great evangelist was a royalist and an Arminian but not an original theologian, and he lived near to the common people who still believed in witchcraft. But it is surprising to find the eminent jurist Sir William Blackstone saying in 1775, 'To deny the possibility, nay, actual existence, of witchcraft and sorcery is at once flatly to contradict the revealed word of God . . . and the thing itself is a truth to which every nation in the world hath borne testimony.' Whereas clergy who denied witchcraft were likely to be accused of unbelief, 'Shame, that one of his cast should be such an atheist'.[1]

Yet despite the zeal with which some Christians, both clerical and lay, sought to base their belief in witchcraft on a Biblical foundation, they were grossly mistaken. For the plain fact is that the Bible knows scarcely anything of true witchcraft, certainly not the New Testament, and the few injunctions found in the Old Testament refer to something else.

This was pointed out at great length by Reginald Scot in his *Discoverie of Witchcraft*. James I did not really touch the points which Scot had raised, for Scot spends eight sections of his book examining the meaning of Hebrew words, and showing that they do not signify witchcraft. Modern scholarship has strengthened his contentions even more.

THE 'WITCH' OF ENDOR

The so-called 'witch' of Endor has frequently been quoted as a clear example of a Biblical witch. Yet the remarkable thing about this notorious lady is that not only is she plainly not a witch, but she is not even called one in the Biblical text. Even Scot overlooks this remarkable fact. Those who hurriedly turn up their Bibles to disprove this assertion (1 Samuel xxviii) will find that the Authorized and Revised Versions both translate 'a woman that hath a familiar spirit'. In fact, the word witch only occurs in the page and chapter headings in the Authorized Version, 'Saul consulteth a witch' and

[1] Richard Steele, writing ironically in the *Tatler*, 28th May 1709.

'Saul seeks to a witch'. These headings are not part of the original text, they are mere interpretations of King James's translators (put in, significantly, in 1611). They are commentaries on the text, which at times interpret or seek to spiritualize the original text.

The Hebrew text says that Saul, in his desperation at the sight of a large Philistine host, and not having found guidance from the prophets or oracles of God, sought out 'a woman that had a familiar spirit'. The narrative vividly describes the seance, where Saul in disguise asked that Samuel shall be brought up from the abode of the dead under the ground. The woman either goes into a trance or consults her control, and she sees Samuel rising up in his prophetic mantle. It is evident that the woman alone saw Samuel for Saul asked her what he looked like. Saul himself only heard a voice, doubtless through the medium herself. At the same instant the woman sees through Saul's disguise and perceives him to be the king.

The whole narrative is indisputably that of a spiritualistic seance, and the Revised Standard Version quite properly calls the woman 'one who is a medium'. That is our modern terminology. The woman is not a witch at all, and the headings of the Authorized Version are alone responsible for having perpetuated this mistake.

It is rather surprising that Sir James Frazer the anthropologist, in his study of this narrative, did not see this point. On the one hand he spoke of the woman as a necromancer, but on the other hand he sticks to the word witch. In rather romantic language Frazer says that the witch 'may have been young and fair, with raven locks and lustrous eyes, or she may have been a wizened, toothless hag, with meeting nose and chin, blear eyes and grizzled hair, bent double with age and infirmity'. And he adds, 'We may safely conclude that this was one of the regular ways in which Israelitish witches and wizards professed to hold converse with the dead.'[1] No doubt, but why call her a witch?

Reginald Scot went much further and said 'that Saul was cousened and abused by the witch, and that Samuel was not raised as is proved by the witch's own talk'.[2] On the other hand there are some credulous and prejudiced modern writers who still believe that the medium of Endor was a witch, because they hold that modern spiritualism is witchcraft. Montague Summers says bluntly, 'Modern Spiritism is

[1] *Folk-lore in the Old Testament*, abridged edn., 1923, pp. 294 f.
[2] Scot, op. cit., p. 83.

merely Witchcraft revived.'[1] But, as we have seen, the spiritism of Endor has none of the marks of classical witchcraft and is not even called such in the Hebrew text.

HEBREW WORDS FOR WITCHES

The medium of Endor is called *ba'alath ob*, a mistress of a familiar spirit or talisman. This does not mean a familiar animal, as in later European witchcraft. It refers probably to the 'control', as modern spiritualism terms it, which is supposed to take charge of the medium and through her mouth gives messages from the dead.

The command in Exodus xxii, 18, 'thou shalt not suffer a witch to live', is translated in the Revised Version as 'a sorceress'. This is quite a different affair. The Hebrew word here used (*kashaph*) occurs some twelve times only, in one form or another, in the Old Testament. Its meaning is not clear and we have to judge its significance from the way in which it is used. The word has been derived by some writers from a root meaning to cut oneself, as did the priests of Baal in a frenzied dance. But other scholars consider it more likely that the word comes from an Arabic root meaning to obscure or to eclipse, used of the sun or moon. From this the Hebrew might mean dark or gloomy, or muttering in a dark and low tone. Magicians are generally associated with darkness, and are given to low mumblings: 'Thy speech shall be low out of the dust' (Isaiah xxix, 4).[2]

It has long been thought that this word 'witch' or 'sorcerer' in Exodus xxii is best understood as 'poisoner'. Reginald Scot maintained this, and this explanation was much quoted in Charles II's time, when capital punishment for witchcraft ceased. Men argued that the Biblical verse did not refer to all manner of magic or witches' assemblies, but only to poisoning. A man who killed his enemy with poison was guilty, of course, of a capital crime. This is still true. But apart from poisoning all the many other activities attributed to witches were not capital offences, or indeed based on actual occurrences. There was no Biblical support for applying capital punishment to them.

James I quoted Samuel's words to Saul, 'disobedience is as the sin of witchcraft' (properly sorcery). Sorcery is linked again with

[1] *History of Witchcraft and Demonology*, p. 269.
[2] *Encylopaedia Biblica*, pp. 2899 f.

whoredom and idolatry in the famous retort of Jehu to Joram, 'What peace, so long as the whoredoms of thy mother Jezebel and her witchcrafts (*keshaphim*) are so many?' (2 Kings ix, 22). Both sorcery and whoredom are connected with the magical and fertility cults of Canaan which so often culminated in prostitution and human sacrifice. The Hebrew prophets declaimed in great indignation against this immorality and magic which undermined true religion and ethics. The man who practises magic uses an evil power, to undermine the righteous by crooked ways and secret arts. He is a man of Belial, a man of blood and wicked ways.

Another Biblical word for witchcraft or wizardry (*qesem*) is more properly translated 'divination'. It is used of obtaining oracles by casting lots. Men wished to know the future and used various means which might help them to discover the unknown or to decide important actions. One of the most popular ways of casting lots was by using arrows, special pointless arrows, originally rods. By the manner in which they fell action was decided. This divination has nothing to do with witchcraft.[1]

These and other types of activity, loosely translated 'witchcraft' or 'wizardry', are in reality magic, good or bad, and sorcery. They are conscious and deliberate practices, that may be intended for useful or for harmful ends. They are not the unconscious or nocturnal witchcraft in which Europeans and Africans have believed.

King James's other Biblical references are no more fortunate. Pharaoh's wise men were simply sorcerers and magicians, and called such in the text. Simon Magus appears only once in the Acts of the Apostles as a magician. But some early Christian writers speak of him as leading a heretical sect in Rome. At the end of his life it was said that Simon tried to fly into the air, but Peter broke the spell, and Simon died of his fall to the ground. Later writers on witchcraft, such as Sprenger, quote this as an instance to show that the Devil can help men to fly and therefore enable witches to fly. But this is adding a great deal to the original story of the magician.

The 'Pythoness' (Acts xvi, 16) was a 'damsel possessed with a spirit of divination' or 'a python'. This was said originally to mean one who spoke through the power of the oracle at Delphi which was embodied in a python. It came to mean a soothsayer, who could make his voice appear to come from another part of the room. As

[1] Ibid., pp. 1118 f.

we should say, a ventriloquist. Whether or not such a person was to be regarded as possessed by a spirit, it is quite different from witchcraft.

TRUE WITCHCRAFT

If the Biblical words for a witch do not describe the sort of person later called a witch, yet there may be some practices which resemble witchcraft. There are a few indications that the European type of witchcraft belief may not have been unknown, to some degree, in Biblical times. But how little there is! It is only to be found in some vague references in the Old Testament, and not at all in the New Testament which preserves a remarkable silence on the whole subject, as if the fresh and fervent religion of its day left no room for the occult.

There is a strange passage in Ezekiel (xiii, 18–21) that cries, 'Woe to the women that sew pillows upon all elbows, and make kerchiefs for the head of persons of every stature to hunt souls.' This sounds like authentic witchcraft belief, as found in other parts of the world, and it is significant that it occurs in a late period of Israel's history, spoken by a prophet who was living in exile in Babylon in the sixth century B.C. Here he would be in contact with new ideas and beliefs, such as may have been little known to the inhabitants of Palestine.

It is not very clear what these evil people do. But one should note that they are women. They hunt souls, 'to slay the souls that should not die', and this they do 'for handfuls of barley and for pieces of bread'. They hunt the souls 'to make them fly', and save other 'souls alive that should not live'. But God 'will let the souls go'.

Quite what is the purpose of sewing pillows on elbows and kerchiefs on the head is not clear. But it is apparent that these women are believed to kill some souls for payment, while other dead souls are restored to life so that they may be used in nefarious designs.

The word rendered 'pillows' may refer to some bands sewn on to the garments, like the phylacteries which were worn by Pharisees at a later date. This would mean that magical strips are sewn on to robes as charms and amulets, either for protection against or for incitement towards demonic forces. The Hebrew literally translated suggests that the women sew these bands on to the hands of God, as if to tie him, but this is hard to credit. It is easier to understand as an action of sewing by these women on to the garments of people who come to them. The word 'kerchief' is uncertain, but it may refer to veils which were worn as protections against evil, or else to prevent the victims seeing what was happening to them.

There are other scattered references in the Old Testament to evil forces, which may mean either the magic arts in general or evil spirits which operate at night. Thus in the Psalms, in particular, we have 'thou shalt not be afraid for the terror by night' (xci, 5). It is at night that evil is thought to be unleashed and then the wicked do their plotting: 'he deviseth iniquity upon his bed' (xxxvi, 4). That this is not mere enmity but could refer to a form of witchcraft is clear from Psalm xi: 'How say ye to my soul, Flee as a bird to your mountain? For, lo, the wicked bend the bow, They make ready their arrow upon the string, That they may shoot in darkness at the upright in heart.' Here the soul is thought to fly like a bird while the wicked shoot at it by night.

Evil men practise what the Hebrew calls *'awen*, a word which includes evil deeds, magic, and sorcery. These are the ones who set 'the snare of the fowler' for the unwary (xci, 3). The just call upon the Lord so that 'the wicked is snared in the work of his own hands' (ix, 16). No doubt many of these verses may be taken in several ways, as the oppression of the poor by the rich, the envy of an enemy at the upright and prosperous, or as the evil deeds of magicians and night-workers. 'The proud have hid a snare for me, and cords; they have spread a net by the way side; they have set gins for me' (cxl, 5). But many of these words, which to western ears sound like plain enmity, are found as technical terms among the Babylonians and neighbours of the Jews. The nets and snares are common words for magic and cursing, and they have a deeper meaning than is apparent on the surface.

LILITH AND NIGHT MONSTERS

Akin to the evil people who work at night are the night monsters in which many ancient peoples believed. Such a creature is Lilith, who seems to have had a fascination for the poet Rossetti:

> *Of Adam's first wife, Lilith, it is told*
> *(The witch he loved before the gift of Eve,)*
> *That, ere the snake's, her sweet tongue could deceive,*
> *And her enchanted hair was the first gold.*

Lilith was, properly, a night-hag, in the popular beliefs of Palestine and Babylon. She was an evil demon who inhabited desert places, and she gets one mention in the Bible: 'The wild beasts of the desert shall meet with the wolves, and the satyr shall cry to his fellow; yea, Lilith shall settle there' (Isaiah xxxiv, 14, Revised Version margin).

According to Jewish tradition the name Lilith was derived from the word for night, *laylah*. The etymology is doubtful, but the belief is clear. Lilith was perhaps the 'terror by night' of Psalm xci, and one ancient commentator on this text says, 'There is a harmful spirit that flies like a bird and shoots like an arrow'. The Babylonians believed Lilith to be a hairy night-monster, especially dangerous to children. Men also were warned not to sleep in an empty house because of the depredations of Lilith, who was like a succubus.

Later Rabbinic legend said that Lilith was Adam's first wife, and together they begat strange children. According to another version Lilith cursed Eve's unborn child and Cain the murderer came forth. Lilith was assimilated to the snake, the author of all evil. There is no trace of such beliefs in the Bible.

Lilith was said by the later traditions to prey on men, and particularly to take on the form of a beautiful woman with flowing hair. There is a connexion here with the Lorelei of later European myth, and with women who lured men to their doom as in the Tannhäuser legend. Teutonic myth embroidered and developed this theme, but its roots are in the east. A modern example of such a story is in *She*, by Rider Haggard.

A whole class of demons took their name from Lilith. A commentary on the priestly blessing goes thus: 'The Lord bless thee in all thy business and guard thee from the Lilin.' These Lilin were thought to be women and dangerous to children.

Another ghoul was Aluqah. 'The vampire (Aluqah) hath two daughters, called, Give, give' (Proverbs xxx, 15). This vampire is mentioned almost casually, but the fact that no explanation is given shows that the reference would be easily understood. She was known to the Arabs as a woman who fed on human flesh. The vampire and the witch were often closely linked in later thought.

In the apocryphal book of Tobit there is Sarah whose seven husbands had been slain by the demon Asmodeus. This is an incubus, probably derived from the name of a Persian fiend. The story probably came from an Armenian original, which it very closely resembles; it was written some time after 200 B.C. Noteworthy in the story is the magical remedy which Raphael gives to drive off Asmodeus. It will be understood how the later writers on witchcraft seized on Asmodeus as a good name to be confessed as a devil who had lain with women. Medieval rabbis had written about Great and Little Asmodeus.

There are, therefore, in the Bible and Jewish books of antiquity, some traces of belief comparable to the later witchcraft belief in Europe. No doubt they formed part of the soil of the witchcraft beliefs, as did Greek and Roman ideas. But the Biblical traces of the belief are scanty, and they are of a different nature from those which were quoted by old believers in witchcraft, such as King James. Frequently they are not clear evidence of witchcraft belief, for the night monsters may be demons of the desert, rather than human beings whose souls wander about in the dark to devour their fellows. Certainly there is not the abundance of belief in witchcraft that might have been expected. The evidence is extremely meagre.

The great Hebrew prophets spoke out strongly against all workers in magic and mischief. 'When they say unto you, Seek unto them that have familiar spirits and unto wizards, that chirp and mutter: should not a people seek unto their God?' (Isaiah viii, 19).

There was little social urge in those times for scapegoats to explain away public ills, for the religion provided for that. The Hebrews had their communal scapegoat, which was sent off to the desert spirits once a year on the great Day of Atonement. Thus the whole people was cleansed annually in this rite from all evil, conscious and unconscious. The New Testament beliefs in the Atonement of Christ served the same purpose.

In the New Testament there is not a trace of belief in witches, unless they are to be vaguely included under the general catalogue of the works of the flesh, 'idolatry, sorcery, enmities' (Galatians v, 20). There was little room for belief in witchcraft under the strong monotheism of prophetic and early Christian teaching, and it withered then as it did later under the surge of modern knowledge.

OTHER NEAR EASTERN BELIEFS

In Arabia one finds some of the ideas common to classical antiquity. In the last chapter but one of the Koran there is a spell against women who breathe or spit on knots: 'I take refuge with the Lord of the Daybreak . . . from the evil of the darkening when it comes on, and from the evil of the blowers among knots, and from the evil of the envious one when he envies.' Another verse of the Koran says that God takes to himself 'during sleep those who do not die', suggesting the absence of the soul from the body in sleep.

The transformation of men into animals is expressed by a special Arabic word (*maskh*). One of the stories in the *Arabian Nights* tells of a jinn who hid his soul in a sparrow's crop, and hid that in a succession of boxes so that no one would be able to harm him. But a man got possession of the sparrow and when he strangled it the jinn fell to the ground in a heap of ashes. And of course there are many stories of flying through the air, on magic horses, carpets, and birds.

Babylonian beliefs in Lilith and night-hags have been mentioned. There were three of them who were believed to be female and to feed on children. Other evil spirits came from the abode of the dead, bringing pest and destruction and flying about by night. Magical texts which have been preserved from Babylon were aimed at enabling priests to control or break the power of those demons who exercise malign influence on sick people. Particularly did ghosts of unburied men prey on those who strayed near tombs. So also did the ghosts of women who died in childbirth. All disease was thought to be due to the acts of evil spirits or sorcerers.

In the clay tablets which have been found among the ruins of the Mesopotamian cities are many incantations and spells designed to protect men against the attacks of demons and sorcerers. It is not easy to distinguish the types of sorcery. Some are clearly concerned with the making of black magic. In the Assyrian laws we read: 'If either a man or a woman have made magical preparations and they have been seized in their hands and charge and proof have been brought against them, the maker of the magical preparations shall be put to death.'

Other incantations are directed against evil women who engage in harmful spiritual practices: 'She in whose heart the word of my misfortune dwells, on whose tongue my ruin is begotten, on whose lips my poison originates, in whose footsteps death stands.' Such persons were supposed to tie the soul of their victim in knots, and the curative charm sought to untie the knot: 'her knot is loosed.'

An exorcism-text denounces the women 'who sit and your witch-craft and your spells against me weave. . . . Tearing of the bowels, burning of the face, and madness (with these), have you bewitched me. . . . You have chosen me for a corpse, you have handed me over to a skull, you have delivered me into the power of a family ghost'.[1]

In ancient Egypt also there were texts used to ward off evil from sick people or from tombs. The idea of injury to the soul is found in the famous myth of Osiris, who was killed by the power of darkness. Another tale of two brothers, tells how one of them hid his heart in an acacia tree, and when his wife had the tree cut he fell down dead. But he revived again when his brother had found his heart in an acacia berry and put it in a cup of fresh water.

Many other beliefs crop up in obscure references in the fragmentary literature of the ancient near east. While the ideas that are known may provide some parallels to certain later European beliefs, yet there is no comparison with the developed witchcraft belief as it appeared in late medieval and Renaissance Europe.

[1] S. H. Hooke, *Babylonian and Assyrian Religion,* 1953, pp. 78–81, 115.

CHAPTER 10

Modern African Witchcraft

The study of witchcraft is particularly interesting and important because witchcraft is still believed to be practised in the modern world. So the study of witchcraft is not merely antiquarian, made up of guesses about the mentality of medieval Europeans, but is one whose interpretation can be greatly eased by a consideration of practices believed in by millions of people today.

It has long been believed that witchcraft abounds in Africa. Reginald Scot said, 'Many great and grave authors write, and many fond writers also affirm, that there are certain families in Africa which with their voices bewitch whatsoever they praise. Insomuch as, if they command either plant, corn, infant, horse, or any other beasts, the same presently withereth, decayeth, and dieth.'

Although beliefs comparable with those of European witchcraft have been known in many parts of the world, it is in Africa that the most careful and extensive study has been made of them. In a number of tribes these beliefs have been studied at first-hand by expert scholars. To the European these beliefs in witches are useful as throwing a great deal of light upon the mental processes of his own forefathers. To the African they are still part of the traditional ideas of his country, and there is little sign of a decrease in witchcraft belief with increasing education.

A comparison of European and African belief, then, may serve a double purpose. It may reveal to Europeans something of the way in which witches are deluded and confess to their imaginary activities. It may help Africans to understand how it is that such widespread and deeply rooted ideas can yet be based upon imagination, and not upon material practices. It is hoped that the foregoing chapters on the fallacies of European witchcraft will already have helped to clear the way for a similar critical study of African beliefs in witchcraft.

This comparison has a practical purpose, therefore, and one that is topical since many people still live in fear of witches. But we must not be understood to imply any close connexion between European and African beliefs. Whether one ever borrowed from the other, or whether both are ultimately derived from some ancient common pool of ideas (some 'archetype of the unconscious'), cannot be said. These are matters of speculation, and quite beyond the scope of the present work. The comparison between African and European witchcraft is made because there are some ideas common to both, and by bringing out these ideas and showing them to be groundless some light may be brought into a dark and complex subject.

THE FEAR OF WITCHCRAFT IN AFRICA

There is no doubt that Africans fear and hate witches, and therefore take stern measures to curb their activities. Missions and governments often claim that their aim is to deliver the African from the fear of witchcraft. This is undoubtedly true. But it is also true that their efforts do not seem to bear much fruit in this sphere, that most educated Africans still believe profoundly in witchcraft, and that there are statements made on many sides that the fear of witchcraft is increasing. The coming of European ideas and customs has unsettled society in Africa, and the increasing insecurity adds to the force of the belief in witchcraft which is held responsible for unknown and incalculable dangers.

Yet while Africans fear witches they do not hunt them out incessantly. Many people are believed to be witches, but as their powers are generally thought to be in abeyance they are not unduly disturbed. Only when there seems to be evidence that the witch is on the prowl, and men sicken, is action taken to restrain the witches' activities. In the olden days most mysterious deaths and diseases were attributed to witches. In modern times lack of success, failure in examinations, inability to gain promotion in office or shop, any strange disease, and especially barrenness in women and impotence in men, is attributed to witchcraft.

When Robert Moffat was in Bechuanaland in 1825 the heir to the throne died of what Moffat called 'Hottentot sickness', i.e. anthrax. But the boy's parents insisted that he had been bewitched by the family of a girl whom he had jilted. The accused family had to flee to a neighbouring tribe to escape an avenging raiding party.

In 1889 Sechele, chief of the Bechuana, baptized by Livingstone forty years previously, had five men executed for witchcraft on the sole evidence of a servant girl. Sechele answered inquiries by admitting the charge, but claiming that proof of guilt was overwhelming, and that he had acquitted many others less guilty.

When the king of the Swazi died in 1890, the Queen Regent pleaded with the British government for permission 'just for one day' to destroy the witches who, it was believed, had killed the king. She submitted to, but resented, Queen Victoria's expressed 'detestation of the practice' of witch-hunting.

In 1937 the Bamangwato chief Tshekedi accused his divorced wife, before the District Commissioner's court, of attempting witchcraft against himself. Together with two magicians she was imprisoned and finally banished from the tribal reserve.

In 1934 a new movement of witch-finders swept over Nyasaland, the Rhodesias, and into the Congo colony. These men, called Bamucapi, used many trappings of European quack medicine together with older witch-hunting methods. They had astonishing success, flourished for a time, and then disappeared.

After the Second World War, a movement of witch-hunters came from Ghana, across Togo and Dahomey, and into Nigeria. Known as Nana Tongo, or Anatinga, these men spread excitement into many villages, enriched themselves and their initiates, and yet were supported by a large body of public opinion, even among the educated, as doing good work in checking the harmful deeds of witches. Their activities were only checked, publicly at least, by prohibitive legislation in 1951.

WHAT IS AFRICAN WITCHCRAFT?

The description of witchcraft in Africa has suffered from distortion, just as it has in Europe. The words: witch, wizard, sorcerer, black magician, witch-doctor, medicine-man, juju-man, fetisher, and so on, are bandied about freely with little attempt at fixing an approximate meaning for them.

What is African Witchcraft?

In his absorbing novel *The African Witch*, Joyce Cary has given a lifelike picture of a woman who lays a spell on her opponents and paralyses the work of the government. But, whatever her charms, this lady is no witch. For she is a known, public figure, who works conscious magic to the furtherance of her ends, and she has none of the characteristics of the true witch.

Joyce Cary is a serious novelist who had worked in Africa, and one expects more from serious writers. One finds, however, Pennethorne Hughes, a writer on witchcraft, saying, 'Christianity fought the religion of the Horned God. It still fights him when it combats the religions and the secret societies of Africa or of the African communities in the Americas. For, substantially, the ritual, and even the appearance of the god of the witches, was that of the High Priest of African cults today . . . their ritual does not consciously parody Christianity in the same way as did the cult in Europe. But the symbolism, the magical processes and the diabolic appearance, must be extremely similar.'[1]

Why 'must'? No African, or anyone who knows anything about either African religion or African witchcraft, would accept that statement for a moment. It assumes that African religions and secret societies are the worship of the Devil, by analogy from this writer's interpretation of European witchcraft as a diabolical cult. Yet the idea of the Devil is foreign to many African peoples. And that the priesthood, ritual, and symbolism of public and accepted religious worship should be associated with the hated, anti-social, and nocturnal witchcraft is demonstrably untrue. There is no logical force in the 'must be extremely similar'. It simply begs the question.

On another page the same writer confuses possession with witchcraft. 'In the witch-master, in Africa today and—as certainly in the medieval witch-cult—there is induced possession, in early days no doubt possession by the cult animal.' Once again this assumes that witchcraft is identical with some diabolical or animal cult. This is not so in Africa, however one may interpret the confessions of European witches. Possession is, indeed, widely practised, but it is done in connexion with public religious ceremonies and not in witchcraft.

One must say for Mr. Hughes that he is treating in the main of European witchcraft, though he does claim to improve on those writers who have made 'no very considered attempt to relate witch-

[1] *Witchcraft*, pp. 91–2.

craft in Europe to the parallel activities of the contemporary African or Polynesian witch-doctor'. But it might be expected that Europeans who live in Africa would have a more accurate conception of the nature of African witchcraft. Yet there is still a great deal of confusion about, and this is evident in the various laws passed by governments that rule over African peoples, and that ought to be able to discriminate what is witchcraft and what is not.

Thus in Nigeria the *Laws* state that 'any person who represents himself to be a witch or have the power of witchcraft' is liable to six months in jail. This ignores the fact that witches do not normally profess to be such except under accusation. Similarly in Uganda the law threatens 'whoever holds himself out as a witch-doctor or witch-finder' with five years' imprisonment. Thus the very doctor who seeks to protect society against witchcraft is made to suffer. This may be well from the European point of view, but Africans do not understand it. Other countries have comparable provisions.

The Tanganyika Ordinance does not mention witch-doctors, but penalizes impartially any pretence to 'occult power or knowledge' with a year in prison or fifty pounds fine. This could apply equally to all kinds of magicians, spiritualists, fortune-tellers, teacup-readers, and the like.

Then in Kenya the 1928 Ordinance blandly penalized any person who pretended to exercise supernatural power! Any prophet or priest, of any religion, might find himself a criminal under such a comprehensive condemnation. Moses or Elijah would not have fared well in Kenya.

Clearly governments have been as much confused about the nature of African witchcraft as has the layman. One must not blame too severely those who attempt to impose European scepticism and legislation direct upon African peoples. One marvels at their temerity. But in recent years research students, often helped by governments, have brought to light some of the conceptions of witchcraft that African peoples themselves possess. We will glance at those for fuller enlightenment.

WHAT AFRICANS SAY ABOUT WITCHCRAFT

In his epoch-making work *Witchcraft, Oracles and Magic among the Azande* (1937), Professor Evans-Pritchard says, 'Azande believe that some people are witches and can injure them in virtue of an inherent quality. A witch performs no rite, utters no spell, and possesses no medicines. An act of witchcraft is a psychic act.'

There are people who are believed to use evil medicines against their enemies, but these are properly called sorcerers. 'They believe also that sorcerers may do them ill by performing magic rites with bad medicines. Azande distinguish clearly between witches and sorcerers. Against both they employ diviners, oracles and medicines.'[1]

By the Azande, who live on the Nile-Congo divide, witchcraft is believed to be a substance in the bodies of witches, a matter that can be discovered by a post-mortem, and that is inherited by children from their parents. Men and women can be witches. They fly through the air at night, giving off a bright light. They steal and eat the souls of their victims, devouring them gradually so that a wasting disease is the outward sign of soul-destruction taking place.

Many other African peoples make similar distinctions, with peculiarities of interpretation in different localities. In Bechuanaland in South Africa people distinguish between 'night witches' and 'day sorcerers'. The former are supposed to be mainly elderly women, who habitually bewitch all and sundry and not just special enemies. They are believed to do this at night, accompanied by other witches and animal familiars, especially owls. The day 'sorcerers', on the other hand, are solitary individuals who do not practise their black arts continuously but only on specific occasions. They may be hired out by someone who wishes to harm a particular enemy, and so they are known and conscious agents of evil who have a palpable apparatus of their trade.[2]

The Basuto use the same word (*baloi*) for witches as do the Bechuana. They distinguish between the anti-social sorcerers, and the more mischievous witches. Witches are women (and a few men) who have the ability to fly and exercise it only at night. They ride on sticks or on fleas, meet in assemblies, and dance stark naked in various places. They have a particular taste for human flesh, especially that of corpses, which they gratify by visiting graves and raising the dead. Sometimes they are thought to capture the newly dead on their way to the spirit world, and to use them as frightening ghosts.

[1] Evans-Pritchard, p. 21.
[2] I. Schapera, *The Bantu-speaking Tribes of South Africa*, 1937, pp. 241 f.

Hence great care is needed to ensure that full funeral ceremonies are carried out.[1]

The Lovedu of the Transvaal have one word (*vuloi*) for witches and sorcerers, but they qualify it with other words to indicate the difference between night-witchcraft and day-witchcraft. All witchcraft is evil and anti-social. The night-witches, mostly women, are born so and inherit the witchcraft from their mothers. They go about naked at night and meet in assemblies. They are believed to cause barrenness in women, to destroy crops, and to cut off parts of the bodies of their victims. They have familiars, such as owls, snakes, and hyenas. The belief differs from that of the Azande in that Lovedu witches are not thought to have any witch-substance, and their souls do not go out alone to work their evil deeds. The whole personality is thought to go away, though a hyena may be left in the witch's image while she is away.[2]

Across the other side of the continent, in West Africa, one finds similar beliefs with minor variations. In Nigeria the Yoruba believe that witches are generally women who fly about at night and meet in secret conclave. They are associated with birds, especially the nightjar which flies about at dusk. They suck the blood of their victims until they die. They are quite distinct from sorcerers and workers in evil magic.[3]

The Ibo of Nigeria hold to belief in witchcraft with great tenacity. Witches consort with one another, flying as balls of fire or night-birds to their meetings. They menace men in health and women in pregnancy. They have to bring a new soul with them on initiation into the witches' guild. They infect other people with witchcraft by putting a special spiritual substance into food so that the person gets a craving for human flesh.[4]

The Nupe of Bida in northern Nigeria believe that women are the most dangerous witches, though some men also are witches. They make themselves invisible at night, recognize and meet other witches, separate their souls from their bodies, and their specific aim is to eat other people's souls. Fire is said to come out of their mouths and tears from their eyes. It is thought, however, that

---

[1] H. Ashton, *The Basuto*, 1952, pp. 293 f.
[2] E. J. and J. D. Krige, *The Realm of a Rain-Queen*, 1943, pp. 250 f.
[3] G. Parrinder, *Religion in an African City*, 1953, pp. 53 f.
[4] C. K. Meek, *Law and Authority in a Nigerian Tribe*, 1937, pp. 79 f.

witchcraft is not hereditary but must be acquired from someone who already has the power.[1]

The Ewe peoples of Dahomey and Togoland think of witchcraft as a being of power that takes up its dwelling in women, chiefly. They wander about at night, walking on their heads, or with feet turned backwards and fire coming out of their eyes and mouths. The witches suck people's blood and take away their souls. They usually suck their own relatives.[2]

Similarly the Akan peoples of Ghana and the Ivory Coast believe that witches change themselves into animals and give off a glowing light like fireflies. Witches are mostly women, and the gift can be inherited or purchased. The witches suck the blood of their victims and divide the body among themselves. The heart is left until the day when they have decided to kill him.[3] It is thought that the Akan word for a witch, *obayifo*, is the origin of the Obeah of Jamaica, taken across by the slaves. But the much-publicized Voodoo of Haiti simply derives from an Ewe word *vudu* meaning 'gods'.

In Sierra Leone the Mende people believe that witchcraft is responsible for any unusual death. A witch is not born a witch, but becomes one by being bewitched by someone else. The presence of a witch-spirit may be shown by autopsy; if the spleen sinks in water it is proof that the deceased had been violated by a witch-spirit. The witches are said to leave their skins during sleep. They may change into rats and eat up the crops, or they may spread disease among men. The witch sucks the blood of her victim from its throat.[4]

The best account of witchcraft in West Africa is that given by Dr. Margaret Field in her *Religion and Medicine of the Gã People* (1937). The Gã live on the Ghana seaboard, and they have been in contact with Europeans for centuries. Dr. Field says that their witchcraft has 'no palpable apparatus connected with it, no rites, ceremonies, incantations, or invocations that the witch has to perform. It is simply projected at will from the mind of the witch. . . . Witches are people mentally afflicted with the obsession that they have the power to harm others by thinking them harm.'[5]

Gã witches are believed to meet in companies at night, while their

---

[1] S. F. Nadel, *Nupe Religion*, 1954, pp. 165 f.
[2] *Africa*, October 1935, pp. 548 f.
[3] Ibid., p. 553.
[4] Ibid., p. 556.
[5] Field, p. 135 f.

mortal bodies remain on their beds. They travel to the assembly by flying, sometimes along those fine cobwebs that are spun out in the night from bush to bush and house to house. Other witches travel on the backs of animals, especially owls, but also snakes, antelopes, and leopards. The witches gather round a pot in which their victims are said to be cooked or their blood contained. Witches are thought to have possessing demons or evil spirits which enter them, and these sometimes get out of control as the witchcraft gets stronger.

There are some curious beliefs held by the Tiv people of central Nigeria, which are at once partly different from those of many other tribes, and illuminating as to the nature of witchcraft belief. The Tiv believe that there is a witchcraft-substance (called *tsav*) which grows on the hearts of human beings and some animals. It is said to look like the liver only smaller, and it may be rounded or notched at the edges. This substance may be red, black, or white, and it can be good or bad.

The owners of this witchcraft-substance may be unaware that they possess it, but it will give them greater personal force and more success in life than if they had it not. All old people are supposed to have this substance, for that is what had enabled them to live to old age. If the witchcraft-substance is good it can be used for personal advantage, and it inspires men to particular feats of talent. But it is potentially dangerous. Only with this substance can a man bewitch another, send him evil dreams, and make poisons to kill him. This bewitching is done at night and only affects one's own kindred.

Tiv witches are said to meet at night and to feed on human flesh. They are carefully organized (which Tiv institutions normally are not). One of their number fetches bodies out of graves, another restores them to life, a third performs the sacrifice. They have cooks who prepare the meat for eating. Yet all this is invisible and spiritual, although, since the most powerful members of society are known from material success and prestige, it may be admitted that they are also the leading practitioners of witchcraft.

All death is believed to be caused by someone's witchcraft-substance, since only persons possessing this are thought to have the power of bringing death. Yet the elders who attend a funeral, and are clearly possessors of witchcraft-substance because of their age, would not admit to having killed the deceased. It is assumed that the victim has been killed by someone who was using his witchcraft-substance for his own benefit rather than for the good of the community.

The Tiv believe that there are anti-social folk who go about spreading death and trouble. At times resentment against them comes to a head, when there are too many deaths, and uprisings occur to suppress them. In 1929 there was a cult called 'Beef' which sought by new ritual methods to force recantation and confession upon accused witches. At other times bewitching is settled by the diviners and the family elders.[1]

GENERAL MARKS OF AFRICAN WITCHCRAFT

The above quick survey of witchcraft belief in different parts of Africa may help to show some of its characteristics, and also the wide distribution of the belief. This does not mean, however, that all African tribes have these beliefs. Many African tribes have not yet been the subject of specialist study, and may never have it before they lose their ancient ideas.

In some African tribes it seems that the type of belief in witchcraft that we have been considering does not exist, or only in vaguely recognizable form. Dr. Nadel, who has written elsewhere of the beliefs of the Nupe of Nigeria, says of another African tribe, the Korongo of the Nuba mountains, in the eastern Sudan, 'The Korongo have no witchcraft beliefs. But they conceive of a certain magic power of similar deadly and obscure agency. Little positive can be said about it. . . . It is certainly owned by grain priests, and possibly also by other individuals (no one is quite certain). It is used against evil-doers who, themselves possessing similar magic, try to interfere with fertility and fertility-rites, and possibly also against other manners of persons, guilty or innocent.'[2]

Some of the peoples of Rhodesia and Kenya also have beliefs which, while regarded by writers on them as witchcraft, appear to be more akin to sorcery. They are said to be conscious actions performed by evil men and women, often at night and harming men invisibly, but also in daytime and by the use of poisons.[3]

---

[1] L. and P. Bohannan, *The Tiv of Central Nigeria*, 1955, pp. 38 f., 84 ff.
[2] *The Nuba*, 1947, p. 307.
[3] See E. W. Smith, *The Ila-speaking Peoples of Northern Rhodesia*, and C. M. Doke, *The Lambas of Northern Rhodesia*.

For the purpose of this study, which does not pretend to be exhaustive and treat of every African tribe, attention will be paid to those beliefs, mentioned in the last section, which are widely distributed and have notable points of comparison with European witchcraft beliefs.

The witchcraft beliefs, then, of many African peoples can be briefly summarized as follows. The witch is generally female. She goes out at night and meets in an assembly with other witches. She leaves her body in her hut and flies to the assembly, often as an owl, other bird, or animal. The witch preys on other people and procures a victim for consumption in the assembly. The blood of the victim is sucked or its members eaten. This causes a wasting disease to his physical body, and the victim lingers until the heart, liver, or some other vital organ is eaten. Children are often thought to be eaten by witches. Any disease may be taken as a sign of their evil machinations. Some people believe that the witch is possessed by a witch-spirit, or has with her some witch-substance, but this belief is far from general.

There is an astonishing resemblance between these modern African beliefs and those of Europe centuries ago. Apart from the peculiar names, such as devils, covens, and Sabbaths, and practices supposed to be perverted from Christianity, like the Black Masses and baptisms, so much of European belief is clearly similar to that of Africa.

Whence comes this similarity? That is to raise a highly debatable question, and one for which there is little solid evidence. It is the thesis of Pennethorne Hughes that witchcraft was 'a widespread survival of palaeolithic emotive religion'. This is said to have 'particularly survived in Northern Europe and in Africa. The African form was, in spite of great powers of hyperaesthesia and magical control, degenerate, as is most African culture.'[1]

This is a hypothesis, but there is little proof of it. Whether African culture was derived from Egypt or elsewhere, or from a common source perhaps on the Upper Nile, is a question hotly debated today. No answer can be given with any degree of certainty. And it cannot be proved either that African culture is degenerate from some much higher level, or that it has only reached upwards so far from a fairly low level.

[1] *Witchcraft*, p. 38 and footnote.

Furthermore, to restrict ourselves to the question of witchcraft and avoid the entanglements of argument about the origins of cultures, it must be noted clearly that in African witchcraft we have to do not with a perverted cult, or with 'magical control', but with a spiritual activity, whether imaginary or not.

WITCHCRAFT TERMINOLOGY

African witchcraft is clearly distinct from sorcery or magic. And since the witch is usually a woman it is useful to restrict this word 'witch' to one who is supposed to be engaged in the nocturnal activities sketched above, even if occasionally a male witch is meant.

A wizard, described by the dictionary as a 'male witch', and also as 'magician and sorcerer', is best regarded as the practitioner of conscious magic, whether through spells or known poison. This may be called evil or 'black magic'. Some African peoples themselves use the word 'black' in speaking of this evil type of magic. For all African tribes believe that there is good magic also, 'white magic'. This latter is helpful and protective. The man who prepares useful magical potions is a respected member of the community, whereas the 'black magician' or wizard works in secret and against the interests of society as a whole.

The nature of the 'witch-doctor' will be discussed later. Suffice it here to say that he is the man who fights witchcraft, by the use of magical and material medicines. The witch-doctor is often medicine-man, leech, herbalist, soothsayer, and diviner all in one. He has useful functions, even if one accepts the point of view that witchcraft is impossible. Only with the coming of colonial legislation has he been branded as a bad lot, equally with the witches themselves. Far different is his honourable status in the eyes of Africans.

The punishment imposed on convicted witches varied, before the coming of Europeans, from death in some places to simple confession in others. Some witch-hunts were undoubtedly cruel, if not organized with the refined tortures of the Inquisition. It is now the duty of the government to protect the members of society from groundless accusation. But legislation has not helped to diminish the belief in witchcraft one whit in Africa. Rather it is said to be on the increase.

Witch-hunters and witch-finders exist, singly or in groups, and adapt themselves to modern methods. The mingling of European nostrums, chemical or astrological, with traditional African remedies is a sign of the times and the inevitable product of the contact of cultures. Witchcraft is still a living force, and it is treated by all methods available, old and new.

CHAPTER 11

Activities of African Witches

After the brief indication of the nature of witchcraft in Africa given in the last chapter, we come to a more detailed consideration of some of the characteristic activities in which the African witches are thought to engage.

The work supposed to be done by witches rests, as in late medieval Europe, upon the general ideas that people have as to the actions of witches, and upon the witches' confessions themselves. We do not commit ourselves to an opinion of the truth of these confessions, if we now speak of their activities as if they were real.

BECOMING A WITCH

Witchcraft is supposed to be either inherited or to be caught. The Ibo of southern Nigeria believe that witches can infect innocent people by putting a spiritual substance into their food. Having partaken of it this person is susceptible to the influence of the witch who then administers a drug to 'make his mouth blunt'. This medicine induces a craving for human flesh and so the neophyte seeks admission to the guild of witches and is told to meet them at night.

Rather similarly the Nupe of northern Nigeria, many of whom are now Mohammedans, suppose that witchcraft is acquired by rubbing a medicine into the eyes or on to the body, and packets of the medicine are supposed to be hidden in the witch's hair or belt. Witchcraft is not hereditary, except in the sense that like a craft it may continue in one family. If anyone wishes to become a witch she is said to go to the female head of the market, who is also supposed to be head of the witches, and is told to meet the other witches under a tree at night. It is believed that both men and women can become witches, but the power of the males is much weaker than that of the females. The men do not eat souls, but play tricks on the unsuspecting and may even be used to give protection against robbers.

The Gã of Ghana think that witchcraft can either be inherited, or else may be imposed upon the witch against her will. It may come to the witch at birth, or as a heritage from a dying relative. Or it may be bought at a very low price. The Gã people are said to think that the witch possession comes from a spirit or a demon, an idea that is rare elsewhere in Africa. The possessing spirit may master its hostess so that she suffers from what a psychologist would call a 'compulsion-neurosis', feeling forced to do things against her better self. Hence the witch may confess to having harmed some person but can find no reason for hating the victim. Many people suffer agonies from fear of becoming a witch, and they dread that some unnatural power is trying to get hold of them for its own purposes.[1]

The Azande of the eastern Sudan have a belief in a witchcraft-substance, which is somewhat comparable to the Gã idea of a witch's demons. They are rather vague as to what sort of substance this is. Some say it is an oval blackish swelling in which small objects may be found, others say that it is red and contains seeds which the witch has eaten in his neighbours' plantations. This substance is said to be discoverable by autopsy, and to be found near the liver or gall-bladder; it may be the bladder or part of the small intestine. A post-mortem examination may be held at the grave of a man who had been accused of witchcraft, the relatives attending as witnesses and the operation being performed by a blood-brother. Gashes are made in the belly, and the intestines are then taken out for examination to see if witch-substance is there. If it is not, the relatives rejoice and put the intestines back. If the substance is there the accusers hang the intestines on a tree.[2]

Azande believe witchcraft to be inherited from parents, the father only transmitting witchcraft to his sons and mothers to their daughters. A man who is proved to be a witch, but whose father was not one, is called a bastard. But the witchcraft may remain in

[1] Field, op. cit., pp. 135 f.
[2] Evans-Pritchard, op. cit., pp. 40 f.

abeyance throughout a man's life; if he does not use his powers then he is not dangerous to his friends. Hence men do not ask the oracles who are the witches in the village, but only when bewitching power is felt do they inquire who is now exercising his faculties.

The Lovedu of Transvaal believe that the 'night-witch' is born a witch, and that he is taught the craft in childhood by his mother. But a witch may keep his powers in reserve and only use them to protect his own crops. The great majority of such witches are female; they drink in the witchcraft with their mother's milk. The mother is said to begin the training, teaching the child to cling to the wall like a bat long before it can walk. Night-witchcraft cannot be bought, nor can it be learnt from someone outside the family. There is no belief in a witchcraft-substance.[1]

Basuto witches are mostly women and inherit their state and their familiars from their parents, usually the mother. They are not as dangerous as are the sorcerers, but they are rather mischievous and immoral. They harm men with their perverted sense of humour. They make horses shy by turning into fireballs, or give children convulsions in their sleep, or give men sexual dreams like the succubi of the Middle Ages. Witches are held responsible for the accidents and fears of the night.[2]

THE WITCHES' ASSEMBLIES

Of great interest, in view of the comparison with Europe, are the meetings and organization of witches, as they are supposed to exist in Africa.

Most Gã witches confess that they belong to companies which meet at night to hold discussions and eat human flesh. The societies are said to be about ten in membership. The company is like a court and has a chief, a messenger, and an executioner. Dr. Field quotes confessions in which witches said they belonged to companies of seven, that they were chief of the company or could name the chief and fellow-witches. Some of the companies are mixed, men and women. At the meetings the witches rival each other in performing marvels. The witch with the most demons, or marvels, is made chief. Since witches are thought thus to meet together, they are

[1] Kriges, op. cit., p. 250.
[2] Ashton, op. cit., pp. 294 f.

believed to be able to recognize one another in the daytime and to be able to tell who are other witches. At the same time, these meetings are spiritual, for it is thought that the witch's body remains on her bed while her soul goes off to the assembly.

The Nupe witches are thought to send out their 'shadow-soul' at night, while their bodies are still asleep in their houses. The witches meet under a tree outside the village, and there they eat souls and work out their plans. There is an order of members and they co-operate in providing a victim in turn. But it is said that rivalry and quarrels are common among witches. Their recognized head (*lelu*) is the woman who supervises the women of the town and the market.[1]

Ibo witches are said to be formed into guilds, so that they can work together to procure victims. Hence they are known to each other and meet at night at an hour indicated by the cry of birds, when they all get up from their beds and go to the place of assembly. An accused witch may be forced to march round the village calling on members of her guild to surrender the parts of their victim that they have taken.[2]

Azande witches are believed to meet together, with elders who are chosen from the older and more experienced members. They have small drums, the membranes of which are made of human skin, and as the drums are beaten to call members to the meeting they give out the call, 'human flesh, human flesh'. The leaders instruct the younger witches and consider their proposals, for a witch is not allowed to kill a man on his own, but his suggestions have to be discussed and accepted by the whole assembly. Then the witches go off to the victim's house, dance around it, and the witch who hates him enters and throws him outside the door where the assembled ghouls worry him and seize parts of his flesh which they take off to cook at their meeting-place. Yet Azande opinion is quite clear that the witch's body remains asleep on his bed, and that it is only the victim's soul, or 'the soul of his flesh', which is taken away. So this cannibalism is not so horrible as it sounds.

The night-witches of the Lovedu are believed to go out at night with their whole being, and not just their souls. Companions remaining in the hut are thrown into a profound sleep, or a hyena may be left in the image of a witch. So witches may be caught, with certain

[1] Nadel, *Nupe Religion*, pp. 165 f.
[2] Meek, op. cit., pp. 79 f.

medicines, and remain immobile till found when they flee away naked. The witches meet in an assembly and know each other. Sometimes they fight witches of other villages and receive wounds which they hide in the daytime and which may prove fatal.

Basuto witches gather together and sing and dance naked. Sometimes they visit a village and send all its inhabitants into a deep slumber while they kill an ox for a feast. But when the dawn comes they remove the spell from the sleepers, resurrect the ox with medicine, and return home. They leave no traces behind, unless it happens that one has gnawed an ox bone too harshly, when the animal will limp the next day. These nocturnal revels are invisible, and yet travellers tell of hearing the witches singing in the distance, and they run away as quickly as possible lest they be captured by the witches. Hence people will not travel alone and unprotected at night.

FLYING AND FAMILIARS

The universal fantasy of flying is found in Africa. Gã witches are believed to fly to their meetings like balls of fire which are said to appear over land and sea. It is possible that the phosphorescence of the waves may have suggested this idea to this coastal people. Many people who see lights in front of their eyes, the sparks and spots of the liverish, may be led to suspect that witches are about or that they themselves are becoming witches. Many others feel worms, snakes, and toads crawling about inside their bodies. As nearly everybody suffers from worms, it is not surprising that they should attribute these uncomfortable feelings to witchcraft.

Those who do not fly as fire are believed to ride on animals, especially on owls, antelopes, and leopards, all nocturnal creatures. Snakes are regarded as witches' steeds, familiars, and doubles, so that a witch may turn into a snake. Some witches say that they wear snakes round their heads or carry them in their private parts. These are fantasies, though there are non-poisonous pythons which are kept tame by some people and are found in some religious cults. Some of the worst witches are thought to have hooks or spurs growing on their heels, a sign of their animal nature.

Ibo witches are believed to appear as balls of fire in the treetops which men can extinguish by the use of the appropriate medicine. They can turn into the smallest insect and so enter tightly closed houses and bite men as flies do at night. They can turn into owls, lizards, vultures, and night-birds. If a night-bird rests on a house men will do all they can to drive it away. Strange bird cries indicate that witches have begun their meeting. The Nupe witches, too, are said to breathe fire from their mouths, and to suck their victims' blood like vampires. It is significant that witches are said to meet in baobab and iroko trees. These trees are pollinated by bats which make a twittering noise like people talking.

The Azande believe that bats can be vehicles of the souls of witches. Particularly is this so when crops are attacked by bats. If a man catches one of these bats he burns it, and places the ashes in beer which people are invited to taste, when the man who sent the bat tastes the beer he vomits and is accused of bewitching the crops. The soul of an Azande witch goes out at night giving off a bright light, like firefly beetles but much brighter. They rub a special ointment into their skin to make themselves invisible. Witchcraft may also be found in animals and birds, if so proved by the poison oracle. Bats, owls, jackals, dogs, and cats may all be witches. The wild animals of the bush may be credited with witchcraft if they are particularly cunning. Especially do wild cats have witchcraft attributed to them, and the males are said to be like incubi to women who give birth to kittens and suckle them like children.

The snake familiars appear again in Zulu and Lovedu belief. Witches send a snake which penetrates the body and kills unborn children. Some say that everybody has a snake in his stomach. The psychologist will easily explain the phallic symbolism of the snake, especially in a tropical country. Other familiars are hyenas, skunks, and owls. The familiars are sent to cause damage to a neighbour's property or to milk his cows. A snake that seems to attack one person only in a crowd must be a witch's snake. The worst of all familiars is a human being who has been killed by the witch and has become his slave. He is kept in a pot or a cave, and he hoes or works evil for his master by night.

The Basuto believe that witches have powerful medicines to make them fly, or they have magic wands on which they ride after the manner of European witches on their broomsticks. One wand is red and the other black. The black one can send men into a deep sleep or raise the dead; the red one can reverse these spells before dawn. Witches can turn themselves into animals: monkeys, snakes,

ows. They frighten men in these shapes and if a man sees
n his hut he knows the witches are after him. Witches'
may also be little men, two or three feet high, with long
rgans like monkeys. These familiars are inherited or
ght, and are sent out by their owners to annoy and harm men,
children, and animals. They may destroy crops, drive out cattle,
and set huts on fire. The little man attracts women and causes various
perversions, like an incubus. These familiars may become semi-
independent of their owners, and they are difficult to get rid of and
may have to be exorcized.

CANNIBALISM AND SOULS

The unnatural cannibalism of which European witches were
accused is also admitted by African witches. Some have confessed
to have killed many people, including their own children, and eaten
them in the witches' assemblies. They describe in detail how that
each witch takes a part of the body, the feet or the hands, and that
when they arrive at the heart the victim dies.

Yet all this is not meant to indicate eating the real flesh; it is all
symbolical. It is the victim's soul which is eaten, and the victim's
body is not harmed, except by disease. Nor is there evidence that
corpses are dug up and devoured by witches, though sorcerers are
known to have done this. The Gã believe that just as the witches'
assembly is spiritual, attended by the souls of the witches only, so
is the eating of their victims. Their witches are said to have a pot
which contains the 'blood' of their victims, but to normal people
this blood would appear as mere water. Similarly when a witch confesses she sometimes makes a pretence of vomiting the blood of her
victims, but this blood is invisible to mortal sight. One is met by
the statement, here as elsewhere, that only those with the right kind
of eyes can see the witches at their work.

Similarly the Ibo witches are said to have to contribute the soul-
substance of their victims on initiation into the guild. The victim is
often a close relative, a child, husband, brother, or cousin. This
may appear unnatural, but there are social and psychological
reasons why relatives should be thought to be killed by witches.
The witch may place a magical preparation in her victim's house to
assist in his capture. She then divulges the name to the chief witch

who wounds the victim with a spiritual arrow. The witches divide the body between them, and when the heart is eaten the man dies. Impotence and barrenness are also caused by witchcraft.

The chief work of Nupe witches is 'the eating of souls'. Every member of the guild has to contribute a human victim in turn. If she cannot get an outsider, because of his protective magic, she brings one of her own family, a child or a brother, for she has more power over them. She brings the body (soul) and the witches divide it among them, and keep on eating till the victim dies. If the witch cannot find a victim she is liable to be killed herself, and divided and eaten in the same manner.

The Azande also insist that the meeting and eating by witches is spiritual. They remove the psychic part of the victim and devour it spiritually. Their assembly drum calls out for human flesh, metaphorically. When they have danced around the victim's hut, they seize and divide him, cooking lumps of flesh in a small witchcraft-pot.

Lovedu witches are supposed to cause mysterious deaths to come upon their victims. No death is regarded as natural. The witches may pour blood over their victims and make them die. Or they may cut off parts of their bodies and put the pieces in sand or corn, which causes great pain to the rest of the body. If a man feels tired and full of aches, it is because a witch has beaten him, or made him hoe his garden, or forced him to ride a bicycle all night, without his conscious knowledge. Witches are supposed to kill men to enslave them. When the shadow is buried the witch retains the real person in a cave or pot and sends it out on nefarious errands.

Basuto witches have a taste for human flesh, and they are held to violate graves to satisfy their craving, particularly new graves which are not sufficiently protected with charms. They can raise the dead and seize the spirit before it reaches the abode of the departed. This is easily done if the full funeral rites have been delayed. With this ghost they frighten people and the relatives of the deceased. With their black wands they can raise the dead, and with their red wands they can reverse the process.

CONCLUSIONS

Some of the above seems remarkably like real cannibalism. It is true that this has taken place in some parts of Africa, though not in most of the areas we have referred to. The societies of leopard-men who indeed and in truth preyed on their fellows are notorious in the forests of the Congo and adjacent areas, but not in most parts of East and West Africa. In Basutoland there are horrible ritual murders, which take place from time to time. But these evil practices are day-light and conscious activities, and are distinguished by the Basuto from the witchcraft which we have described among them above.

It is possible that the notion of witches eating human flesh may be derived from racial memories of what took place ages ago. This is speculative but not impossible. Whatever the case, it is certain that the tribes mentioned insist that the eating done by witches today is as incorporeal as their assemblies.

A further point is that in many parts of Africa there are societies which believe that men can take on animal form, and in which some men dress up in animal skins. The strong belief in reincarnation not infrequently takes the form of metamorphosis, that is, that men change into animals: leopards, monkeys, deer, snakes, and the like. Some think this change only takes place after death. Others think that there are particular people, witches and wizards, who possess the special faculty of changing form. Others again belong to secret societies in which they dress in animal skins to impersonate the dead or totemic ancestors. But these are daylight and conscious activities, and always distinguished from witchcraft.

Some of these beliefs may throw light on European witchcraft. Others are strange to Europe, where the idea of reincarnation has never taken much root.

It has been emphasized that Africans generally believe the witch-craft activities to take place in spirit. However, it must be made fully clear that this does not imply that Africans consider witch-craft to be illusory. Quite the contrary. They are convinced that witches do meet, and actually devour their prey, albeit spiritually. The spirit world is so real that there is never a shadow of doubt in the African's mind that the witches really do all that they are accused of doing.

CHAPTER 12

Witchcraft and Other Practices

When R. S. Rattray was making his monumental studies of the Ashanti people of Ghana, he did his best to enter into the meaning of their religious customs and to expound them to outsiders as sympathetically as possible. As a result, one anthropologist reading Rattray's pages remarked, 'I do not seem to recognize your Ashanti as here portrayed; they seem milk and watery compared with the conception I had formed of them; what about the slaughter at their funeral customs?' Rattray confessed that the same question had worried him. He could not believe that the fine people he knew could become the bloodthirsty savages depicted in the old travel books, with their tales of 'cities of blood'.[1]

Similar questions may have occurred to the readers of this book. It is all very well to say that African women only imagine that they are witches who indulge in spiritual cannibalistic feasts, but is it not true that cannibalism has been practised in Africa? And how can we be sure that the witches are not really guilty of such barbarous practices? Is it truly possible to distinguish witches from cannibals, and to speak somewhat airily of only eating 'the soul of the flesh'? And what of the human sacrifices, the Men Leopards, the Mau Mau? Are not these manifestations of witchcraft, or akin to it?

FUNERAL EXECUTIONS

Rattray solved his dilemma by undertaking a close study of the funeral customs of the Ashanti, a subject that he had not previously investigated. He soon discovered that there had indeed been human

[1] *Religion and Art in Ashanti*, 1927, p. 105.

sacrifices in the past at the funerals of important people. These sacrifices had now practically ceased, but they were the happenings which had aroused the horror of early European visitors and had given the country a bad name.

These human sacrifices were found in many parts of Africa. Indeed, they have been known in most parts of the world—ancient Egypt, Mesopotamia, and many other places. They were not properly speaking 'sacrifices' meant to appease some god, but suicides and executions made for honouring the dead. By far the greater number took place at burial ceremonies, but in some places, e.g. Dahomey, there were annual 'customs' in which the dead monarchs were remembered on the anniversary of their death and more slaves were despatched to serve them.

The reason behind these executions was the desire to honour departed kings and important people. At root, the strong belief in a life after death, in which men would retain the position and glory they had on earth, led logically to the notion that these chiefs would require a similar retinue in the afterlife as they had enjoyed in this mortal existence. They needed court officials, wives, and servants to keep up their prestige in the world to come and to ensure that they would not arrive alone and empty-handed among their forefathers, but would be granted an honoured place in their midst.

Further, those who were killed at such funerals were special classes of people. There were in many African courts specially designated officials whose task it would be to accompany the king at death on his journey to the underworld. In some places they had titles indicative of this, 'one who dies with the king'. They might be ministers of state, wives, sons, or servants. In any case, one effect of their designation to die with the king would be that they were interested in keeping the king alive as long as possible, and in this way palace revolutions would be prevented. They often took their own lives calmly when the king passed away, taking poison, or else they would be strangled by their family without bloodshed.

Other types of people set aside to swell the king's train were criminals who had been condemned to death for some capital offence, but whose execution had been deferred until needed for the king's burial rites. Thus in death they would gain added glory. Others were slaves, or prisoners of war also due for execution. The killing of the latter class was hardly excusable, if the society accepts that it is wrong to kill prisoners of war. They would often be resigned to their fate, but to ensure that they did not protest and so spoil the ceremony they were commonly gagged at their execution.

But it is true that 'blood will have blood'. And in some instances the executioners having begun to shed blood, then worked themselves into a state of frenzy and set about indiscriminate massacres. The streets of towns like Kumasi and Benin were not safe and people fled into the forest until the orgy was over. Hence the descriptions of corpses and heads that the early travellers and punitive expeditions witnessed. In our sensitive days the thought of any public execution is distasteful, but it is not so long since heads were displayed on Temple Bar in London, and we have not yet finally got rid of capital punishment.

However, in all this it is clear at once that there was no connexion whatever between these ritual murders and witchcraft. The witches were never accused of taking part in these executions, which were public and meant to honour the departed monarchs. Whether the witch-cult of Europe was associated with a ritual sacrifice of the monarch every seven years, as Miss Murray has suggested, there is no trace of this practice in Africa. Many African kings lived for forty years or more, and witches were not associated in any way with their burial.

In the ritual murders that accompanied the royal funerals there is no suggestion of cannibalism. It is true that Yoruba kings in Nigeria were supposed to eat the heart of the dead king during the enthronement ceremonies, indeed their very phrase for becoming a king means 'eating the king'. But this was a purely ritual act, after the late king's death, and with the intention of taking over some of his vital power and succeeding directly to him. In any case, it had not the slightest link with witchcraft.

MEDICINAL MURDERS

There are, however, ritual murders notorious in some parts of Africa, which might be thought to have some connexion with witchcraft. At least the work of the murderers bears a resemblance to some of the deeds attributed to witches.

Ritual murders crop up every few years in the British South African colony of Basutoland. These have received a great deal of publicity, not always accurate, but indeed they are a most disturbing feature of Basuto life. It has been suggested that they were not of Basuto origin, but were introduced from some other tribe, but this does not seem to be borne out by the records, which show that these practices have been going on for a century at least.[1]

The murders are often particularly cruel, though generally they are planned to follow a beer-feast when the victim is likely to be drunk. The unwitting victim is decoyed outside the village to a lonely place where he is overpowered, mutilated, and killed. A horrible feature of the practice is that the mutilations are done as far as possible while the victim is still alive, pieces of flesh may be cut off his body or head, eyes, ears, lips, tongue, or bodily organs may be removed, sometimes a whole limb is severed. The wounds may be cauterized with burning stones or hot water.

There seem to be no fixed rules for choosing victims. They may be of either sex, and of any age. Children or adults may be chosen, and in one instance a woman with a newborn baby had both herself and her child to suffer unspeakable agonies before death intervened.

The purpose of the ritual murders is to obtain ingredients for a medicine of invincible power. Hence a human victim, as far better than an animal, is chosen. The living body is preferred to a dead one, and magically potent parts of the body are cut off to provide the most powerful ingredients.

Chiefs, in particular, feel the need of obtaining for themselves such strong magical medicines, which will defend them from all ills and give them success and importance. They are usually inspired and prompted to such deeds by a medicine-man, though it has been hard to prove charges against such people. A number of accomplices are chosen to perform the horrible deed, and they often include one or two members of the victim's own family, with the idea of preventing a blood feud between his family and the executioners.

The government has tried hard to stamp out these murders, and where accomplices have been found they have been hanged, including chiefs if proved responsible. But the executioners have to swear fearful oaths of loyalty and secrecy and they cannot always be traced. The Basuto are very fearful of these murders, and are reluctant to go out or travel at night. Villages have become as quiet as the grave after dark and until dawn.

[1] *The Basuto*, pp. 307 ff.

The Basuto have become very self-conscious about these ritual murders. One tendency that has appeared is to assert that the murders do not occur at all, but that they are figments of the imagination. To this has been added the charge that accusations against chiefs are trumped up and are due to the plots of their rivals. But there seems no doubt that these dreadful murders have actually occurred, for remains of victims have been found in a ghastly state of mutilation.

The Basuto distinguish quite clearly between these ritual murders and witchcraft. The murders are part of the medicinal practices of certain people, and their aim is to procure powerful and 'lively' medicines. Witches are quite different. Witches are mostly women who fly about at night on wands, with which they can cast the living into deep sleep or raise the dead. Witches are cannibalistic, or rather necrophagic, for they are supposed to violate newly-made graves and to capture departed spirits before they reach the abode of the dead. Then they turn them into ghosts to annoy their living relatives. Both the character and the work of witches are quite distinct from ritual murder.

LEOPARD SOCIETIES

In other parts of Africa there are anti-social organizations which appear, or are rumoured to exist, from time to time and carry off human victims. In Sierra Leone there has been fear of a boa-constrictor or Boa Society. Often it appears to be simply rumour, wherein people report that they have been chased by 'cannibals'. Sometimes the fear is so great, and connected with mysterious disappearances of human beings, that special police or soldiers undertake investigations and capture of the criminals. There is the undoubted fact that rarely some anti-social individuals do seek for human victims, so as to obtain the fat that they need for potent medicines.[1]

The Leopard Societies have become notorious for supposedly wicked activities. They have been known in a number of places along the West African coast, usually the deep forest, but by no means in all tribes or countries, and not in the stronger kingdoms. In Sierra Leone the 'Human Leopard' murders were called Tongo-players, from the name of the clubs which officials carried. They

[1] K. L. Little, *The Mende of Sierra Leone*, 1951, p. 233.

seem to have begun about the end of the last century, and at first to have served a useful purpose in putting down anti-social organizations. But power corrupted them and they began to tyrannize the villages over which they had power. People believed that their leaders had the power of turning themselves into leopards, and the society took as its sign a leopard's claw. The head of the society dressed himself in leopard's skins and wore a circle of iron spikes on his head. Many people disappeared mysteriously from their homes, and the government made repeated efforts to suppress Leopard Societies.[1]

In the neighbouring Liberia and French Ivory Coast the leaders of Leopard Societies were said to dress themselves in leopard skins, and to hunt their victims in the way leopards do. They had iron claws fixed on small frames, and clawed their victims so as to give the impression that leopards had indeed eaten them. Neophytes seeking initiation into the Leopard Societies were supposed to bring a human victim with them, generally somebody from their own family. The neophyte during his initiation ceremony was believed to be passed through a leopard skin and so to enact birth from a leopard.

The most powerful secret society of the Ibibio of Nigeria is called Ekkpe, which is the word for a leopard. But, despite some travellers' tales to the contrary, this is not a murdering and cannibalistic society like those of Sierra Leone and the Ivory Coast. The Ekkpe is mainly concerned with the cult of the ancestors and the worship of the spirits of fertility. Named after the leopard, the most feared animal of the forest, it may have had a totemistic origin, though few traces of this remain. Its members perform masquerades dressed in knitted garments which cover the whole figure. Occasionally leopard skins may have been worn, but there seems little evidence of this. Human sacrifices were performed when a chief or notable member died, as in other societies elsewhere.[2]

At Calabar the above society has been confused with a similar organization, Ekkpo, which derives its name from the ancestors and is different in its ritual. The latter society was more brutal than the Ekkpe, beating and killing non-members who intruded on its mysteries, and offering sacrifices to ancestors. In recent times,

[1] F. W. Butt-Thompson, *West African Secret Societies*, 1929, p. 283.
[2] P. A. Talbot, *The Peoples of Southern Nigeria*, 1926, vol. iii, pp. 780 ff.

however, there have appeared new Leopard Societies, which have been suspected of responsibility for killings in remote parts of Calabar province. Bodies have been discovered mauled about as if by leopards.

Mention may be made of the infamous organization of Arochuku among a section of the Ibo people of Nigeria. This was destroyed by a punitive expedition early in this century. In origin the cult of Arochuku was an oracle called the Long Spirit (Long Juju of earlier writers). It had its home in a cave to which men came seeking the advice of the oracle through the priests in charge. As so often happens, the priests found themselves possessed of great power when their fame spread, and they abused it. Disputants who came to consult them brought large presents, and the result often was that one or the other, or both, of the litigants disappeared into the oracle cave, whence they were smuggled out through a secret exit and sold away into slavery. At the end of the slave-trading period much money was still to be made by illicit slaving, and the priests gained both wealth and power.

Clearly all this had nothing to do with witchcraft. The Leopard Societies bore the nearest resemblance to the associations of witches. They were secret, often thought to be cannibalistic, and greatly feared. No man knew what they did and everybody feared the worst. Yet in the minds of most Africans witches were quite distinct from human leopards. Both were hated. But, as there are many spiritual evils, graded according to their potency, so witches and human leopards were regarded as separate from one another. There is no suggestion that the two societies were ever connected in any way. The human leopards were almost always men, the witches were usually women and were never called leopards. The leopards might seize men in the forest and they would simply disappear. The witches could smite anybody with sickness and he would languish perhaps for months visibly on his bed, wasting and consuming as in European witchcraft.

The respectable secret societies, such as the Ibibio Ekkpe, were open to all males and were only secret in the sense that women were supposed not to know their mysteries and rites. The innumerable secret societies of Africa were and still are mostly publicly recognized institutions. Their only connexion with witchcraft is that often, as one of their functions, they were charged with the duty of hunting out witches and breaking their power. More will be said of this in a later chapter.

CANNIBALISM

There is no doubt that cannibalism of various types has been practised by certain African peoples, and not at all by many others. In East Africa, the Nilotic tribes do not practise it, but others, like the Azande, had a reputation for it in the past. Even here the practice seems to have varied with individuals—some liked human flesh and others did not. But about a century ago it is said that human flesh was prepared for food if there had been good success in war. Today, however, the Azande look down on cannibalism, and attribute this to people like the pygmies of the forest who are said to shout at strangers, 'Flesh, flesh!'[1]

In West Africa cannibalism seems to have been practised by some eastern Nigerian and west equatorial tribes. There were various reasons for eating human flesh. There was the magical idea of obtaining and imbibing the inner virtue of the person killed. Medicine would often be made out of part of the body that was not eaten. In this case a woman or child might suffice if the body of a warrior could not be found after a raid.

A great deal of cannibalism was undoubtedly stimulated by the tribal warfare, itself partly encouraged by the slave trade in past centuries. Men preferred fighting to more useful means of gaining a livelihood, and they supplemented their short food supply with the flesh of their conquered enemies. In time people acquired a deplorable taste for human flesh, particularly the more succulent parts of the body.

The flesh was not usually eaten, however, without the performance of ritual. Head-hunting was closely associated with cannibalism. Sacrifices were offered to the enemy's skull to placate his ghost, and also to get him to induce his friends to come to the slayer's town. Plays were performed in which all the village warriors danced around the skull and then it was commonly placed in the owner's house or the chief's house. Then the body would be eaten.[2]

The cannibalistic orgies of the head-hunters might seem to have

[1] Cp. C. G. Seligman, *Pagan Tribes of the Nilotic Sudan,* 1932, p. 497, and Evans-Pritchard, op. cit., p. 278.
[2] Talbot, op. cit., iii, 826 ff.

an even closer resemblance to witches' feasts than other practices we have referred to. It is indeed possible that in some of the detailed and gruesome descriptions made in the witches' confessions, there may be some borrowing from memories of bygone cannibalistic feasts. However, this is dubious. For vivid descriptions of witches' soul-eating is given by peoples who have never indulged in cannibalism, e.g. in western Nigeria and Ghana.

Once again it must be said that witchcraft is always distinguished in the African mind from the physical cannibalism of the head-hunters. The latter were male, usually warriors, who left bones and traces of their meals for all to see. The witches are mostly female, feeding on the spiritual body, and no external evidence of their invisible meals can be obtained, from the very nature of the case.

OTHER CULTS

It should not be necessary to state that the Mau Mau organization of the Kikuyu in Kenya had nothing to do with witchcraft. But the popular press is capable of lumping everything under the name of witchcraft and we must insist on proper definition and delimitation.

The Mau Mau oaths, by which the leaders of this vicious society sought to commit all the Kikuyu to their way, were deliberately meant to include magical and ritual elements which would exercise a fearful influence on the imagination. The use of gourds of blood, the placing of pieces of sacrificial meat to the lips, the piercing of sheep's eyes with thorns, and the like were all procedures linked with black magic and casting of spells. Then, bound by oaths and ritual, the initiate would go out to commit horrible murders.[1]

Quite clearly this is not witchcraft, even if it plays upon similar fears to those which are aroused by witchcraft. The Kikuyu believe both in witchcraft and magic, they know that people can die from the fear of a spell, or can become ill and languish away through breaking an oath solemnly made, or by suffering from the attention of witches. But while results may be comparable, the practices of witchcraft and magic differ from one another.

We have referred to human sacrifice, as connected both with medicinal murder and with funeral customs. Human sacrifices have been made in Africa, as in other continents, for a variety of purposes.

[1] L. S. B. Leakey, *Defeating Mau Mau*, 1954, pp. 80 f.

These purposes are generally magical, for protection of a town or a person, or for acquisition of additional power. Foundation sacrifices have been practised in Africa (as at Jericho, and perhaps old London Bridge). Scapegoats were sacrificed, especially in time of national danger, such as warfare. They were believed to remove evil and disease. Other forms of homicide, such as the exposure of twins, are not sacrificial. All these, and other instances, have no relationship with witchcraft.

Finally, the so-called cults of Horned Gods are not associated with witchcraft in Africa, whatever they may have been elsewhere. Instances, that are quoted by some writers on witchcraft, of masqueraders who wear masks of horned beasts, do not refer to witchcraft at all. The horns or masks are sometimes purely decorative, at other times symbolical of the animal impersonated. Some of these societies persecute witches; they do not represent a god of the witches.

The theory of the dying god, popularized by Sir James Frazer, in which the king may symbolize the deity, be put to death and rise again, is still being debated. Murray says, 'The belief belongs to all parts of the Old World, and survives in Africa into the present century.'[1]

Two things may be said about Africa. Firstly, that many African peoples show no traces at all of such ritual killing of the king. Some of the greatest kingdoms: the Ashanti, Dahomey, Yoruba, Benin, Buganda, Swazi, and Lovedu, had monarchs whose persons were sacrosanct and who lived frequently to ripe old age. Numbers of other African peoples had no kings at all. Secondly, there is no connexion to be traced between such a dying king and the organization of witches, whose characteristics we have insisted upon at the risk of being wearisome.[2]

[1] *The God of the Witches*, p. 158.
[2] See the chapter on Divine Rulers in my *African Traditional Religion*, 1962.

CHAPTER 13

Confessions of Modern Witches

Modern African confessions of witchcraft are as surprising as were those of medieval and renaissance Europe. The confessions sound incomprehensible except as statements of fact, until they are studied in the light of modern psychology. Much of this self-accusation may be paralleled in statements made by neurotic patients.

Sigmund Freud introduced the term 'The Omnipotence of Thought' to explain the superstitions and illusions from which some neurotics suffer. One of his patients had coined this term, the Omnipotence of Thought, 'to designate all those peculiar and uncanny occurrences which seemed to pursue him just as they pursue others afflicted with his malady'. The patient would conjure up the image of some person, or he could come to feel that he was harming others simply by thinking about them. 'Thus if he happened to think of a person, he was actually confronted with this person as if he had conjured him up; if he inquired suddenly about the state of health of an acquaintance whom he had long missed, he was sure to hear that this acquaintance had just died, so that he could believe that the deceased had drawn his attention to himself by telepathic means; if he uttered a half-meant imprecation against a stranger, he could expect to have him die soon thereafter and burden him with the responsibility for his death.'[1]

Such a man, a 'compulsion neurotic', like a witch may be 'oppressed by a sense of guilt which is appropriate to a wholesale murderer, while at the same time he acts towards his fellow beings in a most considerate and scrupulous manner'. Such a person may

[1] *Totem and Taboo,* Pelican edition, p. 138.

never do any physical harm to his friends or foes, and yet, Freud said, 'his sense of guilt is justified; it is based upon intensive and frequent death wishes which unconsciously manifest themselves towards his fellow beings'. Such a theory may give a clue to the confessions of witches.

AFRICAN CONFESSIONS

The best records of confessions of African witches are those carefully set down by Dr. Field for the Gã of Ghana, from hundreds of cases that she examined.

Gã witchcraft confessions contain such remarkable statements as the following: 'I have killed fifty people, including my own brother.' 'I have killed seven children of my own and eaten them with my company.' 'When I bring a victim I take the feet, but when someone else brings the victim I take the thighs.' 'I eat head and waist whenever we eat a human being.' 'I am in a company of seven.' 'I am the least in the company and when a person is killed I get the hands only.'[1]

Witches often confess to having caused barrenness to women or impotence in men. This is a dreadful crime, for fertility is highly esteemed in African society. If one is killed by witchcraft one can always be born again on earth, but barrenness prevents this reincarnation and so is dastardly.

One woman confessed that she had 'taken the womb of another woman'. The witch-doctor asked:

'How long have you had it?'

'About a year.'

'Where have you put it?'

'It is in an earthen pot in my house.'

'Will you let her have it back?'

'I will give it back to her with joy.'[2]

It was understood by both witch and doctor that she was referring not to the actual physical womb of her victim, but to the spiritual substance.

Other witches confessed to having caused blindness, bodily sores, poverty, and debt. Some said that they had taken people's good

[1] Field, op. cit., pp. 139 f.
[2] Ibid., p. 143.

luck away. Others that they prevented men from getting wives, thereby causing them to be held in great contempt by their fellows. One confessed, 'I and my company have killed, spoiled everything, and spoiled people's tempers in our families.'

The cannibalism of witches is freely confessed, as we have seen above. One repentant witch said, 'I am the mother of the child who is now sick. Our company have eaten the body. They gave me my daughter.' Another confessed that the fatal deed had gone too far: 'We have already distributed the parts of the child and have used them, so there is no remedy now.'

An old woman said:

'Four of my children are dead. I killed them. But lately I have killed only one grandchild.'

'How many sons have you?' asked the doctor.

'Only one.'

'Didn't you know that your company were taking away his life?'

'I couldn't know.'

'But you knew that your company suggested to you that you might bring your son to be killed?'

'They put it to me, but I refused. I have never killed more than four children and one grandchild.'[1]

The meetings of the witches, their organization, the cannibalism, all of them spiritual, are confessed to as if they were real happenings. When there is a general witch-hunt the witches vie with each other in recounting their evil deeds. They will name other witches and their leader, on demand.

An interesting example of the omnipotence of thought is seen in the confession of one witch who said: 'I once went to my farm and saw an *Odum* tree and said that I should be glad if it fell down or were uprooted as I would then get my brother to make it into a pounding-mortar to pound *fu-fu* in. Next morning when I went to the farm the tree was on the ground.'[2]

In Ashanti in Ghana there were powerful anti-witchcraft cults in the 1940's. Some of the confessions that have been recorded are as stark as those of the Gä. One witch who was caught by the priest of the cult said that she had brought evil upon her victims: 'I am

---

[1] Field, p. 148.
[2] Ibid., p. 149

the one who made him drive his lorry into the ditch. I was also the cause of the severe illness for which he was taken to hospital.' She confessed to having made a priestess barren after bearing her first child: 'I took away her womb to prepare medicine.' She also confessed to flying on her evil errands: 'This walking-stick is a snake. It is my forerunner any time when I want to fly.... I flew in the night to visit my great-granddaughter.' She had mentioned the latter as one of her accomplices in the spiritual cannibalism.[1]

Miss Ward, who recorded these confessions, insists that it was not real cannibalism but 'spiritual sharing' and 'eating'. She also stresses the relief that came to the accused by the confession. As the confessions were public, they helped to relieve tension and provide an outlet for aggressive feelings. After confession and acceptance by the priest the witch was received back into society by payment of a fine and penance.

A vivid account is given by this writer of public confessions in Ashanti. 'The sanded floor of the fetish place would be surrounded by almost the whole population of the village.... All this was in the heat of the afternoon. Confession was made through the fetish priest, who prompted and questioned the supplicant at intervals. The audience listened intently to each phrase, and in each pause broke into a kind of chanted prayer, beseeching the fetish to accept the confession.'

In this cult, as in others that we shall mention later, the veracity of the confession was tested by sacrificing a fowl. 'When the supplicant indicated that there was no more to be said the fetish priest took a small fowl, slit its throat with a neat movement, and threw it out on to the sand in front of the shrine. It fluttered and jerked, perhaps for half a minute, and then lay still. If it finally died on its back with its feet in the air, that was a sign that the fetish accepted the confession. If it lay in any other position the confession was deemed incomplete, the supplicant was questioned further and urged to omit nothing. Sometimes as many as a dozen fowls might be sacrificed before one of them died the right way up.'[2] There would be a gruelling process in which the priest exhorted the accused to remember his sins, and the crowd besought him to hold

[1] B. E. Ward, 'Some Observations on Religious Cults in Ashanti', in *Africa* vol. xxvi, pp. 54 f.
[2] Ibid., pp. 55 f.

nothing back. The slightest confession of magic would be accepted, provided the fowl died the right way up.

In a new witch-hunting movement akin to the above, to be described in the next chapter, and which swept across western Nigeria in the 1950's, many women confessed. Most of them had not been called witches before the coming of the witch-hunters, nor were they aware of their state. Only a few admitted to having used evil medicines against their enemies. Most of the women, however, believed themselves to be witches after they had been accused as such. Some said that they were members of a witchcraft society and used witchcraft purposely, though not all would admit this. Nearly everyone confessed to having killed some near relative, often their own children or grandchildren. All believed that the witch-hunters had taken away their witchcraft and were glad to have lost it.

The Nupe of Nigeria demand confessions from those who have been accused of witchcraft, and if a woman denies that she has prac- tised it then they think her a liar. But under the strong suggestions of the witch-hunt the woman is no longer sure of herself. Who knows what she or her soul may have done during the night? And does she not indeed have evil dreams and jealous feelings? So she solves her inner conflict by confessing directly to whatever she is accused of, or submitting to an ordeal which will prove her guilt.

The Azande have a somewhat different conception, and Professor Evans-Pritchard says that he has only received knowledge of con- fession from one man, the cleverest but perhaps the least reliable of his informants. In Azande opinion a witch is only important when some mishap occurs. A man may be a witch, but if his powers are only latent then society is not concerned with him. But the Azande believe that witches are well aware of their state, and that in secret they rejoice over the sufferings of their victims. So that they consider it is not possible that a man should be ignorant of his being a witch.

When, therefore, an Azande is accused of being a witch he is surprised. Having always understood that witches knew what they were doing, and not being aware of having harmed anyone else, he is in a quandary. He knows that he has hurt nobody, yet the poison oracle has denounced him. Hence he thinks of himself as an excep- tional case. Everybody believes that witches know each other and work together for their evil deeds, but he is not conscious of having done anything like that. Perhaps in his dreams he had injured others, and the oracle says so. Yet he is not a conscious witch, and does not confess to the crimes ascribed to him, though he submits to the superior power of the oracle.

This provides interesting light upon the question of the sources of information of witches' activities. Clearly these cannot come from the witches themselves, among the Azande, since they do not confess to witchcraft and so do not give information about their supposed practices. These details are furnished by the general myths of society.

The same might be said about the notions of witchcraft elsewhere. They are the opinions about the work of witches held by the generality of men. The confessions only confirm what is already believed, and which is suggested by leading questions, but with additions from the witch's own fertile imagination.

ARE WITCHES CONSCIOUS AGENTS?

This question has been answered for the Azande. People think that witches cannot possibly be ignorant of their condition. If a man is accused, and is not conscious of witchcraft, he regards his own case as quite exceptional.

The Nupe are convinced that the witch must be fully conscious that she is one, and she has a deliberate intention to act as a witch.

Although the visits to other witches are paid by the 'shadow-soul', yet there is held to be a positive evil will behind it all. The witch means and does harm. The Yoruba witches, most of them, did not know they were witches until accused, but then they accepted the verdict of society and confessed.

Dr. Field, after examining over four hundred Gã women accused of witchcraft, said: 'There is no doubt that witches believe that their spirits meet together every night round their witch-pot while their bodies sleep, and this belief dominates their lives. But whether there is any ordinary physical communication between them and whether they ever do in addition have ordinary gatherings in the flesh, *I do not know.*'

She says further that the central reality of witchcraft is medical. Witches suffer from the obsession that 'they have power to harm others by thinking them harm'. Witches may obviously be *queer* persons. Some are neurotics, common in African society. From the

European point of view their deeds are delusions. They cannot do what they are supposed to do.

Montague Summers speaks with bated breath of witchcraft in Africa today, which parallels that in bygone Europe. But he admits that 'it is only their spirit-bodies that attend the magic rendezvous, passing through walls and over the tree-tops with instant rapidity'.[1]

WITCHCRAFT AND DREAMS

Dreams are important in the study of witchcraft, both because of the bad dreams which men attribute to witches, and because some of the delusions of witches are derived from dreams. Various types of dreams are distinguished by African witch-doctors and diviners, but in general it may be said that a bad dream is usually regarded as a witchcraft dream. Nightmares are often thought to be evidence of bewitching, and in them men may believe that they talk with and are enchanted by witches.

In some dreams men think that they are attacked by savage animals, and it is known that witches change themselves into animal form in their soul-hunting. Sometimes men dream of animals or of men changing into animals; these are taken as clear signs of the origin of the dream in witchcraft, and of the predatory action of a witch upon a dreamer's soul. Sleepwalkers or dreamers who cry out or weep are regarded as either being bewitched or themselves witches.

Many of the people who are treated by witch-doctors are obsessed with fears of becoming witches. They believe that at night they are being drawn away, against their own will, to join the company of witches. I knew a woman who was tormented with this fear, and who believed that the chief witch was clinging to her like a leech till she joined their company. She was sick, with unaccountable aches and pains.

There is, of course, a great deal of confusion between the actual dream and the later memory of it, with all the interpretations and additions entailed in recalling and recounting it. There is a big gap between what psychologists call 'the latent content' and 'the manifest content'.

The Freudian theory divided dreams into wish-dreams, anxiety-

[1] *The History of Witchcraft*, p. 163.

dreams, and punishment-dreams. The witchcraft dreams might come under either of the two latter categories. The unrestrained hatred, which seems to 'rise up from a veritable hell', comes out in dream life though it is repressed in the waking state. Little wonder that African women have translated some of their dreaming imagination into the reality of witchcraft confessions.[1]

WITCHCRAFT EXPLAINS MISFORTUNE

Witchcraft is a useful concept to many peoples, because it helps to explain things that otherwise are difficult to understand. It is significant that European belief in witchcraft only received its death-blow with the spread of modern medical and scientific knowledge. We are no longer in need of mysterious explanations of the accidents of life, the aches of the body, or the imaginations of the mind. One had almost said that we no longer need scapegoats—were it not that memories of recent trials, confessions, and persecutions hang heavily upon us.

Africans think and speak of witchcraft very frequently. It is a subject of conversation almost as suitable as the crops or the weather. For everyone believes in witchcraft. Instead of thinking about the damaging effect of cattle disease or vegetable beetles, men speak of the maleficence of witches. I have heard people ascribe the prevalence of malarial fever to witchcraft for many were dying of it. They were scornful when I suggested that living, as they did, in the midst of swamps, fever was bound to be endemic because of the innumerable mosquitoes. What curious ideas the white man has. How can those tiny creatures give fever? But one remembers that Europeans did not associate fever with mosquitoes until towards the end of the last century. Macgregor Laird, with great solemnity, ascribed fever to 'the deadly miasma' and 'the want of excitement'.

Witchcraft is expected in everyday life, just as in Europe one expects measles among children. Not only may all the accidents of village life be credited to witches, but even the educated clerk in the city will put down to their account his failure to get a rise in pay or to pass a Wolsey Hall test. After all, why does an accident happen to one man and not another? Why one day and not the next? Why

[1] For further information on African dreams and soul-wanderings see my *West African Psychology*.

does a house fall down and injure a man, when it might have fallen down many a time when nobody was there? Such a man was clearly injured by witchcraft. 'An enemy hath done this thing.'

At the same time, Africans do not ignore the other causes of misfortune, such as drought which may destroy crops, excessive rainfall which may blight them, or wild beasts which ravage them. But then again witchcraft belief is intertwined with the observation of nature. A man is killed by an animal, but the animal may be a witch in disguise, or he was acting under the influence of a spell. Rainfall may ruin one field and not another. The rain is the agent, but witchcraft is seen as the cause. But a man cannot plead the excuse of witchcraft possessing him, if he has physically harmed his neighbour or lied against his chief. These offences are duly punished.

Among many African peoples all death is regarded as unnatural. At least, any violent or mysterious death is sure to be so regarded. There are many such tragic deaths in a pre-medical society, and all will be attributed to witchcraft or sorcery. Chiefs and rulers, in particular, should not die, as they are semi-divine, so their deaths will be due to witchcraft.

THE SUFFERERS FROM WITCHCRAFT

When a man suffers from misfortune or sickness he asks himself why this has happened. He knows that there are many potential witches, and that to harm him they must be actuated by hatred or jealousy towards himself in particular. So he begins to think of those who might have a grudge against him, either for some offence or through envy at his success, and who are now trying to weaken him.

From this it follows that witchcraft is often suspected among a man's closest acquaintances. 'A man's foes shall be those of his own household.' As those we know best are the ones with whom there may be the greatest friction, so it proves that accusations of witchcraft are often levelled against close relatives, and rarely against those who live at a distance. The latter have not sufficient social contacts to make them feel hatred. The significance of this enmity in the household will be dealt with again later.

When a man believes that he is suffering from witchcraft his feelings may range from anger to terror. If the witch is thought to be destroying the crops or causing the game to go away, the sufferer will have recourse to a witch-doctor or an oracle, to find out who is responsible for the damage.

It is usually thought that it is sufficient to unveil the witch's secret for the harm to be checked. Witches love to work in secret and darkness, and when brought to light they lose their power. This is almost like the modern psychological treatment of bringing complexes to the surface so as to dissolve them.

If a witch is thought responsible for someone's death then more serious action will be taken, and the witch will at least be obliged to flee from the village. The witch may be arraigned before the chief's court and, in olden days, death was often the penalty for a witch accused of killing someone by eating his soul. The work of anti-witchcraft societies will be described next.

Since witchcraft is such a common phenomenon, it may be taken for granted to the extent of no proceedings being taken against its perpetrators, if no useful purpose can be served by concerted action against suspected witches. If the harm done cannot be righted then there is no point in taking any action about it. Witchcraft is one of the facts of life, so one bows to the inevitable. One does not go to the unnecessary trouble and expense of consulting oracles and imposing ordeals if nothing can come of it.

Belief in witchcraft serves as a check upon the hostile words and deeds which men might use in society. For, on the one hand, men are careful not to offend others since they might be witches; one can never tell who is a witch. On the other hand, enmity is an expression of witchcraft, and in expressing hatred so openly one might render oneself liable to an accusation of witchcraft. One arrives at a negative morality—that it is better not to make enemies since hatred is the constant motive of witchcraft.

CHAPTER 14

Modern Witch-hunting

NEW METHODS

Many African religious cults seek to cure witchcraft by exposing the secret activities of its supposed practitioners. This witch-hunting is regarded as a proper proceeding, done for the benefit of society. Governmental laws that forbid such witch-hunting are considered to be absurd. It is the same attitude as that of the charcoal burner in Kipling's *Second Jungle Book,* who regarded the English as 'a perfectly mad people, who would not let honest farmers kill witches in peace'.

There are very ancient methods used by smellers-out, and modernized systems that employ a great medley of cures derived from old and new sources: pagan, Muslim, Christian, Hindu, cabbalistical, and astrological. As an introduction we may look at some modern movements first.

In 1934 a movement of witch-finders swept across Nyasaland, Northern and Southern Rhodesia, and into the Congo country. Dr. Audrey Richards was present in the Bemba country and described what she saw in the number of the journal *Africa* which was devoted entirely to witchcraft (October 1935).

The witch-finders, called Bamucapi, claimed to derive their authority from a certain Kamwende in Nyasaland, but he was a man of mythical powers rather than an organizer of the movement. His disciples were young Africans, dressed in European clothes, and travelling about in twos and threes, getting local assistants to help in the places where they stopped.

When the Bamucapi arrived in a village they would bid the chief call all his people together, and cook a chicken for a communal meal. The men and women were lined up in separate rows and made to pass in turn behind the witch-finder who tried to catch their reflections in a small mirror. They claimed that witches could be recognized as such in the mirror. Any who tried to avoid the mirror, it was said, would be caught at the next visit of the witch-finders and would be called by a mysterious yet compelling drum and forced to go to the graveyard, there to have his crimes unmasked.

When the witch-finders stopped a supposed witch they demanded that he yield up the tools of witchcraft, usually horns, which included all evil charms. If the witch denied having any, they would call out the name of a place to search—the roof, or the granary, and some object would be found there. The people said that the witch-finders must be right, for these witches were the people they had always feared.

Each accused witch had to drink a magic medicine, a reddish soapy powder, to be mixed in a bottle with water. Drinking this medicine was supposed to guarantee complete removal of witchcraft from the area. If any witch returned to his evil practices, having drunk the medicine, his body would swell up to an enormous size and become too heavy to be carried to the grave. It would remain unburied, with all the evils attendant upon such a disaster.

The Bamucapi also sold protective charms and powders, in small cloth bags, against all manner of evils: snakes, wild animals, pests, and misfortunes. These were quite cheap: three and sixpence a time. Very expensive charms were also available, which were said to be infallible for gaining the favour of government officers.

The accused witches surrendered a great variety of magic horns, and the crossroads outside the villages were piled high with the discarded objects. The possession of the horn was regarded as proof of witchcraft. But most people have horns containing magical medicines which are used for all manner of purposes.

Dr. Richards analysed a heap of 135 horns and charms which had been surrendered. The onlookers seemed to consider all these horns as instruments of evil, and pointed out bones from graves or cloths supposedly soaked in children's blood. The analysis, however, proved that most of the horns were innocuous. Of this collection of objects 124 were horns or gourds which had been containers of harmless or good-luck medicines, or even snuff-holders. Or else they were small bags of protective medicine such as many people wear. Of the rest, a few were made of lizard skin or bushbuck horns, and these beasts are considered to be evil. The bushbuck horns are thought to be used by witches for sending the spirit of their victim flying through the air like a torch. There was one piece of a monkey's skull, which the onlookers swore belonged to a human baby. There was a piece of polished wood which was called a lion's bone, by a hunter! And a vulture's skull was said to belong to an owl, because owls are witches incarnate and steal grain from their enemies.

The final analysis showed that only eleven of the 135 objects might have been used for bad magic. Some were even charms that had been used for the good purpose of protection against sorcery. It was clear, therefore, that these witch-finders created a sense of danger among the people, and confused all kinds of charms with black magic and witchcraft. The accused witches were only too anxious to surrender something, no matter what, so that they might be publicly cleared and drink the saving potion. Some old people who had long been suspected of witchcraft walked many miles, so that they might pass the test and be cleared.

The Bamucapi used a mixture of ancient and modern methods. They preached a sermon, quite a new feature in witch-hunting, before beginning the ordeal. They claimed that their power came from Lesa, the Supreme Being whom both pagans and Christians worship. They stressed the necessity of washing away sins. They maintained that their founder, Kamwende, had descended into the grave and had been raised up after two days, paralysed all down one side but having obtained the knowledge of the anti-witchcraft medicine. He was expected to return in power at a second coming. Despite these garbled ideas, the movement was opposed to the Christian missions and was combated by them.

The Bamucapi owed much of their success to their modern methods. The witch-finders were young men, they worked in the open, they sold their medicines in bottles like chemists rather than in the dirty horns of the past, and they used new-fangled teaching. They were successful also because the new fears and insecurities of life seem to put its ills beyond the scope of treatment of the old witch-hunting methods.

Even more recently, since the Second World War and up to 1951, a movement of witch-finding spread in West Africa, from Ghana to Togoland and Dahomey and into Nigeria. These countries have a considerably higher standard of education than have the Rhodesians, yet witchcraft is still greatly feared.

In the Tong Hills of the Northern Territories of Ghana there is a famous shrine, originally of a great ancestor, to which men come for help. For some decades men made an annual pilgrimage from all over Ghana to pray to this spirit. In 1932 the great anthropologist R. S. Rattray described the visit of hundreds of pilgrims, many of whom were dressed in European clothes and had come in motor-cars. They prayed at the shrine for success, money and children, and the removal of blight, misfortune, barrenness, and other plagues of witchcraft.

One feature of this cult was that men could buy a ritual clientship which enabled them to set up a shrine in their own home. So as Nana Tongo (grandfather of the Tong Hills) the cult became very popular in the south of Ghana, particularly as a cure for witchcraft and other misfortunes. Among the Gã, priests who had made the costly annual pilgrimage to the north came back armed with medicines. They would hold ordeals at which accused women would be tested by the reactions of a dying fowl, and fined accordingly and then purified by kola nut being spat all over them.[1]

The witch-finding oracle had continued success and its fame spread far abroad. After the war, a chief of Dassa in central Dahomey, a town in which I lived, sent for this oracle. Its arrival caused great excitement and distress among the churches. Dahomey and Nigeria are neighbouring countries and both are Yoruba-speaking peoples. The oracle spread to Mekaw in Nigeria and thence across to the western provinces of Nigeria, where I met it again. It had now become known as Anatinga or Alatinga, shortened to Atinga. This movement caused such disturbances that eventually the government of Nigeria forbade its use by an order-in-council of 1951: 'The worship or invocation of the juju known as Atinga is hereby prohibited.'

The methods of the Atinga witch-finders are comparable with those of the Bamucapi. Small groups of men would arrive in a village and call on the chief. They would clear an open space round a tree, like a Muslim praying-place, and here would be built an altar of earth around which some danced while others beat drums. During the dancing some would go into a trance (a typical feature of West

[1] Field, op. cit., p. 138.

African religious cults), and they claimed then to have the power of seeing witches. Local youths could also join, and be initiated into the mysteries of the cult and dance.

Only women were rounded up and made to appear before the Atinga witch-finders. The dancers pointed out in their trance those who were witches, mostly old women. The Atinga had prepared in advance a mixture of blood, water, and kola nuts which the witches had to drink to be cleansed. Small pieces of these nuts were sold as protections against witchcraft.

A woman accused of witchcraft was made to confess to the crime, to drink the cleansing potion, and to produce her witchcraft apparatus. This was supposed to be kept in a pot or calabash in which the woman kept her witchcraft-bird, the nightjar, in whose form her soul travelled to the witches' meeting. Many women did confess at once, but there is no record of any witch-bird ever having been surrendered. Several competent European observers witnessed ordeals and examined piles of surrendered objects, but found no birds among them. Many women gave up pots and calabashes, containing medicines of various kinds. Others seized the first object they could find at home, charms and even images of gods. Great masses of these were discarded and burnt, and some were salvaged for local museums. I obtained several myself. There were pieces of old bones, dried skins, and feathers, such as any market sells for magical use.

Women who refused to confess were tried by an ordeal, which was very much the same in Ghana and Nigeria. The woman would be told to bring a chicken, some gin, and money to the chief Atinga. He would pocket the money, pour a small libation of gin on the altar, and cut the throat of the fowl halfway across, leaving the bird sufficient life for it to run about a little. When it finally collapsed, the way in which it lay on the ground, was supposed to indicate the innocence or guilt of the witch. If it died with its breast upwards it was thought to be acceptable to the god and the woman innocent. Any other position proved guilt. But a woman would be allowed to try with several fowls, on due payment. Women who obdurately refused to confess were tortured until they did so, and in a few instances were beaten to death.

The witch-finding movement had great popular appeal in western Nigeria, and when it was finally banned under the Witchcraft

Ordinance there was loud protest, even in the daily newspapers: the government was urged to 'leave our God-sent Atingas to continue their work of ransom'. Many people felt that the work of the Atingas was good, since witchcraft is harmful. Particularly annoyed were those people who had bought the secrets of Atinga themselves at a fee of anything up to a hundred pounds, and were setting up in practice as private witch-finders. Villages that had not been visited by the Atingas were also displeased at not having had their witchcraft removed and their women subjected.

In this witch-hunting it is interesting to note the prominence of youths, in contrast to the age of witch-finders of olden times. Also significant is the fact that many images of gods were surrendered, and temples were violated by roving bands of young hooligans in the aftermath of the prohibition of the movement. It was partly a movement of youth against age, and the old gods have lost their power in this modern world, though potent new gods may come to be adopted. On the other hand, the shrines of the ancestors were respected, as still retaining much of their importance to society.

OLD WITCH-HUNTERS

In the Nupe country of northern Nigeria there is an ancient cult of witch-finders, called Ndako Gboya ('ancestor *gboya*'). This is a society of masked and gowned figures, yet not quite a secret society since it is publicly recognized (although banned officially at times).

The Ndako Gboya is a society of men disguised in very tall cylinders of cloth, anything up to fifteen feet high and fixed on to a ring inside attached to a pole. Strips of coloured cloth are attached to the main tent, and flap in the wind as it moves. This cylinder completely covers the man, supposed to be an ancestral spirit, and as he walks and dances he moves the pole up and down to make frightening gestures.[1]

The masked men dress in a special shrine, and wash themselves with a ritual medicine which endows them with witchcraft power. By possessing this power they can cast out witches. When a village is to be cleansed of its witches, the Ndako Gboya appear early in the morning. There are three or four robed and masked men, with un-masked interpreters who translate the threats and grunts of the

[1] Nadel, *Nupe Religion*, pp. 188 f.

masqueraders. They go around the town or village, looking into its corners, rounding up the people, and dancing in the village square to the accompaniment of drums and dancing.

At night comes the climax when the smelling-out of witches begins, and the women are terrified lest they be accused. During a dance a masquerader will turn to some woman, bending its great height over her in menace, while the assistants seize the suspected witch. She is rushed into the bush and made to pass through an ordeal. She has to dig the ground with her bare hands until the blood comes, and that is regarded as a sign of guilt. In the olden days she was held up to ransom, and was killed if a high price could not be produced. Nowadays she may be chased away from her home and village.

The witch-hunters also used to appear at harvest time, when money was plentiful, and so frighten the women that large sums of money were collected, part of which was given to the Emir of that place. This became such an abuse that in 1921 the society was banned in Nupe province. But the Ndako Gboya are still to be seen, and they have spread far beyond their original home. They appear in the neighbouring Yoruba country, and the masqueraders may even be seen parading the streets of this huge modern city of Ibadan, where I wrote this book.[1]

The Azande do not have witch-hunts like those described above, but they have two principal ways of discerning and combating witchcraft. One is by calling together the witch-doctors for a seance in which they work themselves up into a frenzy. The other way is by consultation of an oracle.

The witch-doctors are called together when a man has some inexplicable trouble, which is therefore referred to witches. Consultation of the oracle might be just as effective, but a public dance of witch-doctors impresses the community, enhances the consultant's prestige, and is a public sign of the war made against witchcraft.

When the witch-doctors assemble together they dance and give messages in a trance, saying that there are dangerous people about. The consultants ask for their names and this requires further dancing, during which the doctor leaps about to the sound of drums, the amulets and bells which he wears making a great noise. Finally he

[1] See my *Religion in an African City*, plate 10.

falls to the ground, then bounds to his feet, and stands in silence till at last he utters the names of those who are bewitching. The accused persons may be folk whom he knows to be enemies of his consultant, or someone against whom the doctor himself has a private grudge. The accused people will later be submitted to the oracle.

Other witch-doctors dance at the same time and give messages to the audience. The seance may last long and have many rambling and partly incoherent messages pronounced by the excited and entranced dancers.

Lovedu witch-hunters in South Africa start their work if required to do so by someone who believes himself to be much troubled by witches. He may call out aloud a warning to the witch in the village, or move away from the village rather than start open action. But then he may consult a witch-doctor, or request smellers-out to inquire of a diviner.

The smellers-out set off towards the place where they know diviners are to be found, often covering considerable distances, but gradually coming nearer home. The diviner will demand a large fee and put various questions to the consultants, finding hidden magical objects and naming persons likely to have practised witchcraft. If he accuses somebody of another clan then the consultants are satisfied. They return home in joy blowing their horns.

The accused witches may be ill-treated and beaten. Their heads are shaved and clothes taken away. Some will leave for the town. Others may not be molested, and a man would not send away a wife accused of witchcraft if in doing so there would be involved the return of cattle given in dowry. Some people are known to be witches but are never accused of witchcraft, and people try to avoid annoying them lest they arouse their anger.

ORDEALS

Witch-doctors who have accused persons brought to them very frequently impose some form of ordeal. Half-severing a chicken's neck, and judging the guilt of the witch from the way it falls is a common method of ordeal in West Africa. It may be used by private witch-doctors as well as by public witch-finding movements.

The chief aim of the ordeal is to expose the identity of the witch and the extent of her power. Witches love darkness, it is believed, and they do their evil work at night. Their power is broken by bringing it into the light of day. Hence one chief requirement is the surrender of the tools of witchcraft, the pot or horn, and often this suffices.

The witch is usually told first to release her victim, by restoring the parts of the spiritual body taken away and by blessing the victim. Then she has to purify herself by ritual washing in medicinal lotions, and sometimes by making a sacrifice of a fowl or an animal. Fines are imposed often and are a source of wealth to the witch-doctor.

Very often the witch is given a drink which is semi-poisonous. If she can vomit the drink without harm to herself then her innocence may be established. The dilution of the poison may depend upon the goodwill of the witch-doctor and the amount of influence the witch can bring to bear upon him.

In many parts of Africa today the poison is administered to a fowl, and its death or survival point to the guilt of the witch. European governments have severely restricted the powers of witch-doctors and chiefs in giving ordeals, and the substitution of the fowl is a compromise from the old administration of poison to the witch. In Rhodesia accused witches are tied up while the ordeal of the fowl decides their fate. The bark of a tree is ground to reddish powder and given to the fowl. It is then watched to see if it will eat, and if it does so then the accused is released. Some accusers are not satisfied with one fowl, and try several in case the first was saved by evil influences.

The Azande use the poison oracle in many events in life and regard its decision as completely valid in law. A red paste is poured into the beaks of domestic fowls, and the spasms that ensue indicate the nature of answers to the questions at issue. Sometimes the fowls die, but they often recover.

In the old days all witchcraft cases were dealt with by the poison oracle. Only men are allowed to consult it, and indeed this oracle is one of the means of keeping the women in their place and making sure that they are faithful to their husbands.

When the poison is administered to the fowl the operator will address questions to the poison, asking it to kill the fowl if the accusation is true. The poison dose may be increased and another fowl may be tried. Eventually the witch is judged, and if guilty she is bound over to cease from troubling the victim.

OLD AND NEW METHODS

One finds in many parts of Africa a mingling of old and new methods of protection against witchcraft. Yet many old methods survive amid new situations.

The Ibibio of eastern Nigeria make sacrifices to witches to protect themselves against their power. They make a plate of bamboo sticks and place on it small portions of rice and palm-oil, and add seven halfpennies or seven kola nuts. They place this offering at the foot of a tree, usually a silk-cotton tree, where witches are thought to gather. There they hope that the witches will devour the meal and will release the bodies that they have been eating. These people have been Christianized and most of their children attend school, yet this ancient form of witch-offering is still practised.

One finds that Christians and Muslims use the arms of their new religion to combat witchcraft, which most of them believe in just as firmly as their ancestors. Is not witchcraft mentioned in the Bible? Mohammedans have diviners who differ very little from pagan diviners, except that they interpret the signs of their oracles by texts from Arabic writings. Charms against witchcraft are made from verses of the Koran.

The orthodox Christian churches do not, in theory, recognize the belief in witchcraft, for the missionaries are sceptical. But increasing numbers of African Christian sects spend a considerable part of their time in combating witchcraft, and they attract to themselves members of other churches who are believed to be troubled by witchcraft.

In Ibadan there was opened in 1956 an 'Occult Tetragram Temple', one of whose chief purposes is to cure barrenness (charmingly called unpregnancy), and to treat women who suffer from this form of bewitching. According to the local press the opening of this temple 'shook the town', and while this is slightly hyperbolical it did have considerable success for a time through its combination of old and new methods. Its leaders have read garbled versions of old European magic and exorcism, and know that the four consonants of Jehovah, the Tetragrammaton, were used as a potent exorcism in the Middle Ages.

The Basuto Christian priest fights against witchcraft by prayer and exorcism. A special service is held at the house of the bewitched person. Hymns are sung, prayers said, and the person is anointed with holy water, while the priest pronounces the words: 'In the name of the Father, and of the Son, and of the Holy Ghost. Christ died for our sins. Amen.'[1]

Zionist prophets among the Zulu regularly combat witchcraft among their followers. The healing includes Biblical invocations, but, like the pagan seances, no healing is regarded as complete until the prophet has found a horn or bottle in the sufferer's hut which is supposed to contain the witchcraft poison.[2]

Thus the new religions seek to meet the needs of people whose ideas have not been greatly changed. It is understandable that Christians in Africa still fear the malevolence of witches, just as much as did Europeans at the time of the Renaissance.

[1] Ashton, op. cit., p. 296
[2] B. G. M. Sundkler, *Bantu Prophets in South Africa*, 1948, pp. 253 f.

CHAPTER 15

Witch-doctors

WHAT IS A WITCH-DOCTOR?

There is a great deal of confusion in books written about Africa over the names to be applied to the different officials in religious matters. The words wizard, sorcerer, juju-man, leech, soothsayer, priest, doctor, and the like are bandied about with little care for precise definition.

No name has suffered more from distortion and misunderstanding than that of the witch-doctor. To many people the witch-doctor is the chief witch, the devil of the magical art. Even colonial governments have legislated against him while leaving worse people unmolested.

Now the truth is that, as one leading authority has put it, the witch-doctor 'is no more a witch than an Inspector of the C.I.D. is a burglar'.[1] For it is a simple fact that the witch-doctor's task is precisely to doctor or heal those who are thought to have been bewitched by other people. Far from being a witch, he is the chief enemy of witches. In legislating against him we have disgraced a respected member of society, and people think that we have helped the forces of evil. If one believes in the reality of witchcraft, then anyone who helps to rid society of its menace is regarded as a power of good.

Dr. Audrey Richards introduces the word 'witch-finder' for these men. It shows one of their functions clearly, but it does not indicate the cleansing part of their task, and it has inevitable associations with the witch-finders of Europe. It is true that the African witch-doctor may resemble some of the Inquisitors or witch-prickers, but

[1] F. H. Melland, *In Witch-bound Africa*, 1923, pp. 199 f.

the inquisition is only a part of his job. The older word witch-doctor expresses the healing function of these men, who seek to cure those that are bewitched, by seeking out and breaking the power of the witches. If the older word can be purged of undesirable associations there is no reason why it should not be retained. In itself it is not misleading.

In the eyes of practically all Africans the witch-doctor is a reputable man. His task is to save our souls from being devoured by enemies, and to break the power of witches on the warpath. It is true that in modern justice accused witches should be protected from baseless charges. Those authorities that have studied the question believe that, in the present transitional stage of society, the powers of witch-doctors should be limited to preventing evildoers and sorcerers from using harmful magic, and that they should not be allowed to punish accused witches.

THE NATURE OF THE WITCH-DOCTOR

The witch-doctor is not a practising witch, but it is true that he may well have certain affinities with witches. He has something of the same spirit. He has to be like witches so that he may overcome them by his more powerful spirit. As Evans-Pritchard put it, 'Only by Beelzebub can one cast out Beelzebub'.

Africans believe in the existence of a spiritual energy, sometimes called 'vital force' or 'dynamism'. This power is latent in many people, animals, and things. It is the power behind religion and magic, linking them into one system. It is the force that gives effect to sacrifices, taboos, charms, and spells. The force of witchcraft can be used by a witch against her enemies, but it can also be used for good against the witch. In a sense it is a neutral, yet highly charged, power and can be turned to good or evil ends like atomic power.

Ghana people believe that witchcraft power can be used for other than harmful ends. The witch can not only harm and impoverish others, but she can also multiply her own crops and possessions. For this reason those who get rich by unknown means, or whose crops prosper while the fields of other people are not so forward, are liable to be accused of witchcraft. Indeed, in societies ridden by belief in witchcraft it is dangerous to do or be anything out of the ordinary, lest undue success or misfortune render one suspect of trafficking with the powers of evil.

The power of witchcraft may be used for the benefit of its owner. But once it is perverted to evil ends it cannot be turned to good again. Once the witch gets a taste of human blood, she acquires a craving that only blood will satisfy. 'It will have blood: they say, blood will have blood.'

The witch-doctor has a power like that of witches. By this power he recognizes those who are using witchcraft, and heals those who are bewitched. But the power is very delicate and is fraught with danger to the possessor. For if the witch-doctor once gives way to the temptation to use his power against an enemy, he is caught inescapably in the grip of his own force and becomes a witch himself. In like manner a priest, whose task it is to protect men against lightning or smallpox, has the power to call down storms or plague upon his enemies. But, priests have told me, if he were once to use this power for his own purposes the evil would return like a boomerang upon his own house and family, destroying them first.

It will be clear from this that the witch-doctor must be an upright man, keeping his hands clean from evil, and wielding his great power solely in the interests of health and the welfare of society.

In the Nupe country of Nigeria the head of the women traders (the *lelu*) is also called the head of the witches. But she is thought of as a 'good witch', who uses her mystic powers for the benefit of the community. She used to employ her powers to prepare medicine to make warriors invincible in battle. She does not practise witchcraft now, but keeps other witches in check. Yet she must have the witchcraft power in order to qualify for her office as female head. In her work of keeping witchcraft under control, she acts rather on the principal of 'set a thief to catch a thief'.[1]

The witch-doctor is usually both a controller of witches and a dealer in magic and herbalism. He is often a diviner, revealing hidden things and foretelling the future. It is as diviner that he is able to detect who are the witches, and as magician he counteracts their evil powers by the application of his medicines and magical spells.

Witch-doctors have special knowledge of medicine and are versed in lore of many kinds. The secrets of these medicines are passed down from age to age, and from one practitioner to another.

[1] *Nupe Religion*, pp. 167 f.

Very often the knowledge is bought with money or services rendered by the apprentice. The diviners naturally have a vested interest in keeping the secrets of their profession, and few Europeans have been able to fathom all their mysteries, or test their claims that they can cure diseases which modern medical science still has difficulty in treating.

At the same time the doctor acquires a considerable knowledge of human nature. He studies the symptoms of those who are bewitched. He learns certain marks that are typical of witches. He comes to recognize the 'compulsion neurotic', as psychology might call him. Like the psychiatrist he watches his patient's symptoms and gleans a good deal from the questions he puts to him.

Some witch-doctors claim to be able to recognize witches by signs that are visible to them alone. Witches may be old, solitary, with bloodshot eyes and hairy faces. Some say that witches have red smoke coming out of their heads which has been interpreted as an aura. Those who cannot see the signs may be told that they have not 'the right sort of eyes'. Special powers are needed 'to see and tell of things invisible to mortal sight'.

Witches are supposed to be able to recognize one another, since they meet for their nocturnal meals. If a witch-doctor possesses some of the witchcraft, he too must be able to recognize witches. But just as a witch's power may be latent and not always active, so it may be with the doctor. In his normal frame of mind he may have difficulty in picking out the witches. But when he dances to the sound of the drums, and is dressed in all his magical array, then his dormant powers come to life. He may go into a trance and be able to name or point out those who are harming their neighbours. His powers of clairvoyance are aroused and witches are no longer able to hide from him.

TRAINING WITCH-DOCTORS

Professor Evans-Pritchard, in *Witchcraft, Oracles and Magic*, has given more particulars of the training of African witch-doctors than any other writer. What he could not see himself was passed on to him by an assistant who deliberately went through all the training of a witch-doctor, under several leading specialists, and then he revealed the secrets to the anthropologist.

Witch-doctors are nearly always men. One rarely hears of a woman practising as a diviner, and when she does it is as an inferior leech with special ailments that she treats, and she is not admitted into the inner secrets of the corporation of witch-doctors. Such a woman would be old. One never hears of a girl or young married woman in such practice. She might be a convicted and cleansed witch, who retained something of the power of witchcraft.

Witch-doctors often co-operate, and several may be seen together at a seance. Here they support one another and do not contradict each other's revelations. But they are not closely united into a trade union. Their corporation is simply mutual assistance, involving little more than dancing together and buying and selling potent medicines among themselves. The pupil learns from an older man, paying him fees, and may go off to others to complete his knowledge.

An Azande youth may approach his tutor directly and ask to become his pupil. If he shows aptitude for the work his training may be short but expensive. But parents may apprentice quite small children to witch-doctors, so that they may be trained from an early age. Here the training is very long and the payment is spread out over years.

The novice is given medicines to eat to make his soul strong and enable him to prophesy. In company with other witch-doctors he meets at the leader's house where magical potions are prepared. He is shown the trees and plants from which these come. He helps to cook and stir them over a fire, and utters incantations over them, praying for protection against evil forces and asking for the gift of recognizing witches. The medicine receives a token payment, of quite a small coin, and then it is tasted by all present and a mixture of oil and ashes is smeared on the bodies of those present.

The chief purpose of the months of ensuing training is to enable the would-be witch-doctor to find out witches, and to resist their attack upon himself. He takes part in communal activities and meals with other doctors, and assists them at seances. At first he makes no effort to divine who are witches, as he is not yet qualified to do so and is a mere imitator of the dances of others. He goes around to other doctors to learn their different medicines and sometimes undertakes long journeys with an older man to obtain some rare remedy.

The Azande believe that there is a witchcraft-phlegm, derived from the witchcraft-substance which is supposed to be in the bodies of witches. Part of the training of a witch-doctor is in the passing of this phlegm from an old man. Witches inherit their substance and it is harmful. Witch-doctors derive their phlegm from medicine and it is beneficial. The phlegm is expectorated by the instructing elder into a small gourd, it is then poured into the novice's throat and he has to swallow it without spitting it out.

The training continues with dances and songs, which anyone can see and copy, and with knowledge of medicines which is passed on privately. The witch-doctor learns to practise sleight-of-hand, so as to be able deliberately to introduce witchcraft objects into or on the skin of his patient and then pretend to have found them there. Conscious fraud is practised, but it is all for a good cause.

The principal Azande rite of initiation is a ceremonial of public burial which the novice has to undergo. The purpose of this is to sever him from his previous life and raise him to a new plane. Such burial and resurrection is found in religious cults in other parts of Africa.[1]

The novice prepares for this rite by observing chastity, and taboos on food before and immediately after the burial. Medicines are put on his body. A mat covers it and earth is heaped on it. But the head and feet stick out of the grave. After dancing and divination gifts are placed at the edge of the grave and the neophyte eventually staggers to his feet and then rests. Meanwhile more dancing takes place and medicines are applied to his body. Finally he is dressed and dances with the rest.

When the final initiation of the new witch-doctor has taken place he adopts a new name, to separate himself from his past life and set up now as a new person. This is his professional name which is used when people consult him for their special needs.

A SEANCE

In the last chapter some description was given of the ordeals and witch-hunting practised in various places. To complete the picture a summary account may now be given of a seance of Azande doctors.

The seance is made up of one or more witch-doctors, dancing and singing to the beating of drums and gongs. During this time

[1] See my *West African Religion*, 2nd edn., pp. 83 f.

members of the audience put questions to particular doctors, who reply by giving a solo dance. Those who are troubled by misfortunes attributed to witches invite the doctors to their houses.

The witch-doctor wears his regalia, a hat decked with feathers, a short skin loincloth, a belt, bracelets and anklets made of seeds, horns and gourds round his waist, and a chain of magic whistles slung across his chest. He meets his fellow doctors and gives greetings in low tones.

A circle is drawn on the ground where the dance is to take place and no one but a doctor may enter it. The line is marked out more clearly with white ashes and horns are stuck in the ground on the line. There is a pot of water which the doctors gaze into so that they may 'scry' or perceive witchcraft. The horns are filled with paste from herbal medicines, which are believed to be the chief aid in the detection of witchcraft.

Drummers stand at the edge of the circle and there is a chorus of boys. Spectators are usually numerous. The consultant invites the public to attend the seance, even though he is paying for it. Those who have questions to ask of the dancers make small offerings of coins or vegetables.

When the doctor has danced alone, following a question, he stops when exhausted and considers his answer. He speaks in a far-off voice, as if the reply is coming from outside himself. As he goes on he gets more confident and multiplies the answer. If it is not fully answered he may dance again. He will give names, if pressed, though he may prefer not to make an enemy by naming a person. But enemies or known rivals of the consultant are easy targets.

In dances the witch-doctors sometimes whip themselves up into great frenzies. In many parts of Africa these are the most sensational performances that can be witnessed, and they sometimes get reported in the popular press in Europe. One meets people, as I have done, who cut themselves with knives in their fury. One is reminded of the priests of Baal who 'cried aloud, and cut themselves after their manner with their knives and lances, till the blood gushed out upon them'.

METHODS OF CURE

The witch-doctors use a variety of cleansing methods to cure those who suffer from witchcraft. These fall into two classes. Firstly those who are supposed to be witches. Secondly those who have been bewitched or are afraid of becoming so.

The witches, as we have said previously, need only to have their identity and power exposed and they are half cured. 'Open confession is good for the soul.' After confessing to witchcraft and restoring the soul of the victim, the witch is cleansed with various remedies prescribed by the doctors and sometimes she has to sacrifice an animal.

The victims are cured by restoring their vitality or bodily members which the witches have taken. Some witch-doctors make a pretence of searching for these stolen members, and finding them hidden in the roof or the cleft of a tree. The bewitched person then receives further medicines, and may remain for a time under the doctor's care.

Some people suffer from the obsession that they are becoming witches. They think that witches are luring them to the nocturnal assemblies, or are introducing a witchcraft-substance into their bodies. This anxious state may result from physical sickness, a wasting disease, or from vivid nightmares which plague the sufferer. Insomnia, added to fitful nightmares, is a fertile ground for this witch fear.

People often consult the witch-doctor without being accused of witchcraft by their friends, enemies, or witch-finders. They have some worrying experiences, which may range from troubled dreams to simple indigestion. They see lights and sparks before their eyes, or feel worms or snakes crawling about in their bodies. The witch-doctor treats these anxious people to the best of his ability. He gives them medicines which have a suggestive, if not a real, physical value. He tries to calm his patient's troubled spirit, shaves off his hair and prescribes baths with medicinal lotions. Slowly the patient's spirit is strengthened, his confidence returns, and he becomes stronger than the evil forces attacking him.

The Ewe people in West Africa have interesting ways of pacifying witch spirits when a person is troubled by them. The witch-doctors tell the patient to provide animal and vegetable gifts and much palm oil. A circle is drawn with ashes and soot in the patient's compound, and the sick person and his family sit in it. The sufferer is rubbed with maize and bean grains which are then put in a calabash. A goat is brought and the patient kneels and touches it, while the doctor calls on the witch to come and accept the offering. The goat is killed and its blood put in the calabash, together with some of its flesh after cooking. Some of the mixture from the calabash is put in small heaps on the ground for the witches, and the rest of the goat's flesh is eaten by the people present. Finally the doctor takes some cowrie shells and touches the calabash with them, asking the witches where they want their gift placing. He names a place, and the manner in which the cowries fall to the ground indicates whether that is suitable. When the right place is found, usually at a cross-roads, the rest of the food in the calabash is left there as a peace offering to the witches.

The witch-doctors are greatly sought after, much feared, but also highly respected. No doubt they do good in restoring confidence in their patients. In some of their methods they are like psychiatrists; indeed is it not the fashion in England to call psychiatrists witch-doctors? No doubt some witch-doctors are extortionate and consciously exploit the credulity of their fellows. That is not peculiar to African religious life.

CHRISTIAN DOCTORS

It is only to be expected that when nearly everybody, Christian, Muslim, and pagan believes in witchcraft the new religions will have their doctors also. There are the Elijahs who rival the priests of Baal.

The Christian diviners are to be found particularly among the native sects that flourish in many places, with their apostles and prophets, and their mixture of Christian and indigenous beliefs. Many people in Europe do not realize how extensive are these off-shoots and secessions from the orthodox missions. In South Africa alone more than 2,000 such sects are known to have existed, though many of them are small and some die out as others arise. In West and East Africa also they are growing and sub-dividing with great rapidity. In one sense they represent an adaptation of Christianity to ancient ways of African life, with all the advantages and dangers attendant upon such adaptation.

The Christian separatist sects use cleansing medicines for the bewitched, just like the herbal remedies of the witch-doctors only issued in modern glass bottles. Or, since it often happens that the sect opposes the use of all medicines, European as well as African, and relies on 'faith-healing', recourse may be had to anointing with oil, sprinkling with holy water, rubbing with ashes, or censing with incense.

Public accusation of witches and confession in church is not uncommon. The prophet or prophetess may diagnose the malady, denounce sin, and demand repentance and ritual washings. Sweeping the house and compound with magical brushes, wearing special clothing and sashes, and taboos of eating pork and other foods all play their part.

Praying over the patient is the most common, with laying on hands and blessing. Repentance is followed by restoration to the Church, and obstinacy punished with excommunication. Different sects vie with each other in offering cures, especially for the evil of a bewitched womb or impotent organ (Sprenger would have understood this!). The sect that can offer a cure to sterility is always sure of a following. Women go to distant hills to fast and pray for children, while others go there to strengthen their prophetic and divinatory powers. Especially do such retreats take place in Lent and Advent.

Christianity, in some of its African forms, struggles with the old beliefs. The Christian prophet is the counterpart of the pagan witch-doctor, regarded as endowed with divine power for this important work, and looked upon with the respect given to the older doctors.[1]

[1] See H. Debrunner, *Witchcraft in Ghana*, 1959.

CHAPTER 16

The Social Setting of Witchcraft

One of the most important questions in the consideration of witchcraft is why the belief prevails in certain types of society. What are the stresses that favour its growth? Why are certain people accused of being witches? Why some classes more than others? If, as seems probable, witchcraft is imaginary (or at least a great deal of it), then why are innocent people accused?

SEXUAL ANTAGONISM

The position of women, and the attitude men have adopted towards them, are important factors. In many parts of Africa only women are thought to be witches, and everywhere women are believed to be in the majority in witchcraft. Complementary to this is the fact that witch-doctors are practically always men.

A good example may be seen among the Nupe of Nigeria. Here both men and women are held to be capable of witchcraft, but the women are the only ones who are really dangerous. The men, like the women, can make themselves invisible and separate their souls from their bodies. But while the female witches seek to eat other people's souls, the males play tricks or exercise a malevolent influence upon their enemies which is rarely fatal. The males may also work good with their witchcraft and protect people from thieves; but the females are always evil. Finally, the males are said to have no specific organization, whereas the females have a very strong coven with a recognized head.

In many places witchcraft is said to be hereditary. It is passed down through the female line, and a son cannot inherit his mother's witchcraft. Since the woman's blood is generally thought to constitute her share in the formation of a child, she is regarded as responsible for the body and the blood while the father passes on the soul. Witchcraft having a special association with blood, this is believed to come down from the mother and to be passed on to her daughter. It is the female who goes around drinking the blood and eating the limbs and soul of her victim.

This being so, the male role is to combat witchcraft by means of witch-doctors and secret societies. Many of the 'secret societies' of Africa have as one of their chief functions the chasing of witches. For example, in the Yoruba country of Nigeria there is a society called Oro. Oro used to be the executive arm of the civil authority, putting criminals to death, but now it is largely engaged in keeping witches away. When Oro comes out, by day or night, no women may leave their houses on pain of death. The voice of Oro is heard in the bull-roarer, a flat piece of wood attached to a cord which the young men twirl around rapidly to make an uneven and terrifying sound. One still hears Oro in the villages, and even in the towns, though here it is much harder to ensure that all women are indoors.

Many of the societies serve to emphasize male prestige, and some of them have an important function in preparing adolescent boys to pass through the initiation into manhood and then to vaunt their powers. But they serve to keep the women in subjection and to harry accused witches. I have heard the Oro society hounding suspected witches from one village to another and giving the poor women no rest.

The fact that women are accused of witchcraft, mainly or exclusively, shows a very deep-rooted sexual antagonism. This is not only true of modern Africa. The same applied to Europe in the late Middle Ages and in the 'enlightened' days of the Renaissance. In Europe, as we have seen, the great majority of the accused were women. The witch-finders were men, most of them celibates. Their morbid preoccupation with the subject of sexual orgies, of which they accused the women and themselves wrote in detail, is an interesting point in their psychology. The subjection of women was one aim of the witch-hunting. The modern emancipation of women may be said to have put the last nail into the coffin of European witchcraft.

KINSHIP STRESSES

In recent years it has become the custom in anthropological circles to consider witchcraft as simply due to kinship stresses and family jealousies. Whether the whole range of belief in witchcraft can be explained away like this is another matter, but certainly jealousy does provide fertile soil for accusations of witchcraft.

It is a remarkable fact, noted by a number of authorities, that witchcraft accusations occur among known, and often related, people. This shows that the belief in witchcraft is not unreasonable, however mistaken it may be, for the sufferer may accuse people who he thinks have good reason to dislike him, or whom he himself distrusts.

We have seen that witchcraft seeks to explain the 'why' of the accidents of life. A man may be bitten by a snake; why was not another bitten instead? Why does it rain on one field and not on another? Why is one man chosen as chief and not his rival? Why do the wicked prosper, building fine houses, having bumper crops, while others equally hard-working fail continually? Surely witchcraft is the reason.

Also accusations of witchcraft are not necessarily random and arbitrary. A man may go to consult a witch-doctor and ask where his sickness has come from, what witch has caused it. But then he, or the doctor, may suggest the names of half a dozen people who may have injured him. The oracle may choose, apparently arbitrarily, between the names, but all were possibilities.

The accusations are reasonable also in that they do not attribute all misfortune to witchcraft. It has its practical side as well. A man bitten by a snake knows that he suffers from snakebite, but he asks also 'who sent the snake?', or 'what witch had taken on a snake's form?' Similarly moral lapses are not attributed to witchcraft, which is not blamed for making a man steal, or lie, or commit adultery. But combining both apparent cause and a reason why, men arrive at the conclusion of witchcraft.

The Azande say, 'Jealousy comes first and witchcraft follows after'. This is a moral conclusion, recognizing that men may possess the power of witchcraft, but only their evil tempers make them use that which might have remained latent or have been turned to good. Jealousy arises especially in family life, where men are in close contact with each other. And as most African societies in the past have been composed of people who live in a small circle of face-to-face relations, naturally they blame those whose enmity they have incurred.

Even so, there are some people within the family circle who would not be accused of witchcraft. A man may suffer from his mother's discipline, but a Zulu son would never accuse his mother of bewitching him. And although some modern Zulu men have accused their fathers of witchcraft, this is regarded as a sign of the degeneration of modern times.[1]

In the main, however, it is agreed by the majority of writers that witchcraft is generally not thought to come from distant enemies. People living far away have not sufficient contacts to produce that irritation and hatred that arise in one's immediate circle. It is those we live amongst who are likely to cause the most friction. 'A man's foes shall be they of his own household.'

When a man is sick he looks around for one who might have caused the illness, and finds her in one of his quarrelling wives. If a child is poorly the anxious mother will think of some lonely neighbour who has petted the child and is jealous of those who have children. African women live in closer contact with other women than they do with the men, and they consult the oracle about their female companions principally.

There are some people who are rarely accused of witchcraft. In many societies noblemen are thought to be above such things. They do not live in close and provocative touch with commoners, and are approached with the respect due to their rank. Moreover, it is as well to keep on the right side of such powerful people and so not to accuse them. Children are also thought to be incapable of witchcraft activity. A girl may be a potential witch, yet her powers do not develop before puberty. Europeans are in a class by themselves. They have strange ways and are different from Africans, apparently unaffected by charms and spells made against them, and so beyond the circle of witchcraft relationship. Only now are they being seen to have feet of clay, and some of them appear to imbibe African superstitions with remarkable credulity.

The greater ease of communications nowadays brings strangers into even remote villages. So they may now be suspected of witch-

[1] M. Gluckman, *Custom and Conflict in Africa*, 1955, p. 92.

craft if they are Africans. The villagers say that they do not feel safe with so many strangers about. In the town where I wrote this there is a modern market which is said to be frequented by witches and ghosts, because there are so many foreigners there.

A potent source of witchcraft conflict in the family is in the mother-in-law complex. The mother-in-law tension is one of the oldest in human society, and some unkind humorist suggests that the first joke was made about mother-in-law fighting a tiger and the tiger getting the worst of it. The Bible speaks in several places of the conflict of 'mother-in-law against her daughter-in-law and daughter-in-law against her mother-in-law' (Micah vii, 6; Matthew x, 35; Luke xii, 53).

During a witch-hunt a young woman will easily accuse her mother-in-law of devouring her children (the wife's), and the mother-in-law, aware of her own maternal envy, will admit it. There is inevitable friction. The young wife is an interloper who has broken the close link of mother and son. Therefore the wife herself may also be accused of witchcraft by the aggrieved parent.

In African society it usually happens that marriage is exogamous. That is to say, that a man must not marry anyone of his own clan. Women enter another family, and sometimes go to another town, when they marry. Hence the wife comes into her husband's family as a stranger. She is regarded with suspicion and unless she quickly bears children she may become disliked. Particularly if her children die at birth, as so often happens, will she be accused of having killed them. Her husband himself may accuse her, for he is not so closely tied to her as to his own blood-relatives. In African society there is not that complete separation from the family, and setting up of a small husband-wife home, that obtains in Europe.

In this situation the wife's closest ties will be with the children she bears, particularly her sons. If she has daughters she is thought to pass on her witchcraft to them, but they will leave the family when they marry. But if she is so fortunate as to have several sons, such as all women long for, then she will be cared for. When she has passed the time of child-bearing she will probably go to live with her eldest son. It is true that a boy's best friend is his mother, and vice versa.

When the witch-finders are at work, it is the young men who are most surprised and concerned if their mothers are accused of witchcraft. The husbands do not seem to bother very much. There are records of young men offering to fight those who accused their mothers of witchcraft, and successfully defending them. It is good to know that natural affection can triumph over superstition.

One of the most frequent sources of conflict in the family is between co-wives. This is one of the evils of a society that allows polygamy. The wives may have their own separate rooms or houses, but they strive for possession of their husband's favours. They accuse each other of eating the souls of other wives or of harming their rival's children. When a child is sick the most obvious vampire is a co-wife, especially if she has no children of her own or none at the time. This enmity is well illustrated in the stories of Leah and Rachel, and Hannah and Peninnah.

There is not the same ideal of romantic love in Africa, at least until modern times, as that which has been so glorified in Europe. A man scarcely knows his wife before the marriage. She comes from another village and it is a family arrangement, and although this may make for stability it does not guarantee compatibility. Then there are the other wives, with their jealousies, especially foreign wives. It is true that a man and wife may grow to love each other, but close and lasting companionship and affection are rare. A man's friends are his fellow men, a woman's are her sons. So women are accused by their husbands of bewitching them or other members of the family.

Very old people are liable to accusations of witchcraft. If they are women, living alone, they are feared as were the old wise women of Europe. Why have they lived so long? Clearly they must have obtained new soul-vitality, most likely from devouring the soul of a tender child. No one will defend them from attack, so they are an easy target for accusation.

UNNATURAL ACCUSATIONS

'Witches kill the people whom it is *not* natural for them to hate,' says Dr. Field. And it is true that many women are accused of and confess to deeds that one can only regard with horror—if they are true.

It was the same in Europe. The stories of kidnapping unbaptized babes, and roasting them for consumption in the Sabbath, are almost unimaginably horrible. Alas! We know only too well today of what abominations the human imagination will conceive. Today we feast upon the macabre and the ghastly, from Grand Guignol to Belsen. Our popular murder stories, real ones in the press and more sophisticated in detective novels, show a morbid preoccupation with cruelty and death.

Apparently the witches' confessions are 'unnatural', but the psychologist will tell us that they are only too human. It is worth quoting again the revealing words of Freud about our dream life. 'Hate, too, rages unrestrainedly; wishes for revenge, and death-wishes, against those who in life are nearest and dearest—parents, brothers, sisters, husband or wife, the dreamer's own children—are by no means uncommon.'[1]

Add to the memories of bad dreams the fact of high child mortality, and the accusation of unnatural deaths is understandable. It is not insignificant that in Europe the rapid decline of witchcraft came in the centuries when medical science was at last successfully combating child mortality. From the seventeenth to the nineteenth centuries the population of England sprang from seven million to forty million. If the children no longer died then a potent source of witchcraft accusation dried up.

The death of belief in witchcraft in Africa may well await such a development. The best way to stop witch-hunts is not simply to legislate against witch-doctors, but to train as many real doctors and midwives as possible. The innumerable sources of infection surrounding the birth of the average baby in primitive huts have to be seen to be believed. In some places the child mortality is seriously estimated at 50 per cent.

It is not 'natural' that women should be accused of killing children for food. But in societies dominated by the fear of witchcraft, people argue from effect to apparent cause. If a child dies someone must have killed it, it is thought. So the mother consults an oracle, which conveniently accuses a co-wife, or the mother-in-law. The latter often accepts the accusation, not because she is guilty but because she knows no better.

It has been said that the problem of death stands at the beginning of every philosophy. In ancient Europe and modern Africa death was often attributed to witchcraft. A post-mortem examination

[1] *Introductory Lectures*, p. 158.

might be taken to prove this. Witchcraft belief thus provided an easy solution for many problems of life and death. The midwives were enemies of the Church, said Sprenger; the witches were direct emissaries of Satan.

AWKWARD PEOPLE

Having said all the above to explain the accusations made about normal people, it may also be allowed that supposed witches are often found among queer and unsociable people. One finds these in all societies. There is the morose individual who always has a grievance, the jealous woman who hates the sight of any other woman near her husband, the shrew who nags and screams and makes the man's home uncomfortable.

There are difficult people who do not fit into any category. Individualists may prefer to go their own way, and live apart from the rest of men. To be 'difficult' may simply mean that one prefers to do one's own cooking and housework. But in a suspicious society the lonely philosopher is easily suspected of alchemy, black magic, and witchcraft.

Christopher Fry puts this point well in his play, *The Lady's not for Burning*, when the accused girl asks,

> *'Why do they call me a witch?*
> *Remember my father was an alchemist.*
> *I live alone, preferring loneliness*
> *To the companionable suffocation of an aunt,*
> *I still amuse myself with simple experiments*
> *In my father's laboratory. Also I speak*
> *French to my poodle. Then you must know*
> *I have a peacock which on Sundays*
> *Dines with me indoors.'*

Undoubtedly some witches are neurotics ridden by fear and anxieties. The ones who are afraid of being compelled to join the witches are often in worse case than those who believe themselves bewitched. They are oppressed with a feeling of guilt, and though they may try to cover this up with mild and gentle behaviour, the hidden complex will at times force its way into social life.

It is often thought that neurosis is a special characteristic of modern European and American civilization, as if its sole cause were the noise and rush of town life. But the tensions which give rise to neurosis are active in most types of society. In all ages one finds those who cry out that the good which they would, they do not, and the evil that they would not, that they do. So the 'compulsion neurotic' feeling urged on towards evil deeds, and safeguarding herself vainly by all kinds of prohibitions and magic, may get relief in the confession of witchcraft. The ease with which some witches confess suggests that they are relieved to get their thoughts clear and be purified and restored to society.

In her later writings Dr. Field has made available the results of some of the first psychiatric studies ever made of Africans accused of witchcraft. Writing more than twenty years since her first book on the subject appeared, and having passed from anthropology to medicine, she reaffirms that while witches are commonly thought to have secret cults, 'no such cult in fact exists'. But she emphasizes the mental illness of her patients, people who would be liable to witch-craft accusations, and treats of depression, anxiety, various psychoses and disorders, down to chronic schizophrenia. Other forms of sick-ness, childlessness, lack of success in business and office, add to the mental anxiety. Of great importance is the ideological background, the belief in possession by alien spirits, the compulsions to action at the supposed dictation of the spirits. In the confessions, while people confess to impossible things, yet they believe in the reality of their confessions, and such acknowledgement can bring relief of mind. Many a woman will confess to witchcraft orgies when she 'has been demonstrably asleep on her mat throughout the night she is supposed to have spent in feasting'. This may be a symptom of mental illness, or the product of a disordered imagination, and it reproduces the ideology of society.[1]

UNSETTLED SOCIETY

The antagonisms of family and sex produce problems in many types of society, but only where the belief in witchcraft is accepted will it be put forward as an explanation of the tensions resulting from quarrels and jealousies. But in certain forms of society other tensions and difficulties come to a head. If witches are believed to

[1] *Search for Security*, pp. 35 f.

exist, then they will be accused of some of the troubles of the times.

Africa today is passing through a turbulent transitional period. Many ages are times of transition, but the twentieth century is particularly so for Africa where many peoples are being forced rapidly through social and industrial revolutions that took centuries to develop in Europe. In a sense, the social struggles of Africa today are comparable with those that shook Europe in the late Middle Ages and the period of the Renaissance and Reformation. As witches and heretics were burnt or hanged in Europe during those hectic centuries, so are they persecuted by modern witch-hunting movements in Africa.

The witchcraft belief is an old one in Africa, and witch-doctors have long practised their arts. But a striking feature of modern times is the comparative impotence of many of the old cults and doctors, and the rise of new movements such as the Bamucapi and Atinga which spread over a wide area. Some of the old people say that there were never so many witches in the old days, which may not be just nostalgia for a good old past, since the young people also say that their elders cannot help them to find protection against modern witches. There is a 'Twilight of the Gods' in Africa. The old cults are either swept away or, very often, slowly dying in the hands of the old people. But new gods are arising, not necessarily Christian or Muslim, but with a veneer of modern ideas covering old beliefs.

It has been said that every tribe believes its neighbours to have more dark and potent magic than its own. Hence the popularity of anti-witchcraft cults that come from distant and mysterious places. The Ashanti neglected their own gods but went a-whoring after those of the Northern Territories. So did their neighbours in Dahomey and Nigeria. The same might be said of the East African movements. When incomprehensible social troubles occur, and the local gods are incompetent to deal with the new forces, then men look around for some new and well-recommended god which will combat the prevalence of witches.

In this century many new influences have played upon African society; especially in the coastal areas, but also even in the most remote regions. European colonial rule once replaced tribal rule, nearly always weakening if not breaking the power of the old chiefs. In recent years African politicians and parties have provided further causes of conflict with the old order. The impact of European trade has increased many times since the establishment of colonialism. It has been accompanied by rapid economic advance for many people, but also by new wants and anxieties. Christianity and Islam have made more progress within the last fifty years than for many centuries previously. Education has been responsible for challenging many old beliefs, and questioning the wisdom of the illiterate elders. Add to these the growth of new coastal and mining towns, the overcrowding of new housing areas, the spread of new diseases, and the upsets of modern wars, and we have fertile ground for the belief in the evil deeds of witches.

Under the manifold changes of modern times there is no doubt that many new anxieties fill people's minds. Anthropologists regard the new witch-finding cults as some of the principal ways in which people seek to explain the ills of life, and adjust themselves to its changes and chances.[1]

The old cults do not meet the new needs. They are fitted to the old village social structure and too rigid to adapt themselves to new ways. The village gods do not fit into modern towns and their priests are out of touch with new ways. Moreover, they are under direct attack from the missions.

The new religions, Christianity and Islam, have, to some extent, provided explanations of the world and of modern ways. Christianity in particular, with its emphasis on education and medicine, has given help and enlightenment. Education, indeed, is one of the greatest panaceas of African life today, regarded by millions as the cure of all ills and almost the sole means of personal, social, and political advance. But Christianity has not reached everybody. Many people have understood it imperfectly. And it often takes no notice of fears such as witchcraft, except to oppose the priests of any new witch-finding movement. Hence new cults arise, with a thin garb of modernism, but working upon the old ideas and intensifying their power.

These new cults, regrettable as they are, yet serve the purpose of allaying the anxieties consequent upon the break-up of the social order. By the stress laid upon public confessions the witches explain the ills of modern life: sickness, barrenness, impotence, in the home and in business. The witches also find peace for themselves, quite

[1] See B. E. Ward, 'Some Observations on Religious Cults in Ashanti', *Africa*, vol. xxvi, no. 1.

frequently, because their confessions cleanse their minds and provide a means of reconciliation with society. They are strictly comparable with the victims of the Communist trials and confessions, in which the accused put themselves right with the omniscient state—but at the cost of life or liberty. In neither case do the trials and confessions excuse the cruelty of so many 'witch-hunts', ancient and modern, African or Russian.

No explanation of witchcraft can be single or simple. It is a complex matter, in which old beliefs are adapted to modern conditions. Both psychological and social factors have to be taken into account. Religious beliefs, too often neglected by the student of society, are of vital importance. Witchcraft is a belief in spiritual evil. When the old religious cults fail, then new ones are sought for. An agnostic attitude simply leaves a dangerous vacuum. Finally only an enlightened and humane faith can abolish the harshness of ignorant faiths.

THE DESIRE FOR A SCAPEGOAT

Society suffers from neuroses as do individuals. To clear itself from guilt society looks about for scapegoats on which to lay its faults.

During the late Middle Ages the Jews, and later the witches, were the scapegoats at whose doors society laid the blame for the terror of the recurrent plagues and the continuing high child mortality. In the twentieth century, the Nazis blamed the German defeat in war upon the still helpless Jews and butchered them with unparalleled barbarity. The modern massacres of Jews are strictly comparable to witch-hunting.

We need not look far for other modern examples. The American Ku Klux Klan is a witch-hunt, this time of coloured people and defenceless minorities. It is significant that the 'unamerican activity' inquiries were commonly called witch-hunts. And in Russia and the Communist states the tyranny of secret police, frequent purges, and artificial confessions follow closely upon the pattern of witchcraft.

Witch-hunts still take place. Where they are suppressed under one name they flourish under another. The dis-ease of society, aggravated by the social and industrial revolutions of our day, favours the growth of fear and superstition. Social and racial conflicts abound, and until they are resolved fear and suspicion will continue.

Witchcraft belief may have had some value in the past. Some of our medical and herbal knowledge may have come from the magical charms of witch-doctors. But the story of witchcraft has too constantly been a tale of cruelty and suffering. The belief may have kept in check the uncharitable feelings that people have towards their neighbours. But the positive evils have been great. The tyranny of men over women, the vengefulness of rivals, the hostility to strangers, the oppression of the weak and the old, the debasement of religion, the lowering of morality and kindness, all have had their part in this dreadful business. One must always remember the obsessions and fears of those who have been accused of witchcraft, and not least their sufferings: sleeplessness, homelessness, public ostracism, torture, death.

CHAPTER 17

The Future of a Tragic Fallacy

'Witchcraft is an imaginary offence because it is impossible,' said Evans-Pritchard. And Dr. Field in West Africa says, 'Since witchcraft is impossible, the fear of witchcraft and activities to counter witchcraft, must be symbolic.'

Few Africans would agree with these sweeping conclusions. Most would say that Europeans, for all their research and sojourn in Africa, have not grasped the secret of witchcraft. Some declare that these are things which the white man is 'incapable' of understanding, for he has not 'the right sort of eyes'.

This does not mean that Africans are gullible and lacking in discrimination. One finds some pagan Africans who are sceptical about the power of certain witch-doctors and have not complete faith in their ways. Some witch-doctors practise fraud and their utterances are not fully reliable, and so the wise men regard them critically. Indeed scepticism is part of the system, so to speak, for it helps to explain unfulfilled prophecies. However, few Africans believe all witch-doctors to be charlatans. Some may be so, but there must be others who are true witch-doctors, else what are they doing in society? Europeans may call some medical men quacks, but few reject all medicines. Doctors are part of the social system and are accepted as useful members of it.

Dr. Field says that 'witches are people mentally afflicted with the obsession that they have the power to harm others by thinking them harm'. The Freudian doctrine of the Omnipotence of Thought shows that men imagine that they can affect their fellows, and even the course of nature, simply by the power of thought.

But does evil thinking harm no one? The jealousy of old against young, the mother-in-law complex, the nursing of grievances, all these are the soil in which flourish envy, malice, and all uncharitableness. Many confessions of witchcraft are imaginary. But there is no smoke without fire, and there are some guilty thoughts which people harbour and which society, blindly and cruelly, seeks to restrain.

Witchcraft 'must be symbolic'. It is a belief which helps to interpret and canalize the dis-ease of society. It is an easy explanation of the ills of life. The competitive individualism of modern times, the fear of other tribes, the uncertainty of existence, all make a breeding-ground in which the ancient witchcraft belief continues to flourish. Many clerks spend considerable sums of money on protective and lucky magic, and even schoolboys resort to charms to pass examinations or influence their teachers, and they may accuse their fellows of witchcraft if they fail.

The African witch-doctor, in old or new guise, keeps his grip on men's minds because he professes to operate in a spiritual realm which they understand and believe in. Because of this some anthropologists would leave the old witch-doctors to continue their work in peace. But we have seen what tyranny and fear so often accompany their operations. The anthropologist C. K. Meek says plainly, 'We cannot lightly discount the fact that diviners, witch-doctors, and ministers of ordeals were frequently bribed to give a favourable or unfavourable decision, and that if they happened to be honest men it was an even chance whether an innocent man was punished or a guilty one escaped.'[1] If witchcraft is illusory the whole work of the witch-doctor is a ghastly mistake.

Evans-Pritchard says that the belief in witchcraft served useful purposes in giving the witch-doctors knowledge of magic, strengthening kinship ties against enemies, and enhancing the power of chiefs who control the oracles.[2] But an illusory belief is very much a second-rate faith. Nadel says more pointedly, 'I presumed no such absolute utility of witchcraft beliefs. I suggested that they resolve certain conflicts or problems: but I did not say that this is a "good" solution or a final one. The aggression invited by witchcraft beliefs is as harmful as anything a society can produce in the way of "disruptive" practices; the relief offered by witch-hunting and witch-punishing is no more than temporary and their capacity to allay

[1] *Law and Authority in a Nigerian Tribe*, p. 341.
[2] *Africa*, October 1935, p. 418.

anxieties no more than illusory: for if witchcraft beliefs resolve certain fears and tensions, they also produce others.' And so he concludes that beliefs in witchcraft are 'the kind of remedy which both becomes a drug and poisons the system. Or, to change the metaphor, we may liken witchcraft beliefs to a safety valve: but let us be clear that the engine which needs it has been badly constructed; nor is the safety valve itself safe.'[1]

What then is the future of the belief in witchcraft in Africa, and what is the cure? Governmental laws have aimed at protecting innocent people from accusation, and they must be praised for that. But because they have not received public consent they have only resulted in driving witch-hunting underground, or making it appear in new guises each of which in turn requires new legislation. The penalties laid upon witch or witch-doctor have not changed the belief in witchcraft, because they have treated the symptoms and neglected the causes. Witchcraft is a spiritual belief and needs to be combated with spiritual weapons as well as material.

Education is certainly needed. Enlightenment as to the processes by which belief in witchcraft develops, and understanding of the soil in which it flourishes, is a necessary first step. But education alone cannot root out such a deep-seated belief. Experienced teachers in Africa have found that students may peer through microscopes to study the apparent causes of disease, but they may still retain their conviction that the 'spiritual part' of the disease comes from a witch.

The spread of a good medical service will do much to reduce the fear of witches killing children and bringing impotence to adults. But disease abounds in tropical countries and it may always be attributed to witches. Death itself is regarded as always unnatural by some peoples, they do not need to ask if witchcraft has done it, all they want to know is the identity of the witch.

Even with a widespread health service there may still be manias which demand scapegoats, of which the persecutions by Nazis and Communists in modern Europe are clear examples. Better economic conditions will go some way towards removing these troubles. But they will never solve the squabbles of family and tribal life. In so far as witchcraft is bound up with the old tribal system, a change of system should ameliorate conditions. But one still finds many

[1] *Nupe Religion*, pp. 205 f.

people in the new towns who live in constant fear of witchcraft. In personal relationships politics and economics are almost powerless.

Religion has been misused, in both Europe and Africa, in the witch persecutions. But religion is the only spiritual force that can give a better faith than that of witchcraft. In the conflict of ideas, which counts so much in the modern world, a pure religion is the only alternative to a debased one. Only perfect love can cast out fear.

In modern Africa Christian faith and morality are slowly replacing old superstitions and evil practices, bringing members of different tribes and families together, and helping men to adapt themselves to the strain of modern life. No doubt a new religion upsets some of the old sanctions, but Meek says again, 'Some of the old ethics will disappear with the old gods, but new gods will create new ethical values'.

It is difficult to say yet whether belief in witchcraft is diminishing much in modern Africa. In Europe it took over a century before the forces released by the Renaissance finally undermined the belief in witchcraft. But against all that makes for tension and unrest there are forces working for good and stability. A slow decrease in witchcraft belief has probably begun, relatively to the other beliefs now spreading. Magic, and the old religions which depended so much upon it, are gradually giving way to modern knowledge and the enlightened and universal religions. The unbalanced social conditions will gradually settle down as people become accustomed to the new ways.

Religion brings in a new force, which not only fills the vacuum created by the collapse of old beliefs, but which also gives a more humane faith, provided that it has high standards and movements of reform from time to time. Such religion gives directions for better social relationships through love of one's neighbour.

The cruelty and misery caused by the belief in witchcraft have been so monstrous and tragic that everything possible should be done to destroy this pathetic fallacy. An enlightened religion, education, medicine, and better social and racial conditions, will help to reduce 'man's inhumanity to man'.

Select Bibliography

(a) EUROPEAN WITCHCRAFT

BOGUET, HENRY, *An Examen of Witches*, 1590, English Translation by E. A. Ashwin, London, 1929.

DAVIES, R. TREVOR, *Four Centuries of Witch Beliefs*, London, 1947.

EWEN, C. L'ESTRANGE, *Witch Hunting and Witch Trials*, London, 1929.

GIFFORD, GEORGE, *A Dialogue concerning Witches*, 1593, new edition, London, 1843.

GUAZZO, FRANCESCO MARIA, *Compendium Maleficarum*, 1608, English Translation by E. A. Ashwin, London, 1929.

HOLE, CHRISTINA, *A Mirror of Witchcraft*, London, 1956.

HOPKINS, MATTHEW, *The Discovery of Witches*, London, 1647.

HUGHES, PENNETHORNE, *Witchcraft*, London, 1952.

HUXLEY, ALDOUS, *The Devils of Loudun*, London, 1952.

JAMES, I., *Daemonologie*, Edinburgh, 1597.

LEA, HENRY CHARLES, *A History of the Inquisition of Spain*, vol. iv, London, 1907.

LEA, HENRY CHARLES, *A History of the Inquisition of the Middle Ages*, vol. iii, New York, 1906.

LEA, HENRY CHARLES, *Materials towards a History of Witchcraft*, Pennsylvania, 1939.

MATHER, COTTON, *The Wonders of the Invisible World*, London edition, 1862.

MURRAY, MARGARET ALICE, *The Witch-cult in Western Europe*, Oxford, 1921.

MURRAY, MARGARET ALICE, *The God of the Witches*, no date, London.

MURRAY, MARGARET ALICE, *The Divine King in England*, London, 1954.

NOTESTEIN, WALLACE, *A History of Witchcraft in England*, Washington, 1911.

POTTS, THOMAS, *The Trial of the Lancaster Witches*, 1613, edited by G. B. Harrison, London, 1929.

REMY, NICHOLAS, *Demonolatry*, 1595, English Translation by E. A. Ashwin, London, 1930.

SCOT, REGINALD, *The Discoverie of Witchcraft*, London, 1584, new edition, London, 1930.

SPRENGER, JAMES, *Malleus Maleficarum*, 1484, English Translation by Montague Summers, London, 1928.

SUMMERS, MONTAGUE, *The History of Witchcraft and Demonology*, London, 1926.

SUMMERS, MONTAGUE, *The Geography of Witchcraft*, London, 1927.

TAYLOR, JOHN M., *The Witchcraft Delusion in Colonial Connecticut, 1647–1697*, New York, 1908.

WILLIAMS, CHARLES, *Witchcraft*, London, 1941.

(b) AFRICAN WITCHCRAFT

Africa, Journal of the International African Institute, Vol. VIII, No. 4, October 1935.

ASHTON, EDMUND HUGH, *The Basuto*, London, 1952.

BUTT-THOMPSON, FREDERICK WILLIAM, *West African Secret Societies*, London, 1929.

DEBRUNNER, HANS, *Witchcraft in Ghana*, Kumasi, 1959.

DOKE, CLEMENT MARTYN, *The Lambas of Northern Rhodesia*, London, 1931.

EVANS-PRITCHARD, EDWARD, *Witchcraft, Oracles and Magic among the Azande*, Oxford, 1937.

FIELD, MARGARET JOYCE, *Religion and Medicine of the Gã People*, London, 1937.

FIELD, MARGARET JOYCE, *Search for Security*, London, 1960.

KRIGE, EILEEN JENSEN and JACOB DANIEL, *The Realm of a Rain Queen*, London, 1943.

LITTLE, KENNETH LINDSAY, *The Mende of Sierra Leone*, London, 1951.

Select Bibliography

MEEK, CHARLES KINGSLEY, *Law and Authority in a Nigerian Tribe*, London, 1937.

MEEK, CHARLES KINGSLEY, *Tribal Studies in Northern Nigeria*, London, 1931.

MELLAND, FRANK HULME, *In Witch-bound Africa*, London, 1923.

NADEL, SIEGFRIED FERDINAND, *Nupe Religion*, London, 1954.

PARRINDER, GEOFFREY, *West African Psychology*, London, 1951.

PARRINDER, GEOFFREY, *Religion in an African City*, London, 1953.

PARRINDER, GEOFFREY, *West African Religion*, 2nd edn., London, 1961.

RATTRAY, ROBERT SUTHERLAND, *Religion and Art in Ashanti*, Oxford, 1927.

SCHAPERA, ISAAC (editor), *The Bantu-speaking Tribes of South Africa*, London, 1937.

SMITH, EDWIN WILLIAM and DALE, ANDREW MURRAY, *The Ila-speaking Peoples of Northern Rhodesia*, London, 1920.

SUNDKLER, BENGT, *Bantu Prophets in South Africa*, London, 1948.

WAGNER, GUENTER, *The Bantu of North Kavirondo*, London, 1949.

WILLOUGHBY, WILLIAM CHARLES, *The Soul of the Bantu*, New York, 1928.

WILSON, GODFREY and MONICA, *The Analysis of Social Change*, Cambridge, 1945.

Index

DATE DUE

MAR 18 2001	
APR 02 2001	
APR 23 2001	
MAY 08 2003	